a
bird's-eye view of the
Bible

by
Mary Williams

redemptorist
publications

a

bird's-eye view of the

Bible

© Copyright Mary Williams 2004

Published by **Redemptorist Publications**
Alphonsus House, Chawton, Hampshire, GU34 3HQ UK
Tel. +44 (0)1420 88222, Fax +44 (0)1420 88805
email rp@rpbooks.co.uk, www.rpbooks.co.uk
A Registered Charity limited by guarantee.
Registered in England 3261721.

First published January 2011

Design by Eliana Thompson

ISBN 978-0-85231-383-1

A CIP catalogue record for this book is available from the
British Library

Printed by Nuffield Press Limited, Oxford, OX14 1RL

A Bird's-Eye View of the Bible by Mary Williams About the Author Acknowledgements Contents A Bird's-Eye View of the Bible by Mary Williams About the Author Acknowledgements Contents A Bird's-Eye View of the **about the author** About the Author Acknowledgements Contents A Bird's-Eye View of the Bible by Mary Williams About the Author Acknowledgements Contents A **about the author** Bible by Mary Williams About the Author Acknowledgements Contents A Bird's-Eye View of the Bible by Mary Williams About the Author Acknowledgements Contents A Bird's-Eye View of the Bible by

To St Mary's Church, Marshalswick, St Albans, and all who wish to learn more of the Bible, with thanks to those who have taught me both in a formal capacity and in the school of life.

Sadly, Mary Williams died before this book was published, but was delighted that it had been accepted by Redemptorist Publications.

Mary had wide experience in education. She was also a lay minister in St Albans Diocese from 1979 until 2003 when she moved to Solihull. She held degrees from Cambridge University in Science and Theology, a London M.Th. degree, and the Diploma in Pastoral Studies from Birmingham University, as well as a Cambridge University Certificate in Education.

After secondary school teaching, she moved into adult work, first as a Chaplain's Assistant with the RAF, then as Head of Religious Studies in the College of All Saints, Tottenham, and finally as a Course Director on the St Albans Diocese Ministerial Training Scheme, preparing men and women for ordained and lay ministries. As a Hospital Chaplain she also worked among those with learning difficulties and in a Medical Rehabilitation Centre.

She had a love of the environment and concern for the issues it precipitates. Her chief relaxations were overseas travel, especially freelance in the developing world and in Israel/Palestine, and a deep interest in her large number of great-nieces and nephews.

This book developed out of an invitation from the Revd Richard Pyke, Vicar of St Mary's, Marshalswick, St Albans, who invited Mary Williams to take responsibility for the housegroups. Sounding people out, it became clear that what was required was a course on the Bible – and if it could show the unity of the Bible, all the better!

Investigation led Mary to feel that she would have to write such a course herself, and so *A Bird's-Eye View of the Bible* came into being. The housegroups took two years to work through the material, so the whole thing is thoroughly tried and tested.

St Luke's, St Albans, with a differing background, also used the material. Both St Mary's and St Luke's made useful suggestions, encouraging the publication of this book, as did also the Rt Revd Christopher Herbert, former Bishop of St Albans. Mary expressed gratitude to them and to the many others who have helped in the production of *A Bird's-Eye View of the Bible*.

Mary noted that particular thanks were due to Theo and Rachel Christophers, Jeff Crosby, Chris Lowry, Coralie Parsons and the Revd Peter Rich, who all commented on the text and made valuable suggestions, and to Jonathan Pyke and Matthew Burden.

Chris Bromley, with her superb desktop-publishing skills, brought *A Bird's-Eye View of the Bible* into a useable form before publication, and Mary expressed gratitude both to her and to her husband, Michael, who released her for this work, and supported Mary and Chris in many practical ways.

Finally, Mary wished to thank Canon Dennis Stamps, Ministerial Development Officer in St Albans Diocese, and his predecessor, Canon Anders Bergquist, for advice on publication.

Redemptorist Publications would like to add their thanks to Mary Williams' family, who worked faithfully after her death to bring about Mary's dream of publishing *A Bird's-Eye View of the Bible*.

A Bird's-Eye View of the Bible by Mary Williams About the Author Acknowledgements **contents** Bird's-Eye View of the Bible by Mary Williams About the Author Acknowledgements Contents A Bird's-Eye View of the Bible by Mary Williams About the Author Acknowledgements **contents** Bird's-Eye View of the Bible by Mary Williams About the Author Acknowledgement Contents A Bird's-Eye View of the Bible by Mary Williams About the Author Acknowledgements **contents** Bird's View of the Bible by Mary Williams About the Author Acknowledgements Contents A Bird's-Eye View of the Bible by

* Chapters in italics are for background reading. See page 6.

id Testament Abraham Moses Liberator Teacher The Law David The Shepherd King The Covenant Solomon
nificent The New Testament St Luke's Gospel Salvation History The Roman Empire Galatians Christian Paul Apo
e Gentiles The Pro **part one** Hosea The Exile The One and Only God Stories of Creation The Psalms The Wisd
ature Daniel The Passion Resurrection Jesus The Old Testament Abraham Moses Liberator Law David The Sheph
The Covenant Galatians The Roman Empire Acts of the Apo **introduction to the book** the Gentiles The
ment Abraham Moses Liberator Teacher The Law David The Shepherd King The Covenant Solomon the Magnific

The Book and You

What the book aims to do

The book is intended for groups, though it could also be used by individuals. It seeks:

- to enable you to find your way round the Bible by using its index;
- to help you perceive the over-arching unity of the Bible;
- to appreciate how human understanding of God develops over the biblical period;
- to explore the relevance of the Bible to situations today;
- to appeal to the whole person, heart as well as head!

These aims may seem ambitious! But you will find that, as you progress, the aims are imperceptibly being met in the most exciting way.

Who is the book for?

The book seeks to cater for:

- those with little or absolutely no knowledge of the Bible;
- those with some knowledge (though perhaps rather muddled), who wish to deepen it and piece it together into more of a unity;
- those with little time of their own between housegroup meetings;
- those with more time, who wish to dig deeper.

What the book consists of

The book explores the history and literature of the Bible, from both the Old and New Testaments.

The book is extremely flexible. If it is being used by a group, the group may decide to do more than one section at a time, or to take several sessions over a particular section of the book.

In the contents list, some chapter headings are in italics. These chapters provide background and information for the Bible study chapters. If the book is being used by a group, you may prefer to read these sections at home before group meetings.

In parts two and three, "History Embedded in Literature", the emphasis is on the history rather than the literature. In parts four and five, "Literature Spun from History", the emphasis switches primarily to the literature, which is more diverse as the issues broaden.

The layout of the book aims to be user-friendly, each session following a common pattern. First, an introductory background sets the topic to be studied in its context, accompanied by pictures and maps where helpful. Then follow the suggested passages to be read, alongside points to consider as you read them. Finally, possible issues for discussion are suggested. These show how the Bible can speak with relevance and power to current issues today.

Using the book as a group

If a group is using this book, it is good to check that people have read the relevant background chapter, and then read through the suggested passages and consider the points raised.

After the "Possible Issues for Discussion", the group might like to pray about the issues raised.

Old Testament Abraham Moses Liberator Teacher The Law David The Shepherd King The Covenant Solomon gnificent The New Testament St Luke's Gospel Salvation History The Roman Empire Galatians Christian Paul Ap he Gentiles The Prophets Amos Hosea The Exile The One and Only God Stories of Creation **part one** The Wis rature Daniel The Passion Resurrection Jesus The Old Testament Abraham Moses Liberator Law David The Shep g The Covenant **introduction to the book** of the Apostles Philippians Paul Apostle of the Gentiles Th tament Abraham Moses Liberator Teacher The Law David The Shepherd King The Covenant Solomon the Magnif

A note on possible issues for discussion

You may not want or be able to cover all of these. If this is being used by a group, the group can decide which questions they are particularly interested in. In any case, you will find that several of the issues recur in different contexts as you progress through the course.

All you need is a Bible

However, if you do not already possess one, it can be bewildering to know which one to buy that will be the most useful for you.

There are Bibles that are more traditional, stressing the most accurate translation (the Revised Standard Version and New Revised Standard Version; also the New English Bible and Revised English Bible), whereas others cater more for the general reader. (These include the Good News Bible and the New International Version – many people like the Good News Bible with its helpful line drawings.) If using this for group study, it is good to have a mixture of versions in the group, so that different slants of meaning can be compared.

Don't be afraid to ask for help in choosing the Bible that best suits you. But do have an up-to-date one – not your great-grandmother's dusted down! (For further information see "Versions of the Bible", page 13.)

Quotations in the text are from the New Revised Standard Version of the Bible, unless otherwise stated.

You may find it helpful to have some reference books, such as Bible commentaries which provide an introduction and comments on the biblical text. William Neil's *One Volume Bible Commentary* is particularly helpful and readily available; it could also be used later on to explore passages not contained in this book. The *New Jerome Biblical Commentary* provides detailed help; it is authoritative, up-to-date and very readable but, however, it is much more expensive.

The book and you

The book is devised to meet different people's needs, so do not be put off by it before you start. It is important that you take from the book what you want – what suits you.

Use it as a well or bran tub. Draw from the well however much you individually need. Exploring the bran tub may reveal certain unexpected surprises. Above all, go on and on questioning. Much of the Bible was written in answer to questions. It's also the best way to learn.

Old Testament Abraham Moses Liberator Teacher The Law David The Shepherd King The Covenant Solomon nificent The New Testament St Luke's Gospel Salvation History The Roman Empire Galatians Christian Paul Apo he Gentiles The Pro **part one** Hosea The Exile The One and Only God Stories of Creation The Psalms The Wis rature Daniel The Passion Resurrection Jesus The Old Testament Abraham Moses Liberator Law David The Sheph The Covenant Galatians The Roman Empire Acts of the Apo **introduction to the book** the Gentiles The ament Abraham Moses Liberator Teacher The Law David The Shepherd King The Covenant Solomon the Magnifi

Reference Section

THE BIBLE AS A LIBRARY

Books of the Bible

One way of categorising the books of the Bible is shown in the diagrams below in which they are presented as a library.

An alternative categorisation is shown on the following two pages.

OLD TESTAMENT LIBRARY

5	Books of **Law**	L
10	Books of **History**	H
4	Books of **Stories**	S
4	Books of **Poetry**	P
2	Books of **Wisdom**	W
14	Books of **Prophecy**	PR

NEW TESTAMENT LIBRARY

4	**Gospels**	G
1	Book of **History**	H
21	**Letters**	LE
1	Book of **Prophecy**	PR

Old Testament Abraham Moses Liberator Teacher The Law David The Shepherd King The Covenant Solomon gnificent The New Testament St Luke's Gospel Salvation History The Roman Empire Galatians Christian Paul Ap the Gentiles The Prophets Amos Hosea The Exile The One and Only God Stories of Creation **part one** The Wis erature Daniel The Passion Resurrection Jesus The Old Testament Abraham Moses Liberator Law David The Shep g The Covenant **introduction to the book** of the Apostles Philippians Paul Apostle of the Gentiles Th tament Abraham Moses Liberator Teacher The Law David The Shepherd King The Covenant Solomon the Magnif

Old Testament *(categorised according to the Jewish scriptures)*

GOD'S COVENANT OF LAW WITH ISRAEL

CATEGORY	BOOKS		CONTENTS
THE LAW ("Torah" in Hebrew) or Pentateuch ("Five Scrolls")	Genesis		Creation, patriarchs and family sagas. Moses and the Exodus. Rule of life (10 commandments) and laws for daily life and religion.
	Exodus		
	Leviticus		
	Numbers		
	Deuteronomy		
FORMER PROPHETS	Joshua		History of conquest of Canaan, united kingdom and divided kingdoms, up to fall of Jerusalem and exile.
	Judges		
	1 and 2 Samuel		
	1 and 2 Kings		
LATTER PROPHETS			
MAJOR	Isaiah		Prophets whose messages are written down. God's revelation through personal and national experiences results in a growing discernment of God's character. The prophets challenge the people to keep God's Covenant in every aspect of life: personal, family, commercial, political and international; and also in worship.
	Jeremiah		
	Ezekiel		
and **"THE TWELVE"**	1. Hosea	2. Joel	
	3. Amos	4. Obadiah	
	5. Jonah	6. Micah	
	7. Nahum	8. Habakkuk	
	9. Zephaniah	10. Haggai	
	11. Zechariah	12. Malachi	
THE WRITINGS	Ruth		History and historical stories.
	1 and 2 Chronicles		
	Esther		
	Ezra		
	Nehemiah		
	Job		Hymns, prayers, wise writings about faith and daily life.
	Psalms		
	Proverbs		
	Ecclesiastes		
	Lamentations		
	Song of Songs (or Song of Solomon)		Love song.
	Daniel		Apocalyptic literature (revealing "what is hidden"); also Wisdom literature.

The Apocrypha *(See also the following page)*
These Jewish books are found in some Bibles between the Old and New Testaments. They were written in Greek, mostly between 200 BC and AD 70.

The Apocrypha contains some important texts, notably the Wisdom books of the Wisdom of Solomon, and Ecclesiasticus (or the Wisdom of Jesus, the son of Sirach), and the historical books of 1 and 2 Maccabees.

New Testament

GOD'S COVENANT IN JESUS CHRIST WITH ALL PEOPLES

CATEGORY	BOOKS	CONTENTS
GOSPELS ("Good News")	Matthew	The Good News of the life, teaching, death and resurrection of Jesus Christ.
	Mark	
	Luke	
	John	
HISTORY	Acts of the Apostles	Birth and growth of early Church.
LETTERS (Epistles)		
From Paul	Romans	All deal with Christian belief and behaviour in daily life.
	1 and 2 Corinthians	
	Galatians	
	Ephesians	
	Philippians	
	Colossians	
	1 and 2 Thessalonians	
	1 and 2 Timothy	
	Titus	
	Philemon	
Unknown author	Hebrews	
"Catholic" (or "General") letters to Church universal from…	James	
	1 and 2 Peter	
	1, 2 and 3 John	
	Jude	
APOCALYPSE (revealing "what is hidden")	Book of Revelation	God's final victory in spite of all.

Old Testament Abraham Moses Liberator Teacher The Law David The Shepherd King The Covenant Solomon
nificent The New Testament St Luke's Gospel Salvation History The Roman Empire Galatians Christian Paul Apo
he Gentiles The Prophets Amos Hosea The Exile The One and Only God Stories of Creation **part one** The Wis
rature Daniel The Passion Resurrection Jesus The Old Testament Abraham Moses Liberator Law David The Shep
; The Covenant **introduction to the book** of the Apostles Philippians Paul Apostle of the Gentiles The
ament Abraham Moses Liberator Teacher The Law David The Shepherd King The Covenant Solomon the Magnifi

HOW THE BIBLE HAS COME DOWN TO US

The canon of scripture

Much is still unknown about how the books of the Bible reached us in their present form. The question revolves around the "canon" (from Greek *kanon*) – this word means "rule" or "principle". The question is, why just *these* books in our Bibles? And why in just *this* order?

The formation of the Old Testament and Apocrypha
The earliest texts and their organic development over the centuries

Though the Old Testament spans some 2,000 years of history, the earliest written records were not made until less than 1,000 years BC. History of the preceding centuries is therefore embedded in the earliest literature. The prophet Jeremiah dictates his prophecies onto a scroll (c. 605 BC). This is burned by the king, so Jeremiah then dictates an expanded edition (see Jeremiah chapter 36).

Over time, many texts were edited or added to, to make them more applicable to new situations in which the people now found themselves, or to give a new slant to past events. Even so, "updated" texts still generally retain and reveal their earlier origin. Examples of organic growth of Old Testament texts may be seen in the description of the crossing of the Red Sea (page 25), and also in Psalm 89, where an expansion of the original Psalm in honour of King David (verses 1-36) grapples with what sense can be made of God's promises to David, now that there is no longer a king.

The Old Testament becomes "fixed"

The first part of the Bible to be "fixed" – perhaps around the time of the scribe Ezra (date debatable; possibly around the end of the fifth century BC) – was probably the Pentateuch (i.e. the first five books of the Old Testament). By the time of Jesus, there was the Pentateuch ("the Law"), and a body of historical and prophetic books ("the Prophets"). It is still unclear, however, whether the threefold standard division of the Jewish Bible into Law, Prophets and Writings dates from before or after the time of Jesus.

The Greek "Septuagint"

The history of the Old Testament canon is further complicated, because it "crystallised" along two somewhat different routes.

Following the exile, an increasingly large number of Jews lived outside Israel. Called the "Dispersion" (or "scattering", see page 49), they adhered to the Jewish religion, but were surrounded by Greek culture and spoke Greek. From the middle of the third century BC onwards, authorised Greek translations of the Hebrew Old Testament books were prepared in Alexandria in Egypt for the use of such Jews who formed a large minority of the city's population.

This so-called Septuagint version, often represented as LXX, because it was said to have been carried out by 72 translators, was hugely successful. St Paul was brought up on it and found it established throughout his missionary journeys, so that it became the scriptures of the Christian Church. It was the standard Bible also of all other New Testament writers. The Septuagint contains also certain books originally written in Greek (i.e. not translations of Hebrew texts), so that it possesses rather more books (and in a different order) than the (later?) Hebrew canon of the Old Testament.

Old Testament Abraham Moses Liberator Teacher The Law David The Shepherd King The Covenant Solomon gnificent The New Testament St Luke's Gospel Salvation History The Roman Empire Galatians Christian Paul Ap he Gentiles The Pro **part one** Hosea The Exile The One and Only God Stories of Creation The Psalms The Wis rature Daniel The Passion Resurrection Jesus The Old Testament Abraham Moses Liberator Law David The Shep g The Covenant Galatians The Roman Empire Acts of the Apo **introduction to the book** the Gentiles The ament Abraham Moses Liberator Teacher The Law David The Shepherd King The Covenant Solomon the Magnif

Christian translations of the scriptures

Early Christian translations of the Bible generally followed the Septuagint (i.e. Greek) version. The most famous of these translations is the Vulgate (meaning "spoken language") by St Jerome around AD 380. This became the official version of the Western Latin-speaking Church.

At the Reformation in the sixteenth century, the Reformers were anxious to get back to what they saw as the original sources. They therefore opted to follow the shorter Hebrew canon, and gave the name Apocrypha (meaning "what is hidden") to those books which were in the Greek Bible, but not in the Hebrew one.

The Roman Catholic and Orthodox Churches have always continued the early Christian practice of reading all the books of the Greek canon. The Lutheran Church, and other Churches of the continental Reformation, only accepted the authority of those books that were in the Hebrew canon. The Church of England steered a middle course, saying the Apocryphal books are "read for example of life and instruction of manners, but no point of doctrine shall be established thereby" (Article 6 from "The Thirty-nine Articles", which are printed at the back of the *Book of Common Prayer*).

The formation of the New Testament

The New Testament books were all written in Greek, and we understand better how their selection and order came about.

Paul himself, when dictating one of his letters, would have been totally unaware that he was writing "scripture", which would acquire an authority equal to or greater than the authority of Isaiah or Ezekiel. But by the end of the first century AD his writings were treasured by Christians.

The second century saw a great sifting of Christian writings, as the Christian communities determined which should be regarded as the divinely inspired words of God to his Church. On the one hand, many "Gnostic" (or secret) revelations were excluded. On the other, the Church included many books against the wishes of Marcion, a wealthy late-second-century shipowner and amateur theologian; he included only the Gospel of Luke and letters of Paul in his New Testament, and thought the Old Testament ought not to be read by Christians at all.

The process of selecting and editing was substantially complete by the mid fourth century. One of its most interesting and important features is that it left us a fourfold portrait of Jesus in four separate Gospels. The Church deliberately decided not to harmonise the stories into one single Gospel, although some private attempts were made to do so.

Differences between Greek and Hebrew texts

As well as differences in the number and order of books, there are also differences of text between the Greek and Hebrew traditions. (For example, Greek Daniel contains many expansions, including the song that the Three Children sing in the fiery furnace: "Bless the Lord, all ye works of the Lord: praise him and magnify him for ever.")

In 1947, the Dead Sea Scrolls were discovered; they are the remains of a library of a strict Jewish community on the shores of the Dead Sea. These scrolls give us, for the first time, Hebrew biblical manuscripts from around the time of Jesus which are 1,000 years older than the previously oldest known standard medieval manuscripts of the Hebrew Bible. However, they do not resolve which version of biblical books is the original: "short" and "long" texts of Jeremiah turn up in the same cave.

Old Testament Abraham Moses Liberator Teacher The Law David The Shepherd King The Covenant Solomon nificent The New Testament St Luke's Gospel Salvation History The Roman Empire Galatians Christian Paul Apo he Gentiles The Prophets Amos Hosea The Exile The One and Only God Stories of Creation **part one** The Wis rature Daniel The Passion Resurrection Jesus The Old Testament Abraham Moses Liberator Law David The Sheph The Covenant **introduction to the book** of the Apostles Philippians Paul Apostle of the Gentiles The ament Abraham Moses Liberator Teacher The Law David The Shepherd King The Covenant Solomon the Magnifi

VERSIONS OF THE BIBLE

The versions differ, depending on:

(a) the lack of agreement over Old Testament content (see preceding discussion);

(b) whether the Old Testament translation is made from Hebrew or Greek;

(c) sometimes, too, the theological position the translators occupy – e.g. whether to translate Isaiah 7:14 as "a virgin shall conceive and bear a son" or "a young woman shall conceive and bear a son" (the more literal translation).

AV   Authorised Version, 1611; in USA, called the King James Version

RV   Revised Version, 1881–85: minor updating of language of AV for clarity

NEB   New English Bible: the first modern translation in contemporary English (NT 1961 and 1970; OT and Apocrypha 1970)

REB   Revised English Bible (1989 revision of NEB): adds inclusive language

RSV   Revised Standard Version (1946–52); scholarly accurate translation

NRSV   New Revised Standard Version (Anglicised version 1989–95): adds inclusive language

GNB   Good News Bible (1976): uses everyday natural English for those for whom English is a second language. Helpful line drawings

NIV   New International Version (1978 USA; 1979 Britain): used by mainly conservative churches; excludes the Apocrypha. It aims at clear and natural English

JB   Jerusalem Bible (1966): a Roman Catholic translation, so books of the Apocrypha are integrated among books of the OT

NJB   New Jerusalem Bible (1985): adds inclusive language

Further notes on versions:
Both **JB** and **NJB** use the sacred name Yahweh for God in the OT.

Printed versions of **REB** and **NRSV** are available both without the Apocrypha, and also with it in a separate section.

RSV and **NRSV** contain an enlarged Apocrypha as recognised in the Eastern Churches and which is printed separately. They therefore provide an acceptable version in Protestant, Roman Catholic and Eastern Orthodox Churches.

A note on the gender of God

Traditionally, in both biblical and subsequent Christian civilisations characterised by male domination, God has been referred to as "he".

In some quarters today, there is a move to right the impression this gives that God is male by substituting the noun "God" for the pronoun; this, however, makes for somewhat cumbersome language.

Images of God in the Bible illustrate both masculine and feminine characteristics. The story of creation itself describes God as making man and woman in "our image" (Genesis 1:26-27). This indicates that both man and woman reflect God's image, the more so when they are united. Further examples show how Hosea sees God as a mother carrying Israel like a child and teaching him to walk (Hosea 11:1, 4). Jesus too likens God to a woman searching for a lost coin (Luke 15:8-10), and himself to a hen gathering her chicks under her wing (Luke 13:34).

Both genders are therefore subsumed in God, though God also transcends gender. For the sake of simplicity and common usage, this study uses the pronoun "he" for God.

Old Testament Abraham Moses Liberator Teacher The Law David The Shepherd King The Covenant Solomon gnificent The New Testament St Luke's Gospel Salvation History The Roman Empire Galatians Christian Paul Ap he Gentiles The Pro **part one** Hosea The Exile The One and Only God Stories of Creation The Psalms The Wis rature Daniel The Passion Resurrection Jesus The Old Testament Abraham Moses Liberator Law David The Shep g The Covenant Galatians The Roman Empire Acts of the Apo **introduction to the book** the Gentiles Th tament Abraham Moses Liberator Teacher The Law David The Shepherd King The Covenant Solomon the Magnif

HISTORICAL TIME CHARTS

The dates given are as accurate as possible. However, dates before the time of David (c. 1000 BC) are bound to be approximate, and there is vigorous disagreement among biblical scholars as to what exactly happened, and when.

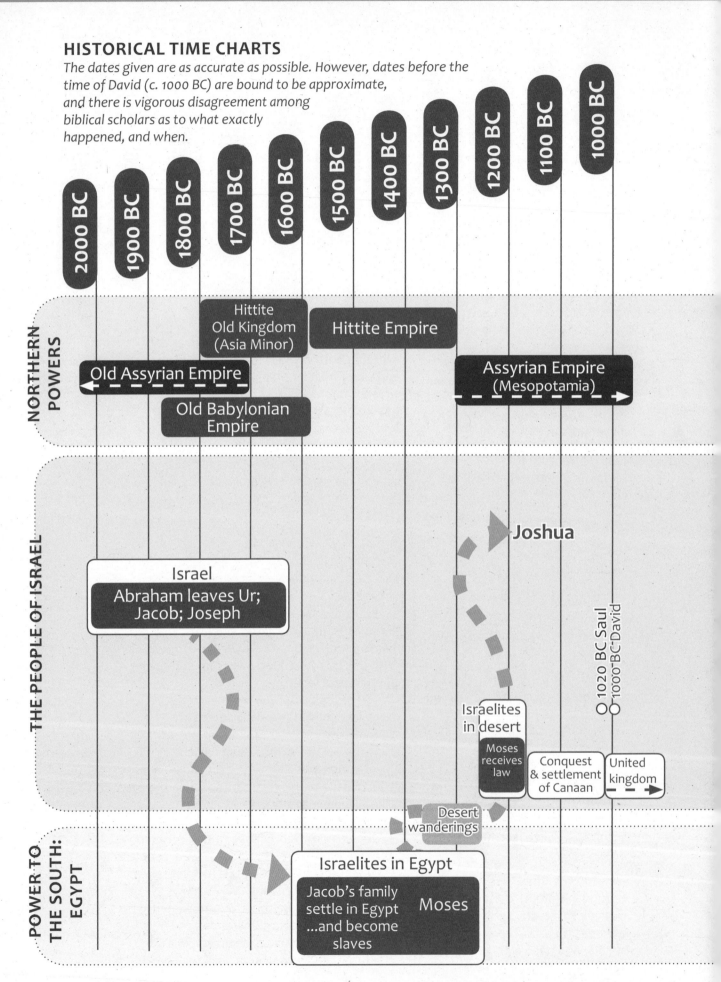

Old Testament Abraham Moses Liberator Teacher The Law David The Shepherd King The Covenant Solomon
gnificent The New Testament St Luke's Gospel Salvation History The Roman Empire Galatians Christian Paul Ap
he Gentiles The Prophets Amos Hosea The Exile The One and Only God Stories of Creation **part one** The Wis
rature Daniel The Passion Resurrection Jesus The Old Testament Abraham Moses Liberator Law David The Shep
g The Covenant **introduction to the book** of the Apostles Philippians Paul Apostle of the Gentiles Th
tament Abraham Moses Liberator Teacher The Law David The Shepherd King The Covenant Solomon the Magnif

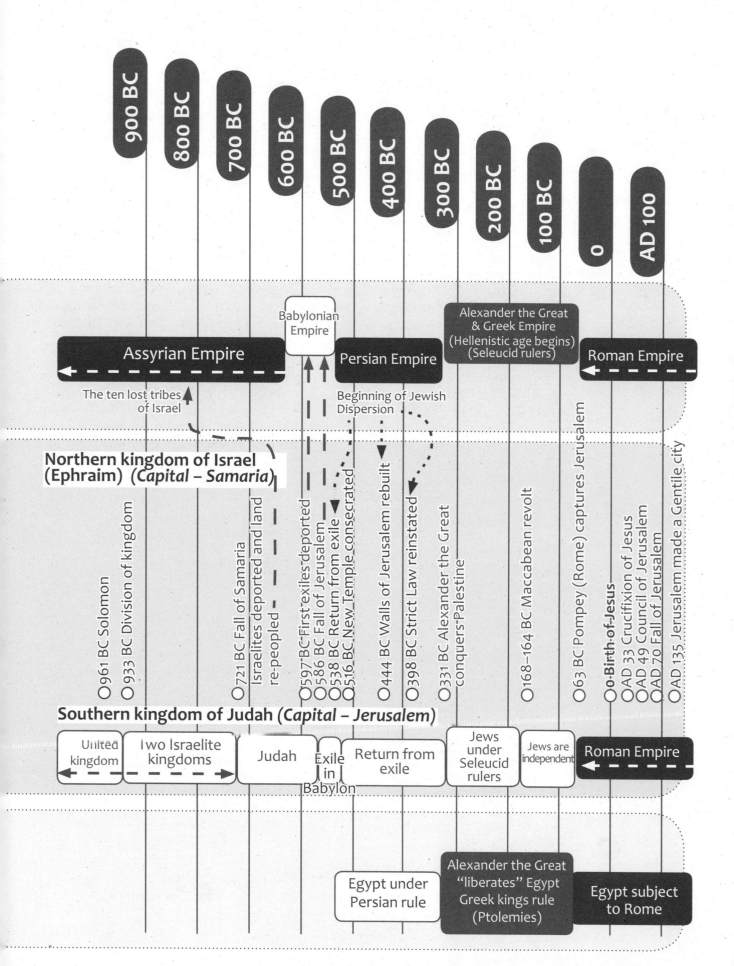

Old Testament Abraham Moses Liberator Teacher The Law David The Shepherd King The Covenant Solomon
nificent The New Testament St Luke's Gospel Salvation History The Roman Empire Galatians Christian Paul Apo
he Gentiles The Pro **part one** Hosea The Exile The One and Only God Stories of Creation The Psalms The Wis
rature Daniel The Passion Resurrection Jesus The Old Testament Abraham Moses Liberator Law David The Sheph
The Covenant Galatians The Roman Empire Acts of the Apo **introduction to the book** the Gentiles The
ament Abraham Moses Liberator Teacher The Law David The Shepherd King The Covenant Solomon the Magnifi

A Brief Introduction to the Bible

The developing revelation of God

The Bible relates the developing revelation of God. It is not *God* who changes – he is "the same yesterday and today and for ever" (Hebrews 13:8). But people's *ideas* of God change, depending on who they are, where they are and when they are living.

Sometimes quite ordinary people rise to quite extraordinary heights and then pass on their insights to the rest of us – as did the prophets and (as you will see later in the session on Philippians) as did Leonard Wilson, whose daughter said there was "nothing special" about him. So our corporate idea and experience of God continues to grow, for we can never know God completely. The word "God" itself implies he is beyond our total comprehension.

Jesus reveals as much of God as it is possible for us to comprehend, and so the revelation is in one sense complete. But we nevertheless continue to learn as we unpack ever more of the meaning of the revelation of God in Jesus for us, and as the Holy Spirit continues to lead us on into the truth of each new situation (John 16:12-13). So God continues gradually to unfold himself to us in many ways today. One way is when a verse or passage of the Bible suddenly becomes live for us.

The nature of biblical revelation

The overarching theme is to come to know God individually in a personal sense, and corporately through living together. God's dealings with an individual or a nation start with *where they are* (and not where God might wish them to be), thus enabling them to know God individually and corporately in their own lives.

Very gradually, a notion evolves that *love* is behind and under *all* things (in spite, so often, of events that appear to contradict that). Humanity's destiny is to grow in knowing and experiencing that love.

The Old Testament shows how, through Abraham and Moses, God entered into a Covenant with a particular people, through which they perceived something of God's character and requirements. Eventually, a very few came to recognise that even suffering can be a means of growth and revelation.

The Covenant is fulfilled in the New Testament through Jesus' life, death and resurrection, making possible new life for all who enter into it through baptism.

The word "covenant" means an agreement, or promise, or relationship which is legally binding and may be compared with marriage.

God continually invites us (like Abraham and Mary and all those in biblical times) to cooperate with the divine purpose, which reaches its culmination in the freedom and love revealed and made available to all through Jesus. St John invites each individual to share his experience of being "the disciple whom Jesus loves".

We are shown what it is to be loved *unequivocally* by God *as we are now*, and as we have it in us to become. Experiencing the depth of such love, which reaches right down into the heart, has a powerful transforming effect. It marks the distinction between "knowing about" God and actually "knowing" God personally.

Old Testament Abraham Moses Liberator Teacher The Law David The Shepherd King The Covenant Solomon gnificent The New Testament St Luke's Gospel Salvation History The Roman Empire Galatians Christian Paul Ap he Gentiles The Prophets Amos Hosea The Exile The One and Only God Stories of Creation **part one** The Wis rature Daniel The Passion Resurrection Jesus The Old Testament Abraham Moses Liberator Law David The Shep g The Covenant **introduction to the book** of the Apostles Philippians Paul Apostle of the Gentiles Th ament Abraham Moses Liberator Teacher The Law David The Shepherd King The Covenant Solomon the Magnif

Looking at the Bible as a whole

To help in perceiving the distinction, yet unity, of different sections of the biblical narrative, it may be understood as a drama, comparable to a play of Shakespeare's.

Prologue	Genesis 1–11
Act 1	Genesis 12 (Abraham to the end of the Old Testament)
Act 2	The Good News of Jesus Christ (the Gospels)
Act 3	The early Church (the Acts of the Apostles and the Letters or Epistles)
Epilogue	The book of Revelation

The Prologue and the Epilogue are outside history proper, thus placing the historical Acts 1, 2 and 3 within the context of eternity, which is the backcloth against which Acts 1, 2 and 3 are staged.

When, therefore, in Part 2 we start with Abraham, we are starting with the earliest recorded historical person in the Bible – even though we cannot be exactly sure of his date.

In Part 4, we consider the early chapters of Genesis (the Prologue), which consider the perennial (eternal) questions humanity asks:

> who made me?
> what sort of being am I?
> what is the purpose of life?

The Epilogue proclaims God's final and ultimate victory over all.

The time spread of the books of the Bible

The Bible contains 66 books (39 in the Old Testament and 27 in the New).

The Old Testament (OT) spans 2,000 years of history before Christ, but was actually written down during the time from 1,000 years before Christ.

The New Testament (NT) was all written from around AD 49 to not later than AD 120 – i.e. in less than 100 years.

For different ways of categorising the books of the Bible, refer to the Reference Section ("The Bible as a Library", pages 8-10). (Note that the books of the Apocrypha are written from a Jewish angle, even if written in the first century AD.)

The Bible and truth

(a) The Bible as history
Most historical accounts are written from a particular viewpoint – generally that of the victor (in a dispute or war).

Biblical history is written by those who believe in God. Therefore individuals' lives or national events are assessed as to how they match up to, or thwart, God's will and purpose for his people.

(b) The Bible as literature
The Bible contains many different types of literature. There are straightforward historical accounts (although always told or evaluated from a religious angle), such as the stories of David. There are also letters, poetry, proverbs, parables, prophecy, myths and apocalyptic literature.

All these convey religious truth, though through different literary forms. Sometimes it is more helpful to ask: "What is the truth contained in this story?", rather than just "Is it true?" (which generally means "Is it literally true?").

Old Testament Abraham Moses Liberator Teacher The Law David The Shepherd King The Covenant Solomon nificent The New Testament St Luke's Gospel Salvation History The Roman Empire Galatians Christian Paul Apo he Gentiles The Pro **part one** Hosea The Exile The One and Only God Stories of Creation The Psalms The Wis rature Daniel The Passion Resurrection Jesus The Old Testament Abraham Moses Liberator Law David The Shepl The Covenant Galatians The Roman Empire Acts of the Apo **introduction to the book** the Gentiles The ament Abraham Moses Liberator Teacher The Law David The Shepherd King The Covenant Solomon the Magnifi

For example, "My Love is like a red, red rose" (Robert Burns) we recognise as poetic rather than literal truth, and Aesop's fable of the race of the hare and the tortoise (in which the hare takes a rest on the way, enabling the plodding tortoise to win) conveys a truth about life in a way similar to the parables of Jesus and the stories in Genesis 1 to 11.

Some passages contain such depth of insight that they can be understood at different levels. (Such passages include Isaiah chapter 53; the parables of Jesus, for which he so rarely gave interpretations; and St John's Gospel.)

(c) The Gospels
The Gospels are not straight history or biography, but a quite unique form of literature. They present a quite unique event – God incarnate among us.

The word "gospel" means "good news" – good news indeed!

A minimal time chart of biblical times to the present day – *very* approximate!

2000 BC	Abraham	(actually any time between 2000 and 1600 BC)
1500 BC	Moses	(probably 1250 BC)
1000 BC	David	
500 BC	Exile in Babylon	(actually 586-537 BC)
0 BC/AD	Jesus	
AD 500	Byzantine Empire	(actually 320s to Crusades)
AD 1000	Crusades	(actually 11th to 13th century)
AD 1500	Turkish Empire	(actually 13th to 20th century)
AD 2000	Today	

Old Testament Abraham Moses Liberator Teacher The Law David The Shepherd King The Covenant Solomon
gnificent The New Testament St Luke's Gospel Salvation History The Roman Empire Galatians **part two** Ap
he Gentiles The Prophets Amos Hose **history embedded in literature** of Creation The Psalms The Wis
rature Daniel The Passion Resurrection Jesus The Old Testament Abraham Moses Liberator Law David The Shep
g The **old testament** The Roman Empire Acts of the Apostles Philippians Paul Apostle of the Gentiles Th
tament Abraham Moses Liberator Teacher The Law David The Shepherd King The Covenant Solomon the Magnif

Introduction to the Old Testament

THE FERTILE CRESCENT

Note how the crescent follows the major rivers and coastline, skirting the deserts of Arabia, Sinai and the Sahara. This explains why it is called the Fertile Crescent. (The area of the Nile delta is called Goshen.)

The land of Canaan/Israel/Palestine is the same in size as Wales. Its importance derives from its strategic situation at the crossroads of Europe, Asia and Africa.

Situated between the major political and military powers – to the north, Mesopotamia, and to the south, Egypt – it lay on the trade routes, while warring armies of the major powers clashed on its soil.

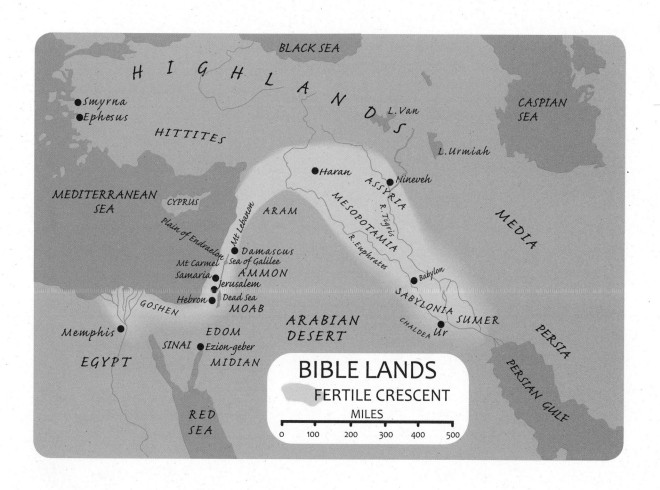

19

Old Testament Abraham Moses Liberator Teacher The Law David The Shepherd King The Covenant Solomon
nificent **part two** tament St Luke's Gospel Salvation History The Roman Empire Galatians Christian Paul Apo
ne Gentiles The Prophets Amos Hose **history embedded in literature** of Creation The Psalms The Wisc
ature Daniel The Passion Resurrection Jesus The Old Testament Abraham Moses Liberator Law David The Sheph
The Covenant Galatians The Roman Empire Acts of the Apostles Philippians Paul Apo **old testament** The
ament Abraham Moses Liberator Teacher The Law David The Shepherd King The Covenant Solomon the Magnifi

A brief survey

The historical section of the Old Testament from Genesis chapter 11 onwards starts with Abraham, a native of Ur, situated near the Persian Gulf.

Abraham set out on a long geographical and spiritual journey in search of the true God. The foundation for the unfolding revelation was made in God's threefold promise to Abraham:

- to give him a land (the land of Canaan);

- to give him descendants (in spite of his and his wife's advanced age); and

- through his descendants, to bless the whole world (Christians would say, through Jesus).

God entered a Covenant with Abraham to this effect, and Abraham, the man of faith, believed it and accepted it.

The Covenant was ratified and further developed with Moses, the liberator of his people from slavery in Egypt, and the teacher of the Law that God gave for his people.

The conquest of Canaan took place slowly, with the Hebrews, a nomadic people, living alongside the Canaanites, an agricultural people – except when they clashed. Gradually, the Hebrews absorbed the Canaanite people. However, the Canaanite religion of Baal, the god of agriculture, lived on as a constant challenge to the worship of the God of the Hebrews.

David's conquest of the Canaanite city of Jerusalem united the twelve Hebrew tribes under himself as king.

The Hebrew kingship was not an absolute monarchy as in the surrounding countries, since it was based on the Covenant. This meant that both God and the people had rights which the king had to accommodate. The shepherd king therefore best describes the desired model of Hebrew kingship.

Solomon, whose reign started so promisingly, later forgot this nature of kingship, resulting in the twelve tribes becoming split. Ten broke off to found the prosperous northern kingdom of Israel (sometimes called Ephraim), which lay on the international trade route. Its capital was Samaria, and a new line of kings was established. The two remaining mountainous tribes in the south (Judah and Benjamin) formed the kingdom of Judah. Jerusalem continued as their capital, and their kings were descended from David.

The failure of both kingdoms to live up to the demands of the Covenant finally led to their downfall. Israel fell to Assyria in 721 BC, and the Israelites were carried off and became absorbed by the Assyrians. When Judah fell to Babylon in 586 BC, the Jews remained distinct in exile. It was here, in a foreign land, that the belief evolved that the God of the Hebrews was indeed the God of the whole universe.

Some fifty years later, under Persia, the Jews were permitted to return to Judah. The return, however, was spasmodic. From the time of the exile, we enter the age of the Dispersion, referring to the spread of Jews into foreign countries.

The Old Testament era drew to a close with the first *religious* persecution of Jews from 168 to 164 BC. This resulted in the writing of the book of Daniel, which includes for the first time belief in a partial resurrection of the dead.

Old Testament Abraham Moses Liberator Teacher The Law David The Shepherd King The Covenant Solomon gnificent The New Testament St Luke's Gospel Salvation History The Roman Empire Galatians **part two** I Ap he Gentiles The Prophets Amos Hose **history embedded in literature** of Creation The Psalms The Wis rature Daniel The Passion Resurrection Jesus The Old Testament Abraham Moses Liberator Law David The Shep g The **old testament** The Roman Empire Acts of the Apostles Philippians Paul Apostle of the Gentiles Th tament Abraham Moses Liberator Teacher The Law David The Shepherd King The Covenant Solomon the Magnif

Abraham – The Father of Us All

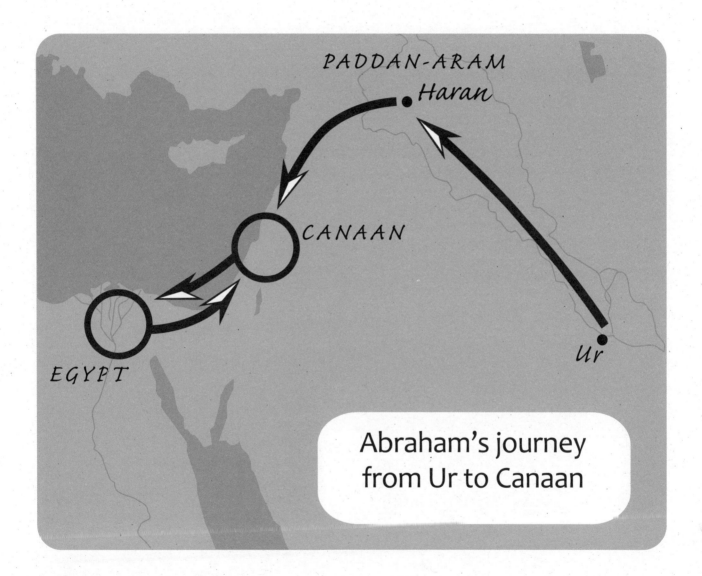

Abraham's journey from Ur to Canaan

Abraham is the first truly historical person we meet in the Old Testament, living sometime between 2000 and 1600 BC. It was, however, for religious reasons his story was remembered – he is pre-eminently the man of faith and trust in God, and therefore of obedience to him. Ur, his native city, had a highly developed civilisation, and Abraham was a rich man and tribal chief. But something in Ur dissatisfied him – possibly the command to worship the Sun-god – and he set out to seek his freedom, and to search for the true God. He was therefore open to God.

SUGGESTED READINGS AND POINTS TO CONSIDER AS YOU READ

Abraham's family	Genesis 11:31-32
God's promise to Abraham	Genesis 12:1-5
• What are the three strands of God's promise to Abraham – the promise to which God will always remain faithful? • What is Abraham's response (look at verse 4)? *The response is put in three succinct consecutive words (in versions other than the New English Bible, Revised English Bible and Good News Bible): "So Abram went."* *It reminds us that we have freedom to serve or reject God: he will never force us.* *(Abraham's response at the beginning of the Old Testament is paralleled by Mary's unconditional response to the angel Gabriel in Luke 1:38 at the beginning of the New Testament.)*	
Birth of Isaac *Note that Isaac means "laughter" (Genesis 18:12-13, see 17:17).*	Genesis 21:1-7
Sacrifice of Isaac *(the binding of Isaac in Jewish tradition)*	Genesis 22:1-19
• Read the passage carefully; note the build-up of suspense. *(NB Other religions practised sacrifice of the firstborn son. Might this have influenced Abraham?)* • Was Abraham right to be ready to sacrifice Isaac? • Was he right in believing God was calling him to do this? • In what ways do you think God "speaks" to us? • Why do you think this passage is important? *(Mount Moriah is identified with what later became the Temple Mount in Jerusalem, sacred to Jew, Christian and Muslim, all of whom regard Abraham as the "father"/founder of their faith.)*	
New Testament assessment of Abraham *Note how in Romans 4:16c-17a Abraham is described as "the father of us all" (Romans 4:3, 16-22).*	Hebrews 11:8-19

Old Testament Abraham Moses Liberator Teacher The Law David The Shepherd King The Covenant Solomon gnificent The New Testament St Luke's Gospel Salvation History The Roman Empire Galatians **part two** Ap he Gentiles The Prophets Amos Hose **history embedded in literature** of Creation The Psalms The Wis rature Daniel The Passion Resurrection Jesus The Old Testament Abraham Moses Liberator Law David The Shep The **old testament** The Roman Empire Acts of the Apostles Philippians Paul Apostle of the Gentiles Th ament Abraham Moses Liberator Teacher The Law David The Shepherd King The Covenant Solomon the Magnif

POSSIBLE ISSUES FOR DISCUSSION

1   How do we understand promises today?

Are they "for ever"?

2   In what ways do people still search for freedom and for God, even at considerable personal cost, as did Abraham?

3   "Abraham believed God" (Romans 4:3).

But Abraham's (and Sarah's) laughter at the idea of a son in their old age (Genesis 17:17 and 18:12-13) suggests his faith contained an element of scepticism as he searched after the true God.

Hans Küng (a German theologian) has said: "Doubt is the shadow cast by faith", and "Faith is like the sea; the further into it you go, the deeper you get."

Can faith be "proved"?

Can faith ever be 100%?

4   Abraham learnt a new truth about God in his readiness to sacrifice Isaac.

If we also are ready to act on what we think God requires of us, may we too sometimes learn new truths which we otherwise would not know?

Old Testament Abraham Moses Liberator Teacher The Law David The Shepherd King The Covenant Solomon gnificent The New Testament St Luke's Gospel Salvation History The Roman Empire Galatians Ap he Gentiles The Prophets Amos Hose **history embedded in literature** of Creation The Psalms The Wis rature Daniel The Passion Resurrection Jesus The Old Testament Abraham Moses Liberator Law David The Shep The **old testament** The Roman Empire Acts of the Apostles Philippians Paul Apostle of the Gentiles Th ament Abraham Moses Liberator Teacher The Law David The Shepherd King The Covenant Solomon the Magnif

How the First Five Books of the Old Testament Were Written

How the First Five Books of the Old Testament Were Written

Consider how today we acquire and process information and ideas in daily life:

e.g.

- reports of an accident from the angle of different witnesses;
- different newspaper accounts reporting the same incident;
- the internet;
- Chinese whispers, and the resulting muddle which may result from mishearing.
- Do you say "Northern Ireland" or "the north of Ireland"?

- What difference of understanding do these uses convey?
- "Bad" King John (who gave us Magna Carta): has he been stereotyped?

These examples all show that storytelling depends on who you are, where you are and when you live.

Scholars have carried out detective work on the Bible to discover how it came to be written.

> "Biblical criticism", from the Greek word *krisis* which means "judging" or "assessing", is the process by which scholars "weigh up" the internal clues present in the literature itself.

For the first 1,000 years of Old Testament history (from 2000 to 1000 BC), the stories were handed down by word of mouth, probably around the campfire at night. This is called the **oral tradition**; it depended on who you were and where you were – so that though the stories might have much in common, they differ in detail.

The "classical" theory of how the books of the Law of Moses came to be written

Date BC	Name of Text	Name for God in text	Where written
950–850	J (Jahwist)	Yahweh (LORD) (Jehovah)	Judah
c. 750	E (Elohist)	Elohim (God)	Ephraim (Israel)
621	D (Deuteronomist)	LORD your God	Jerusalem (Judah)
c. 540	P (Priestly writers)	LORD	Exiles in Babylon

J & E becomes JE

J E & D becomes JED

JED becomes P

Example of combination of sources

In the crossing of the Red Sea (see notes on page 28), the Priestly editor (c. 540 BC) describes dramatically how Moses enabled the crossing – but the earlier J writers (950–850 BC) give the natural cause of the crossing (Exodus 14:21b).

EXODUS 14: THE J VERSION FROM THE NEW REVISED STANDARD VERSION

21b: The LORD drove the sea back by a strong east wind all night, and turned the sea into dry land;

24:     At the morning watch the LORD in the pillar of fire and cloud looked down upon the Egyptian army, and threw the Egyptian army into panic.

25:     He clogged their chariot wheels so that they turned with difficulty. The Egyptians said, "Let us flee from the Israelites, for the LORD is fighting for them against Egypt."

27b: At dawn the sea returned to its normal depth. As the Egyptians fled before it, the LORD tossed the Egyptians into the sea.

Compare this to the Priestly version where over the centuries Moses has become a larger-than-life figure.

EXODUS 14 : THE P VERSION FROM THE NEW REVISED STANDARD VERSION

21a: Then Moses stretched out his hand over the sea.

22:     The Israelites went into the sea on dry ground, the waters forming a wall for them on their right and on their left.

23:     The Egyptians pursued, and went into the sea after them, all of Pharaoh's horses, chariots, and chariot drivers.

26:     Then the Lord said to Moses, "Stretch out your hand over the sea, so that the water may come back upon the Egyptians, upon their chariots and chariot drivers."

27a: So Moses stretched out his hand over the sea, and

28:     the waters returned and covered the chariots and the chariot drivers, the entire army of Pharaoh that had followed them into the sea; not one of them remained.

29:     But the Israelites walked on dry ground through the sea, the waters forming a wall for them on their right and on their left.

Resonances between the story of creation and the crossing of the Red Sea

1. In Genesis chapter 1, which gives the Priestly version of creation, God divides the waters under the firmament from those above (verses 6-8).

    This concept is echoed in the Priestly version of the walls of water divided at the Red Sea.

2. Just as God created the world in the P (Genesis 1:1 – 2:4a) and JE (Genesis 2:4b-25) stories of creation, so the Exodus and Covenant at Mount Sinai are the point where God creates his own special people.

Different sources
These texts (J, E, D and P) show

(a) reinterpretation in the light of new situations, which indicates:
(b) a development in the people's understanding of God.

Current scholarship is less certain than the "classical" theory about delineating the various component parts. Instead, it is more interested in the final text as we now have it. (See page 53, which refers to the Gospels, but a similar movement has also taken place with regard to Old Testament texts.)

Moses' death is described in Deuteronomy chapter 34. To name the books of the Law after Moses does not therefore mean he wrote them, but that they are written "in tune" with Moses' teaching.

Similarly, the Psalms, only some of which David wrote, are all named after him as in the spirit of David, the psalmist. Solomon, renowned for his wisdom, lends his name to subsequent Wisdom writings. This is how later authors claim authority for their writings. There was no law of copyright.

Old Testament Abraham Moses Liberator Teacher The Law David The Shepherd King The Covenant Solomon
nificent The New Testament St Luke's Gospel Salvation History The Roman Empire Galatians **part two** Apo
e Gentiles The Prophets Amos Hose **history embedded in literature** of Creation The Psalms The Wis
rature Daniel The Passion Resurrection Jesus The Old Testament Abraham Moses Liberator Law David The Shep
The **old testament** The Roman Empire Acts of the Apostles Philippians Paul Apostle of the Gentiles The
ament Abraham Moses Liberator Teacher The Law David The Shepherd King The Covenant Solomon the Magnifi

Moses – Liberator and Teacher

Abraham's descendants, encountering famine, went down to Egypt and in due course became slaves serving Pharaoh Rameses II on his massive building projects. Moses, saved at birth by Pharaoh's daughter and brought up as an Egyptian prince, feels his Hebrew blood coursing when he encounters God in the burning bush at Mount Sinai (also called Mount Horeb).

He returns to lead his people to freedom and, after ten plagues, Pharaoh releases them. The Hebrews are spared from the tenth plague (in which the angel of death kills Egypt's firstborn sons) by placing the blood of a lamb killed in sacrifice on their doorposts and this, together with the escape over the Red Sea, becomes remembered as the "Passover" (otherwise called the Feast of Unleavened Bread), the annual Jewish springtime feast of deliverance from slavery to freedom.

During the Hebrews' forty years in the wilderness, at Mount Sinai God offers to be their God – they have now seen him in action, so know something of him. The people

agree, and freely enter into a Covenant/ Testament of union with God and each other, which is binding on each side and is sealed with blood. So the twelve tribes become one people.

The Hebrew language used only consonants without vowels. It is likely that Moses led the Hebrews from the Nile Delta (Goshen) over the Sea of Reeds where the Suez Canal runs today, rather than towards the natural barrier of the Red Sea. Without the vowels, the two words are indistinguishable in Hebrew.

On Moses' death, Joshua (the name becomes Jesus in New Testament Aramaic) leads the people over Jordan into the Promised Land.

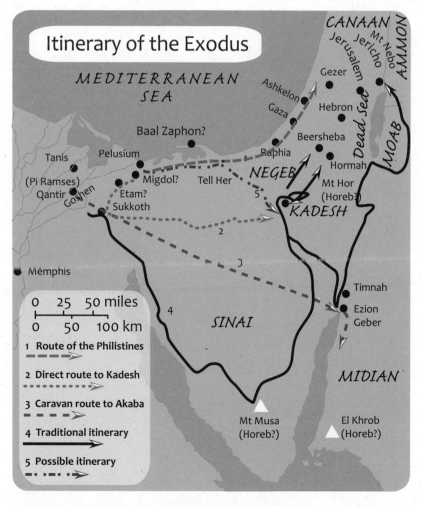

Itinerary of the Exodus

MEDITERRANEAN SEA

CANAAN
AMMON
Jerusalem Jericho Mt Nebo
Gezer
Ashkelon
Gaza
Hebron
Beersheba
Dead Sea
MOAB
Raphia
Baal Zaphon?
NEGEB
Pelusium
Hormah
Tanis
Migdol? Tell Her
Mt Hor (Horeb?)
(Pi Ramses)
Qantir Goshen
Etam?
Sukkoth
5
KADESH
2
3
Memphis
Timnah
Ezion Geber

0   25   50 miles
0   50   100 km

4   SINAI

MIDIAN

Mt Musa (Horeb?)
El Khrob (Horeb?)

1 **Route of the Philistines**
‐ ‐ ‐ ‐ ▶

2 **Direct route to Kadesh**
··········▶

3 **Caravan route to Akaba**
‐ ‐ ‐ ‐ ▶

4 **Traditional itinerary**
——————▶

5 **Possible itinerary**
‐ ·‐ ·‐ ·▶

Old Testament Abraham Moses Liberator Teacher The Law David The Shepherd King The Covenant Solomon
nificent **part two** tament St Luke's Gospel Salvation History The Roman Empire Galatians Christian Paul Ap
e Gentiles The Prophets Amos Hose **history embedded in literature** of Creation The Psalms The Wis
ature Daniel The Passion Resurrection Jesus The Old Testament Abraham Moses Liberator Law David The Shep
The Covenant Galatians The Roman Empire Acts of the Apostles Philippians Paul Apo **old testament** The
ament Abraham Moses Liberator Teacher The Law David The Shepherd King The Covenant Solomon the Magnifi

SUGGESTED READINGS AND POINTS TO CONSIDER AS YOU READ

God's revelation and Moses' call at the burning bush At the burning bush, Moses meets God in a profound religious experience. God says he is the God of Abraham, Isaac and Jacob, and reveals his name (i.e. his character) as **I AM** (equally validly translated as **I WILL BE**). The Hebrew consonants are **YHWH**, for Yahweh, a name too sacred for Jews to utter. • What do you think God's name tells us of his character? Moses jibs at his call and makes several excuses. • What are they?	Exodus 3:1-15,19-21
The Passover *Note how verse 39 explains the alternative name for the Passover Festival.*	Exodus 12:1-13,29-39
Crossing of the Red Sea The Sea of Reeds, a marsh north of the western arm of the Red Sea, is sometimes passable. • What, for the Priestly writers (sixth century BC), enabled the crossing? • How does this compare with the earlier J writers' version (tenth century BC)? • What is the natural cause in J's account? • Do the writers still see this as a miracle?	Exodus 14:5-29
Covenant at Mount Sinai	Exodus 19:1-8
The Ten Commandments	Exodus 20:1-17
Sealing of the Covenant with blood (The altar, representing God, is sprinkled and then, after their assent, the people are also sprinkled, so forging the union between God and his people.) For the Hebrews, blood symbolised life, which only God could give. The last three references show how the Covenant/Testament/Agreement is entered into. It becomes legally binding by being ratified by blood so as to be life-giving.	Exodus 24:3-8

Old Testament Abraham Moses Liberator Teacher The Law David The Shepherd King The Covenant Solomon
nificent The New Testament St Luke's Gospel Salvation History The Roman Empire Galatians **part two** Ap
e Gentiles The Prophets Amos Hose **history embedded in literature** of Creation The Psalms The Wis
ature Daniel The Passion Resurrection Jesus The Old Testament Abraham Moses Liberator Law David The Shep
The **old testament** The Roman Empire Acts of the Apostles Philippians Paul Apostle of the Gentiles The
ament Abraham Moses Liberator Teacher The Law David The Shepherd King The Covenant Solomon the Magnifi

POSSIBLE ISSUES FOR DISCUSSION

1 Are religious experiences (like the burning bush) still experienced today?

   Have you any examples of religious experiences of your own?

   Are such experiences trustworthy?

2 God revealed his name, so that Moses could know his character and describe him.

   How might you describe God today?

3 How would you describe a miracle? What are its characteristics?

   Would you describe the crossing of the Red Sea as a miracle?

4 Are there other aspects of society you might have expected the Ten Commandments to cover?

   Can you discern the nature of the society in which they originated – that of male property-holders in which women are regarded as a "possession"?

5 By New Testament times, the rabbis had codified the Law into 613 equally important commandments, though some still possibly adhered to the idea that the Ten Commandments were special. If so, perhaps Jesus was being asked if he supported 10 or 613 laws when questioned as to which commandment was greatest (Matthew 22:34-40; Mark 12:28-34).

   Jesus rejects either option. Instead, he summarises the Law by picking two separate verses from the Torah, and claiming they fulfil all its demands: "You shall love the Lord your God, and your neighbour as yourself" (Deuteronomy 6:5; Leviticus 19:18).

   How does Jesus in this answer transform the Ten Commandments?

   Note though that Luke shows some lawyers had already reached this conclusion (Luke 10:25-28).

Old Testament Abraham Moses Liberator Teacher The Law David The Shepherd King The Covenant Solomon
nificent **part two** tament St Luke's Gospel Salvation History The Roman Empire Galatians Christian Paul Ap
he Gentiles The Prophets Amos Hose **history embedded in literature** of Creation The Psalms The Wis
ature Daniel The Passion Resurrection Jesus The Old Testament Abraham Moses Liberator Law David The Shep
The Covenant Galatians The Roman Empire Acts of the Apostles Philippians Paul Apo **old testament** The
ament Abraham Moses Liberator Teacher The Law David The Shepherd King The Covenant Solomon the Magnifi

Examples of religious experience

1. The Religious Experience Research Unit based in Oxford has collected a great number of accounts of a lighting up of awareness. Typical of many is an experience recalled by a man in his mid-fifties who said in an interview:

   "I think perhaps I was six. I was taken to a park in the evening to enjoy a firework display. It was summer. There was a crowd of people by the lake... Against the darkening sky, before the fireworks were set alight, I remember seeing these trees, poplar trees they were, three of them. It's very difficult to say exactly what happened because the order of this experience is of its own kind. There was a breeze and the leaves of the poplars vibrated, rustled. I believe I said to myself, 'How beautiful, how wonderful those trees are.' I think there was awe and wonder, and I remember comparing the luminousness – that's a grown-up word, of course – the marvellous beauty, the haunting oppressive power of those trees with the artificiality of the surroundings, the people, the fireworks, and so on. Oddly I kind of knew that this was something extraordinary at the moment it occurred. It was as simple as that, just seeing these trees, but it was the event of my childhood... I knew then it was going to last. And so it has... What happened was telling me something. But what was it telling? The fact of divinity, that it was good? – not so much in the moral sense, but that it was beautiful, yes, sacred."

   A Matter of Life and Death,
   John V. Taylor, 1986 © SCM Press.
   Used by permission of Hymns Ancient & Modern Ltd.

2. I am reminded of a passage in Bishop Anthony Bloom's book, *School for Prayer*, in which he tells of an old lady who came asking for his counsel: though she had prayed continuously for fourteen years she had never sensed the presence of God. How could she learn the secret? He gave her wise advice, and later she told him of her first experience. She had gone into her room, made herself comfortable, and begun to knit. She felt relaxed and noticed with content what a nice-shaped room she had, with its view of the garden, and the sound of her needles hitting the arm-rest of her chair. And then she gradually became aware that the silence was not simply the absence of sound, but was filled with its own density. "And", she said, "it began to pervade me. The silence around began to come and meet the silence in me... All of a sudden I perceived that the silence was a presence. At the heart of the silence there was Him."

   The fascination of that account lies in the woman's simple recognition that her awareness of God came together with her deeper awareness of the familiar things around her. It must always be so. The Holy Spirit is the invisible third party who stands between me and the other, making us mutually aware.

   The Go-Between God,
   John V. Taylor, 1992/2002 © SCM Press.
   Used by permission of Hymns Ancient & Modern Ltd.

The Law

The Law

The meaning of the word Law

Much misunderstanding arises because the Hebrew word *Torah* is not the exact equivalent of the Greek New Testament *Nomos*, or the English word, Law, by which it is translated.

To the Hebrews, *Torah* includes the whole content of God's Covenant revelation to his people, including its nature and purpose, which was taught to the people through prophets and priests. Much of its content is therefore in narrative form, though a secondary part refers to the human response to God. This latter, if codified into specific requirements, could acquire a legal status, which is the meaning of *Nomos*.

The *Law/Torah* (contained in the first five books of the Old Testament) thus consists of:

(a) narratives of early Hebrew history (found in Genesis, Exodus, Numbers);

(b) commandments and laws relating to both social and cultic (i.e. worship) situations (in the latter part of Exodus, Numbers chapters 1–20, Deuteronomy and Leviticus).

The narrative accounts contain no prescribed punishments, remaining true to the lack of legalism originally intended.

The Ten Commandments (Exodus 20:1-17; Deuteronomy 5:6-21) seem to have occupied a special place within the Law. They reflect the circumstances of a particular society, and are obviously not in themselves a complete moral code. However, it is not surprising that Christian tradition has continued to cherish them.

Insofar as the Ten Commandments represent the human response to God's gratuity, they became enlarged and adapted to fit evolving historical situations and worship.

The development of the Law

After the fall of Jerusalem in 586 BC, followed by the devastating exile in Babylon (where initially the Jews felt it was impossible to worship God), they asked searching questions about God's Covenant, the Law and why this tumultuous disaster had occurred. Had God finally given up on them?

The answer some of them reached was that they had failed God by failing to keep the Law; the Law they came to understand as a contractual relationship derived from the small print, as it were, of the Covenant. It then became easy to distort the Law into a religion of *works* which depended upon *them*, rather than on a relationship with God of joy, delight and separateness based on his amazing love and goodness.

This legalistic understanding of *Torah* could be encountered in New Testament times, and is frequently challenged by Jesus and Paul. (See Galatians: pages 63-66.)

The prophets, the Covenant and the Law

The prophets warned against a legalistic understanding of the Law, and sought to recall Israel to her original Covenant relationship. Jeremiah foretells a new Covenant written on the human heart (31:31-34), while Hosea (2:16, 19-20) and Ezekiel (16:8, 60) liken the Covenant relationship to the union of marriage between God and his people.

An example of a law

Leviticus 13 describes the law relating to leprosy. The priest's role is central, both in diagnosing the condition which, if positive, results in isolation from society, and also in confirming any cases where leprosy has been cured.

The priest is also involved in cases of leprosy in clothes (13:47-50) and leprosy in houses (14:35-57). Today we might ascribe such conditions to mildew and rising damp!

Clearly, therefore, "leprosy" here is not an exact medical condition; rather, it refers to conditions of change and decay. The book of Leviticus is very concerned about managing boundaries and transitions, and the priests have a special role in helping the people to negotiate them.

Old Testament Abraham Moses Liberator Teacher The Law David The Shepherd King The Covenant Solomon
nificent The New Testament St Luke's Gospel Salvation History The Roman Empire Galatians **part two** Apc
e Gentiles The Prophets Amos Hose **history embedded in literature** of Creation The Psalms The Wisc
ature Daniel The Passion Resurrection Jesus The Old Testament Abraham Moses Liberator Law David The Shepl
The **old testament** The Roman Empire Acts of the Apostles Philippians Paul Apostle of the Gentiles The
ament Abraham Moses Liberator Teacher The Law David The Shepherd King The Covenant Solomon the Magnifi

David – The Shepherd King

The "conquest" of Canaan was slow, with the Hebrews living on the hills under a series of leaders or "judges", and the Canaanites in the valleys. The Philistines, an advanced civilisation, lived along the coastal plain and frequently led sorties inland.

> The Philistines possibly came from Crete.

Samuel is often described as the last of the judges and first of the prophets. He tended the ark, the portable throne of God made at Mount Sinai and containing the Ten Commandments (Exodus 25:10-22), which journeyed with the people, symbolising God's presence with them.

Rather than a series of intermittent leaders, the Hebrews began clamouring to be "like other nations" and have a permanent leader, a king. Samuel regarded this as disloyalty to God and warned them against a king's probable excesses, but nevertheless under God's guidance complied with their request. Saul, the first king, was considered a failure because he disobeyed God's requirements; David was chosen as the next king-elect.

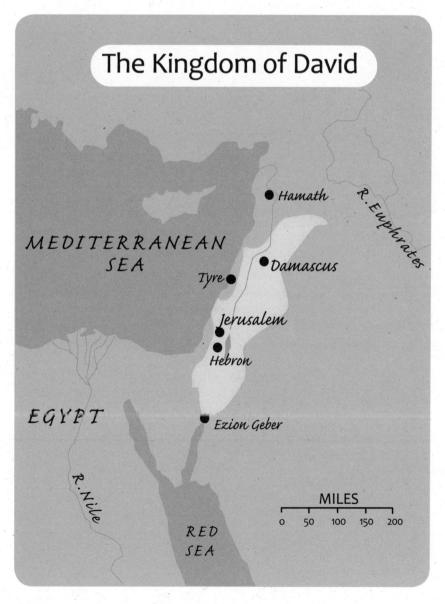

The Kingdom of David

- Hamath
- R. Euphrates
- MEDITERRANEAN SEA
- Damascus
- Tyre
- Jerusalem
- Hebron
- EGYPT
- Ezion Geber
- R. Nile
- RED SEA

MILES
0   50   100   150   200

33

Old Testament Abraham Moses Liberator Teacher The Law David The Shepherd King The Covenant Solomon
gnificent **part two** tament St Luke's Gospel Salvation History The Roman Empire Galatians Christian Paul Ap
he Gentiles The Prophets Amos Hose **history embedded in literature** of Creation The Psalms The Wis
rature Daniel The Passion Resurrection Jesus The Old Testament Abraham Moses Liberator Law David The Shep
g The Covenant Galatians The Roman Empire Acts of the Apostles Philippians Paul Apo **old testament** Th
tament Abraham Moses Liberator Teacher The Law David The Shepherd King The Covenant Solomon the Magnif

SUGGESTED READINGS AND POINTS TO CONSIDER AS YOU READ

David (a shepherd boy from Bethlehem) is anointed to become king in due course	1 Samuel 16:1-13
David kills Goliath The Hebrew king's task was to lead his people in keeping God's Covenant. David is described as "a man after [God's] own heart" (1 Samuel 13:14). Can you see why from the first two readings? • How did David's experience as a shepherd prepare him for his future kingship? • Does Psalm 23 also shed light here? These first two stories, each containing details of David's family (16:6-10; 17:12-16), give different accounts of his rise.	1 Samuel 17:1-52
David (an outlaw) spares Saul's life • Why did David spare Saul's life? • What does this tell us about his concept of Hebrew kingship?	1 Samuel 24:1-22
David is anointed king, unites the kingdom, captures Jerusalem and makes it his capital David chooses Jerusalem, a Canaanite city between the northern and southern parts of his kingdom, to be his capital. • How does he seize it from the Jebusites?	2 Samuel 2:1-4a; 5:1-10
David brings the ark to Jerusalem • Why does David regard it as important for the ark to be in Jerusalem?	2 Samuel 6:12-15, 17
David wants to build a temple	2 Samuel 7:1-13
David's great sin concerning Bathsheba and Uriah	2 Samuel 11:1-27
and the challenge by Nathan, the prophet, to David • What is David's great sin? Why, as king, is it so heinous? • How does Nathan challenge David? • How does David respond and what does this tell us about him?	2 Samuel 12:1-18, 24

Old Testament Abraham Moses Liberator Teacher The Law David The Shepherd King The Covenant Solomon
gnificent The New Testament St Luke's Gospel Salvation History The Roman Empire Galatians **part two** Ap
he Gentiles The Prophets Amos Hose **history embedded in literature** of Creation The Psalms The Wis
rature Daniel The Passion Resurrection Jesus The Old Testament Abraham Moses Liberator Law David The Shep
The **old testament** The Roman Empire Acts of the Apostles Philippians Paul Apostle of the Gentiles Th
ament Abraham Moses Liberator Teacher The Law David The Shepherd King The Covenant Solomon the Magnif

POSSIBLE ISSUES FOR DISCUSSION

1   How do we assess others?

    – by outward appearances, rather than seeing the **real** person?

2   The prophet Samuel rejected Saul as king, because Saul disobeyed God's commandment to slaughter all the Amalekites (1 Samuel 15:1-33).

    Do you think God rejects people in this way?

    Christians in the early Church suggested the Philistines (the Hebrews' traditional enemies) and Amalekites were really symbols, or allegories, for spiritual demons and powers of wickedness.

    Is this a satisfactory way of:

    (a) avoiding moral responsibility?

    (b) ensuring God is on the side of the Hebrews?

    Do we today ever use comparable explanations:

    (a) for situations in society?

    (b) for international situations?

3   What is prejudice?

    David doesn't immediately recognise himself in Nathan's parable.

    Is it easier to see faults in others rather than to recognise our own?

    (Compare Matthew 7:3-5; Luke 6:41-42.)

4   Would **you** say David was "a man after God's own heart"?

    Why do you think God did not reject him after his great sin?

The Covenant

The Covenant concept was commonly used for ordinary transactions in the ancient Near East. In the Bible, the concept becomes central, and essentially refers to the relationship freely entered into between God and his people. It is a completely gratuitous, undeserved initiative from God, intended to result in a relationship of joy and blessing, which however requires a response from humans if the relationship is to persist and flourish. The Covenant relationship (described on pages 16 and 20) is "an agreement, or promise, or relationship which is legally binding, and may be compared with marriage". Parties entering into such a relationship were not necessarily on an equal footing.

"Testament" is another word for Covenant. Thus, in the Bible, the Old Testament refers to the Covenant relationship established principally with Abraham and Moses, while the New Testament grows out of the New Covenant initiated through the death and resurrection of Jesus Christ.

The Covenant in the Old Testament

God renews his Covenant on several occasions. In biblical order, these are:

1   The Covenant with Noah, made after the Flood (Genesis 9:8-17).

In this Covenant, God promises never again to destroy the earth and its creatures. It is therefore a universal Covenant made between God and the whole of creation, both humans and creatures. It is sealed and "signed" by the rainbow – God's gloriously coloured bow which is set aside, never again to be used aggressively against the earth.

2   God's Covenant with Abraham is in the form of a threefold promise (Genesis 12:1-3):

> "Abraham" means "father of a multitude".

(a)   God will give Abram a land for him and his descendants;
(b)   Abram's descendants will be great, as the stars in the sky or the sand on the seashore (Genesis 22:17);
(c)   through Abram's descendants the whole world will be blessed.

In his response ("so Abram went", Genesis 12:4), Abraham accepts God's promise.

However, Abram understandably wonders how the Covenant is to come about since he and his wife are childless and beyond childbearing age. God therefore further ratifies his promise by sealing the Covenant with a sacrifice Abram is asked to make (Genesis 15:1-11, 17-20).

In the final ratification of the Covenant (Genesis 17:1-14), Abram's name becomes Abraham, and God demands the circumcision of every male of eight days old – "so shall my covenant be in your flesh an everlasting covenant".

Isaac is finally born to Abraham (aged 100) and Sarah (Genesis 21:1-7).

> Circumcision among Semitic peoples is known to be an ancient rite; now for Abraham and his descendants it carries special significance.

3 God's Covenant with Moses at Mount Sinai (or Horeb) is based on God's promise to the whole Hebrew people that he will become their particular God (Exodus 19:1-8; 20:1-17; 24:3-8). Having seen God's character through his rescue of them from slavery in Egypt, they have the required knowledge to decide if this God should be the god of their choice. (As yet, each tribe is thought to have its own tribal god.)

The people are invited to keep the Law as their response to this Covenant, to which they agree. The Covenant is thereupon sealed with sacrifice: Moses sprinkles blood (representing God-given life) from the sacrificial animals on the altar (representing God); he then reads "the book of the covenant" to the people. On the people's assent, the remainder of the blood is sprinkled on them. Thus God and his people are bound by blood in a life-giving relationship.

(A certain amount of repetition indicates that different strands of written tradition have been woven together. Another tradition [Exodus 31:18; 32:15-20; 34:1-4, 27-28] refers to the tablets of stone on which the commandments were carved.)

4 God's Covenant with David promises David a rich posterity (2 Samuel 7:11-13), while 2 Samuel 23:1-7 describes idyllically the life of a people whose king is in a Covenant relationship with God.

Psalm 89:1-36 expresses similar sentiments about David, the chosen of the Lord, and his Covenant relationship with God. However, a total reversal of mood in verses 38-52 indicates the people's orderly life has become shattered; the nation has hit hard times; Jerusalem is destroyed; there is no longer a king. God, it seems, has rejected his part of the Covenant (verses 38-39). The Psalmist (perhaps an exile in Babylon after the fall of Jerusalem in 586 BC) agonises, "What's happened? What has gone wrong? Has God broken his promise to David?" David is now a past figure (v. 49).

This indicates how the Psalm grew, as a later generation struggled to make sense of life in a changed world.

The development of the Covenant in Hebrew understanding

The original universal Covenant with Noah gradually became narrowed down, through Abraham and his "tribe", through his descendants at Mount Sinai, to the king of Israel, pre-eminently David. Finally, it resides in one individual descendant of David, Jesus, who inaugurates the New Covenant through his death and resurrection. This Covenant which brings forgiveness is foreshadowed at the Last Supper in the wine as Christ's shed lifeblood of the New Covenant (1 Corinthians 11:25; Mark 14:23-24; Matthew 26:27-28. Also, Luke 22:20, which is omitted in some versions).

But the understanding of the Covenant gradually changes too. God's promise to Abraham is one of limitless blessing. It is unconditional, and accepted as such in a contractual agreement of which circumcision is the sign. At Sinai, God freely and gratuitously chooses the Hebrews as his people in a totally selfless act. The Law is given as a way whereby the Hebrews can respond to this invitation.

This promise and gratuitous choice by God reveal his quite amazing goodness and generosity. The Covenant relationship was intended to be one of joy between God and his people, called to be separate from all others.

Later, after the fall of the kingdoms of Israel and Judah, and the destruction of Jerusalem in 586 BC, resulting in the Babylonian exile, the people were utterly traumatised. What had happened? Weren't they still God's chosen people?

The answer of many was that they had broken the Covenant relationship, forgetting this was intended as a relationship of joy based on God's generosity. In legalising the people's response, the Covenant was turned into a religion of works and legal obedience to God. Thus the Covenant could come to be understood as depending on the Hebrews and their acts, rather than on the amazing generosity of God.

But the original sense of the graciousness of God's Covenant was kept alive, especially by the prophets. Jeremiah chapters 30–31 celebrates God's new Covenant in a beautiful passage which Jesus may have had in mind at the Last Supper.

In New Testament times, a lawyer quotes two separate verses from the Torah, "You shall love the Lord your God..." (Deuteronomy 6:5) and "You shall love your neighbour as yourself" (Leviticus 19:18), as God's requirements for his people in keeping the Covenant.

THE COVENANT RELATIONSHIP IN THE BIBLE

Universal covenant with Noah

Covenant with Abraham

Covenant with Moses

Covenant with David

Jesus inaugurates New Covenant

The people of the New Covenant become increasingly inclusive until they are universal

See book of Acts (pages 67-71)

Old Testament Abraham Moses Liberator Teacher The Law David The Shepherd King The Covenant Solomon nificent The New Testament St Luke's Gospel Salvation History The Roman Empire Galatians **part two** I Apo e Gentiles The Prophets Amos Hose **history embedded in literature** of Creation The Psalms The Wis ature Daniel The Passion Resurrection Jesus The Old Testament Abraham Moses Liberator Law David The Shep The **old testament** The Roman Empire Acts of the Apostles Philippians Paul Apostle of the Gentiles The ament Abraham Moses Liberator Teacher The Law David The Shepherd King The Covenant Solomon the Magnifi

Solomon – The Magnificent

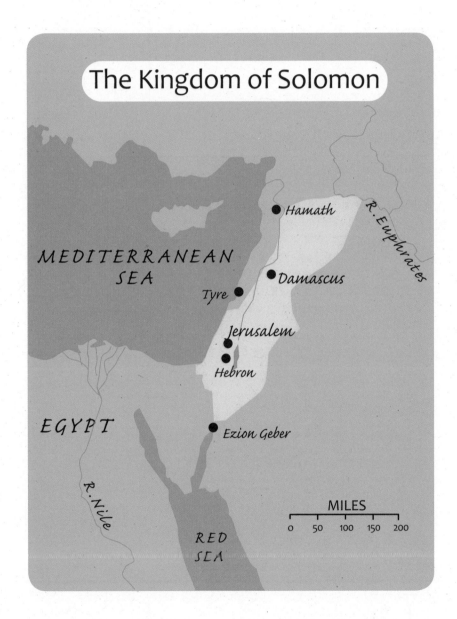

Solomon, renowned for his wisdom, splendour and wealth, succeeded his father, David, as king.

Under him, the kingdom achieved its widest-ever boundaries (1 Kings 4:24). He carried out a massive building programme, including an elaborate palace and the Temple of God. However, the resulting slavery, forced labour and heavy taxes precipitated rebellion at the end of his reign.

Old Testament Abraham Moses Liberator Teacher The Law David The Shepherd King The Covenant Solomon
nificent **part two** tament St Luke's Gospel Salvation History The Roman Empire Galatians Christian Paul Ap
he Gentiles The Prophets Amos Hose **history embedded in literature** of Creation The Psalms The Wis
rature Daniel The Passion Resurrection Jesus The Old Testament Abraham Moses Liberator Law David The Shep
The Covenant Galatians The Roman Empire Acts of the Apostles Philippians Paul Apo **old testament** Th
ament Abraham Moses Liberator Teacher The Law David The Shepherd King The Covenant Solomon the Magnif

SUGGESTED READINGS AND POINTS TO CONSIDER AS YOU READ

Solomon's prayer for and practice of wisdom	1 Kings 3:5-14, 16-28; 4:34
Extent of the kingdom	1 Kings 4:20-21, 24
Solomon's daily provisions and wealth	1 Kings 4:22-23, 26; 9:26-27; 10:14-15, 23
Solomon builds the Temple	1 Kings 5:1-12; 5:18 – 6:2, 38c
The ark is placed in the Holy of Holies	1 Kings 8:1, 6, 9 (see 6:19)
Solomon dedicates the Temple When the Temple is completed, Solomon places the ark, God's throne, symbolising his presence, in the Holy of Holies (a windowless, perfect cubic room, symbolising God's perfection). At the dedication, God's glory descends on the Temple in the form of a cloud. Can you think of any other Bible passages where a cloud symbolises God's presence?	1 Kings 8:10, 12-14, 27
Solomon builds palaces and other civic buildings	1 Kings 7:1, 2a, 6a, 7-8
Visit of the Queen of Sheba	1 Kings 10:1-9
Causes of discontent What causes of discontent does Solomon's reign precipitate?	1 Kings 4:7; 5:13-17; 9:15, 20-22; 11:1-9
Rebellion of Jeroboam As Solomon increasingly becomes an absolute monarch "like other nations", so he forgets his duties as the shepherd-king of his people under God's Covenant. (Compare the challenge to be a shepherd-king [rather than a despot] that the prophet Nathan makes to King David over Bathsheba and, later in the northern kingdom of Israel, that the prophet Elijah makes to King Ahab over Naboth's vineyard [1 Kings 21:1-29]. In each of these instances the king repents.)	1 Kings 11:26-40

A cubit was measured from the elbow to the fingertip, about 17 inches or 445 mm.

Sheba was probably Yemen, possibly Ethiopia.

Old Testament Abraham Moses Liberator Teacher The Law David The Shepherd King The Covenant Solomon gnificent The New Testament St Luke's Gospel Salvation History The Roman Empire Galatians **part two** Ap the Gentiles The Prophets Amos Hose **history embedded in literature** of Creation The Psalms The Wis rature Daniel The Passion Resurrection Jesus The Old Testament Abraham Moses Liberator Law David The Shep g The **old testament** The Roman Empire Acts of the Apostles Philippians Paul Apostle of the Gentiles Th tament Abraham Moses Liberator Teacher The Law David The Shepherd King The Covenant Solomon the Magnif

POSSIBLE ISSUES FOR DISCUSSION

1 How successful is Solomon in achieving the ideals at the beginning of his reign?

2 It is said: "Power corrupts; absolute power corrupts absolutely."

Do you agree?

Was this true of Solomon?

3 Where does ultimate authority lie in our society today?

- in the European Union?
- in the power of multinationals or banks?
- in Parliament?
- in the electorate?
- in the Church?
- in the family?
- in the individual?

Was the answer the same at the end of the 1939–45 war?

Old Testament Abraham Moses Liberator Teacher The Law David The Shepherd King The Covenant Solomon nificent **part two** tament St Luke's Gospel Salvation History The Roman Empire Galatians Christian Paul Apo e Gentiles The Prophets Amos Hose **history embedded in literature** of Creation The Psalms The Wisc ature Daniel The Passion Resurrection Jesus The Old Testament Abraham Moses Liberator Law David The Sheph The Covenant Galatians The Roman Empire Acts of the Apostles Philippians Paul Apo **old testament** The ment Abraham Moses Liberator Teacher The Law David The Shepherd King The Covenant Solomon the Magnific

THE DIVIDED KINGDOM

On Solomon's death, the kingdom became divided into:

a. The southern kingdom of Judah (occasionally called Israel because of God's choice of his people, Israel), which consisted of two tribes: Judah and Benjamin. Its capital was Jerusalem, and its first king was Rehoboam, son of Solomon.

b. The northern kingdom of Ephraim, or Israel, consisting of ten tribes. Its capital was Samaria, and its first king was Jeroboam, who was not related to David, and who set up shrines of golden calves at Bethel and Dan to prevent pilgrimage to Jerusalem.

> Kings of the southern kingdom of Judah were always descended from David.

While the two kingdoms coexisted, the northern kingdom, Israel, was the more prosperous as it had access to the international trade routes.

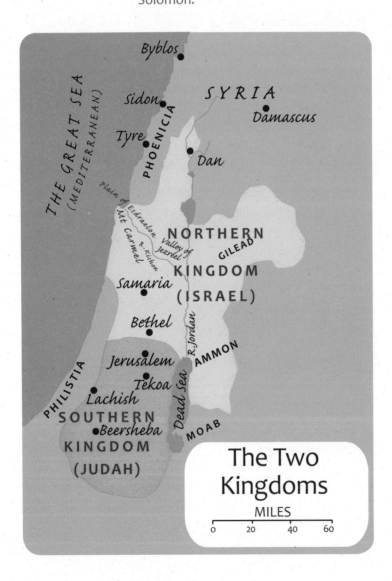

The Two Kingdoms

MILES

0   20   40   60

Old Testament Abraham Moses Liberator Teacher The Law David The Shepherd King The Covenant Solomon
nificent The New Testament St Luke's Gospel Salvation History The Roman Empire Galatians **part three** Ap
he Gentiles The Prophets Amos Hosea **history embedded in literature** of Creation The Psalms The Wis
rature Daniel The Passion Resurrection Jesus The Old Testament Abraham Moses Liberator Law David The Shep
The **new testament** The Roman Empire Acts of the Apostles Philippians Paul Apostle of the Gentiles The
ament Abraham Moses Liberator Teacher The Law David The Shepherd King The Covenant Solomon the Magnif

Introduction to the New Testament

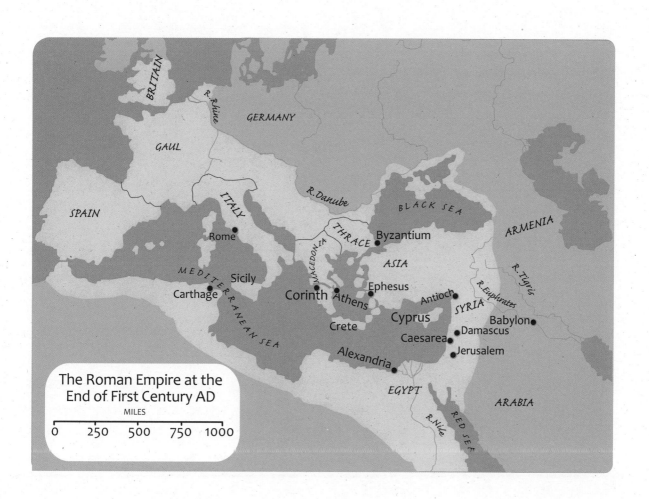

The Roman Empire at the End of First Century AD

MILES

0   250   500   750   1000

Old Testament Abraham Moses Liberator Teacher The Law David The Shepherd King The Covenant Solomon
nificent **part three** ament St Luke's Gospel Salvation History The Roman Empire Galatians Christian Paul Ap
e Gentiles The Prophets Amos Hose **history embedded in literature** of Creation The Psalms The Wis
ature Daniel The Passion Resurrection Jesus The Old Testament Abraham Moses Liberator Law David The Shep
The Covenant Galatians The Roman Empire Acts of the Apostles Philippians Paul Ap **new testament** Th
ament Abraham Moses Liberator Teacher The Law David The Shepherd King The Covenant Solomon the Magnif

BACKGROUND TO NEW TESTAMENT TIMES

THE LAND
The whole land, roughly the size of Wales, is composed of distinct districts.

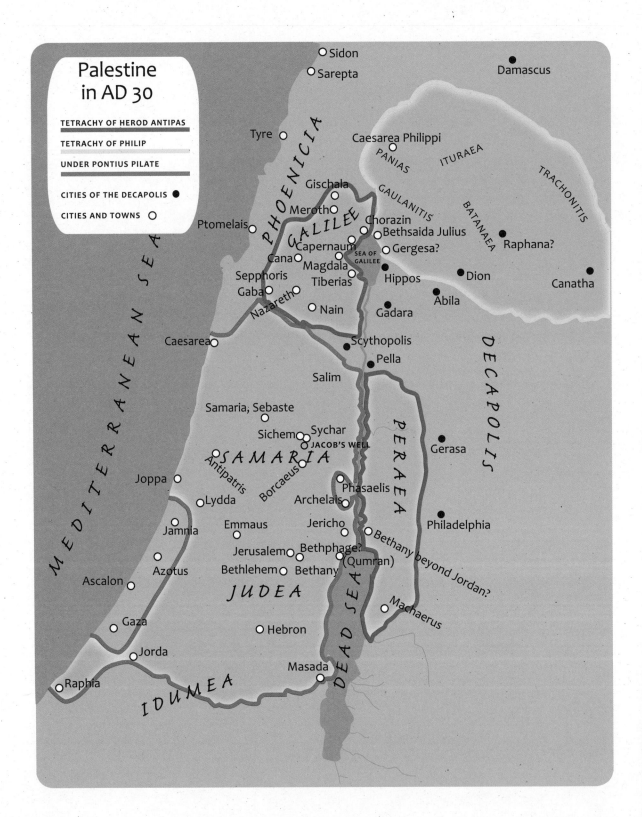

Old Testament Abraham Moses Liberator Teacher The Law David The Shepherd King The Covenant Solomon
gnificent The New Testament St Luke's Gospel Salvation History The Roman Empire Galatians **part three** Ap
he Gentiles The Prophets Amos Hosea **history embedded in literature** of Creation The Psalms The Wis
rature Daniel The Passion Resurrection Jesus The Old Testament Abraham Moses Liberator Law David The Shep
The **new testament** The Roman Empire Acts of the Apostles Philippians Paul Apostle of the Gentiles The
ament Abraham Moses Liberator Teacher The Law David The Shepherd King The Covenant Solomon the Magnif

Galilee

The Sea of Galilee (also known as the Sea of Tiberias or lake of Gennesaret) lies under the slopes of snow-capped Mount Hermon (3030 m); the lake (300 m below sea level) is approximately 13 miles long and 7 miles wide.

The region of Galilee consists of fertile agricultural land, and a thriving fish industry operated in New Testament times. The region was populated mostly by Gentiles (Isaiah 9:1), and the people were sturdily independent; they had been forced to accept the Jewish religion under Judas Maccabeus (164 BC).

Galilee lay on the great trade route (the Way of the Sea) which linked Egypt with Syria and the north. Traversing the narrow coastal plain, the road turned inland round the northern shore of the Sea of Galilee and on to Damascus. Galileans therefore met and dealt with tradesmen from many countries, and were in no sense narrowly Jewish.

Judea

In the south, the dry limestone hills of Judea lie 28 miles east of the Mediterranean, above the deep rift valley of the Jordan which pours its waters into the Dead Sea, lying some 400 m below sea level. Jerusalem (700 m) is situated on the edge of the Judean wilderness which drops steeply some 15 miles down to Jericho, the Jordan valley and the Dead Sea.

Judea was not on the great international trade route. Life centred round the city of Jerusalem with its Temple worship; this became the focus of pilgrimage for Jews worldwide at festival times.

Samaria

Samaria, lying between Galilee and Judea, consists of the hill country to the north of Judea. As the northern kingdom of Israel, the territory had fallen to the Assyrians in 721 BC; some of its people had been deported and the area was resettled by Assyrians, so that Samaritans were of mixed blood. They had built their own rival temple on Mount Gerizim. For such reasons, they were despised by strict Jews.

Samaria lay on the direct route from Galilee to Judea, though travellers often followed the Jordan valley instead, resulting in the steep climb up through the Judean wilderness to Jerusalem.

The rulers of Palestine

In 63 BC, the Roman general Pompey entered Jerusalem, and Palestine became part of the Roman Empire. Herod the Great (Matthew 2:1-19), nominated as a puppet king by Rome, ruled with considerable success from 37 to 4 BC, carrying out vast building programmes and introducing Graeco-Roman culture (gymnasia, theatres, stadia) throughout Palestine. He built the huge seaport of Caesarea as his capital, and restored the ancient city of Samaria, renaming it Sebaste (meaning Augustus, after the emperor). (The names of these two cities indicate Herod's policy of maintaining good relations with Rome.)

However, Herod was despised by most Jews because he promoted Gentile culture, and also because, though he professed the Jewish faith, he was of mixed blood (coming from Edom to the south of Judea). Under Caesar Augustus

Old Testament Abraham Moses Liberator Teacher The Law David The Shepherd King The Covenant Solomon
gnificent **part three** ament St Luke's Gospel Salvation History The Roman Empire Galatians Christian Paul Ap
e Gentiles The Prophets Amos Hose **history embedded in literature** of Creation The Psalms The Wis
rature Daniel The Passion Resurrection Jesus The Old Testament Abraham Moses Liberator Law David The Shep
The Covenant Galatians The Roman Empire Acts of the Apostles Philippians Paul Ap **new testament** Th
ament Abraham Moses Liberator Teacher The Law David The Shepherd King The Covenant Solomon the Magnif

(27 BC – AD 14), peace (the Pax Romana) was restored throughout the Empire. Augustus became recognised as a god, and temples were everywhere erected to him, including those built by Herod. The Jews, with their strict monotheistic religion, refused point-blank to worship Caesar.

To appease growing Jewish unrest, Herod embarked in 20 BC on a massive rebuilding of the Temple in Jerusalem; it was only recently completed (AD 63) before it was destroyed by Rome when Jerusalem fell in AD 70.

On Herod's death, the expanded territory was divided between his sons, known as tetrarchs rather than kings (Luke 3:1). Archelaus (Matthew 2:19-23), who ruled in Judea, was so cruel that in AD 6 Rome deposed him, and henceforth Judea was governed directly by a Roman governor called the procurator. Philip ruled over territories (mostly Gentile) to the north-east of Galilee until his death in AD 34, while Antipas was tetrarch of Galilee and Transjordan until he was deposed in AD 39. (It is this Herod who is referred to several times in the New Testament: Luke 3:19-20; 9:7-9; 13:31-33; 23:6-17.) He built his capital on the Sea of Galilee, naming it Tiberias after the Emperor Tiberius (AD 14–37).

A phylactery is a small box.

The scriptures and the Law (or Torah)
Central to Jewish religious observance is the record of God's revelation contained in the Law consisting of the first five books of the Old Testament (the Pentateuch.) These books had reached their final form by the end of

the fifth century BC. By the end of the third century BC, the prophetic books were also regarded as divine revelation; the New Testament phrase "the Law and the prophets" refers to these two blocks of literature. By the end of Old Testament times, almost all of the remaining books of the Old Testament were accepted as divine revelation.

The Shema is the commandment found in Deuteronomy 6:4-5.

Jewish parties
- The Sadducees were a priestly aristocratic party centred round the Temple in Jerusalem. They recognised that their continued position of privilege depended on maintaining peaceful relations with Rome; they were therefore determined to suppress any uprising. They did not believe in the resurrection of the dead.

- The Pharisees claimed their religious descent from the *Hasidim*, or "Pious Ones", who, in 168–164 BC, had remained loyal to the Law and resisted the attempts of Antiochus IV to stamp out the Jewish religion, even at risk of martyrdom. This experience led to belief in a resurrection of the dead. A non-priestly party, they were found throughout Palestine. They opposed violence against Rome.

The Law was central to the life and practice of the Pharisees. They obeyed the directions of Deuteronomy 6:8-9 literally, wearing a phylactery on the forehead and arm containing

Old Testament Abraham Moses Liberator Teacher The Law David The Shepherd King The Covenant Solomon
gnificent The New Testament St Luke's Gospel Salvation History The Roman Empire Galatians **part three** A
he Gentiles The Prophets Amos Hosea **history embedded in literature** of Creation The Psalms The Wi
rature Daniel The Passion Resurrection Jesus The Old Testament Abraham Moses Liberator Law David The Shep
g The **new testament** The Roman Empire Acts of the Apostles Philippians Paul Apostle of the Gentiles Th
tament Abraham Moses Liberator Teacher The Law David The Shepherd King The Covenant Solomon the Magni

the "Shema", which they also fixed to the doorpost. By New Testament times, rabbis (teachers of the Law) had codified the Law into 613 precepts of equal importance. This oral tradition was intended to interpret the written Law in the contemporary situation. Such precepts were, however, impossible for ordinary people to keep, and some Pharisees fell prey to rigorous legalism.

- Scribes and lawyers

  A scribe was an educated man, versed in the interpretation of the Law; he was able to pronounce over disputes concerning the Law. Scribes were mostly Pharisees, but the Sadducees also had their own scribes. Lawyers were students of the Law.

- The Essenes are not mentioned in the New Testament, but are known chiefly for their community at Qumran on the Dead Sea, whose scriptures were discovered in caves in AD 1947. Believing Jewish society corrupt, they withdrew to live in isolated communities sworn to secrecy, in order to concentrate on keeping the Law in preparation for the Messianic age.

- Zealots

  These advocated violence against Rome in defence of their faith, represented by the Temple and the Law. One of the Twelve, Simon, is described by Luke as "the Zealot" (Luke 6:15; Acts 1:13), and by Mark (3:18) and Matthew (10:4) as "the Cananaean", which is Aramaic for Zealot.

- The Sanhedrin (Jewish council)

  This council of seventy-one members, based in Jerusalem, was chaired by the High Priest. It held considerable autonomy under Rome, although it had lost its power to pass the death sentence. It consisted mostly of Sadducees and Pharisees.

Messiah means "God's Anointed One".

The Messiah and the kingdom (or reign) of God

Popular Jewish thought looked forward to an ideal ruler who would establish God's kingdom of righteousness in the world. It was believed that he would be a descendant of David, and many thought he would also reinstate the kingdom of David.

Many Jews believed that God's agent in bringing about the Kingdom of God would be the Messiah. However, while some expected the Messiah to be a human being, perhaps of Davidic descent, others looked for a supernatural being who would usher in God's kingdom, and whose coming would mean the conquest of evil.

Old Testament Abraham Moses Liberator Teacher The Law David The Shepherd King The Covenant Solomon
nificent **part three** ament St Luke's Gospel Salvation History The Roman Empire Galatians Christian Paul Apc
e Gentiles The Prophets Amos Hose **history embedded in literature** of Creation The Psalms The Wis
ature Daniel The Passion Resurrection Jesus The Old Testament Abraham Moses Liberator Law David The Shepl
The Covenant Galatians The Roman Empire Acts of the Apostles Philippians Paul Ap **new testament** The
ament Abraham Moses Liberator Teacher The Law David The Shepherd King The Covenant Solomon the Magnifi

The Temple

The Temple in Jerusalem was the centre of Jewish worship, religion and pilgrimage, and in New Testament times it was the only place where sacrifice could be offered.

The enormous Temple platform, open to the sky, occupied about one-fifth of the city; named the Court of the Gentiles, it was open to all. Situated at the western side was the Temple building itself, surrounded by a fence with notices in Greek, which read:

"Let no foreigner enter
within the screen
and enclosure surrounding
the sanctuary.
Whoever is taken so doing
will himself
be the cause that death
overtakes him."

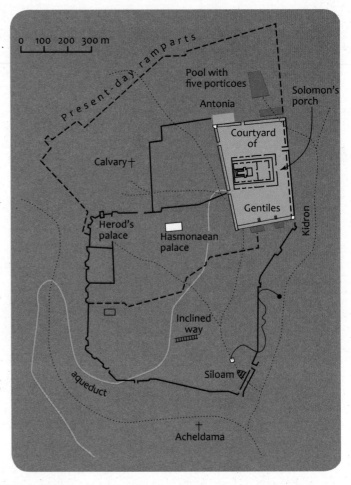

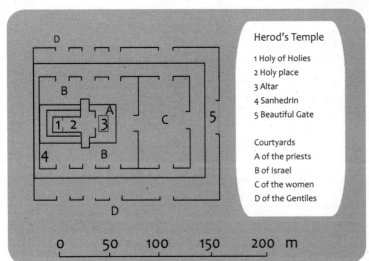

Herod's Temple

1 Holy of Holies
2 Holy place
3 Altar
4 Sanhedrin
5 Beautiful Gate

Courtyards
A of the priests
B of Israel
C of the women
D of the Gentiles

At the eastern end of the building was the Court of the Women, where public worship was held (with women in the gallery). A flight of steps led to the Court of the Israelites (men only), and further steps to the Court of the Priests. Inside this court stood the actual Temple house, approached by a flight of steps and through an elaborate porch.

The building consisted of two rooms, each a perfect cube. The first one, the Holy Place, contained the seven-branched candlestick, the table for the shewbread and the altar of incense. A richly woven curtain, 18 cm thick, separated it from the Holy of Holies; this was completely empty, and entered only once a year by the High Priest on the Day of Atonement. In front of the Temple house stood the huge rough-hewn stone altar of sacrifice, where offerings were constantly burning.

Old Testament Abraham Moses Liberator Teacher The Law David The Shepherd King The Covenant Solomon nificent The New Testament St Luke's Gospel Salvation History The Roman Empire Galatians **part three** Apo e Gentiles The Prophets Amos Hosea **history embedded in literature** of Creation The Psalms The Wis ature Daniel The Passion Resurrection Jesus The Old Testament Abraham Moses Liberator Law David The Shepl The **new testament** The Roman Empire Acts of the Apostles Philippians Paul Apostle of the Gentiles The ament Abraham Moses Liberator Teacher The Law David The Shepherd King The Covenant Solomon the Magnifi

The synagogue

Synagogues were gatherings for worship from the exile onwards, when Jews could no longer meet at the Temple. When synagogues came to be built, they served primarily as worship centres, but were also used for educational and judicial purposes. A minimum of ten men are required for synagogue worship to proceed.

> Synagogue is Greek for "congregation".

Some times and seasons

The Jewish year is based on a lunar calendar.

The three main feasts of Passover, Pentecost and Booths (or Tabernacles) are also known by their earlier agricultural names of the Feasts of Unleavened Bread, of Weeks, and of Ingathering. They commemorate the Exodus from Egypt, the giving of the law to Moses and the great autumn harvest festival.

The annual fast day required by the Law, the Day of Atonement, is a corporate day of repentance. It falls in late September or early October.

The Jewish day runs from sunset (around 6 pm) to sunset.

The Sabbath, the seventh day of the week (Saturday), is holy and a day of rest. It reflects God's rest after completing his work of creation (Genesis 2:2-3).

Jews of the Dispersion

From the Babylonian exile onwards, Jews were found living outside Israel. By New Testament times, there were Jewish quarters in most Roman cities; in Alexandria and Rome they formed substantial minorities. Surrounded by Greek culture and speaking Greek, but Jewish in religion, Jews who were able to made pilgrimage to Jerusalem for great feasts such as the Passover. Because Jewish unrest throughout the Empire could potentially cause such havoc, all Jews everywhere were exempt by Rome from military service because of their refusal to fight on the Sabbath; they were also exempt from worship of the Roman emperor as divine.

God-fearers and proselytes

The monotheistic Jewish religion with its high ethical content appealed to many Gentiles, who wished to become associated with it. Gentile proselytes became full Jews through proselyte baptism, circumcision and full adherence to the Law. However, circumcision was abhorrent to many Gentiles, and these became God-fearers, attending synagogue worship and following the Jewish ethical code.

Proselytes and God-fearers provided a special target for Paul in his Gentile mission since, as seekers after truth, they were more open to new ideas.

Old Testament Abraham Moses Liberator Teacher The Law David The Shepherd King The Covenant Solomon
gnificent **part three** ament St Luke's Gospel Salvation History The Roman Empire Galatians Christian Paul Ap
he Gentiles The Prophets Amos Hose **history embedded in literature** of Creation The Psalms The Wi
rature Daniel The Passion Resurrection Jesus The Old Testament Abraham Moses Liberator Law David The Shep
g The Covenant Galatians The Roman Empire Acts of the Apostles Philippians Paul Ap **new testament** Th
tament Abraham Moses Liberator Teacher The Law David The Shepherd King The Covenant Solomon the Magnif

THE NEW TESTAMENT

The word "Gospel" means "good news"
– the good news that Jesus is the long-
awaited Messiah.

> Messiah (Hebrew) = Christ
> (Greek). "Messiah" means
> "Anointed One" – anointed
> with God's Spirit to fulfil God's
> purposes, as set out in the
> Covenant, but never achieved
> by ordinary people. There was,
> however, no agreement as to
> how the Messiah would fulfil his
> role or who he would be.

The Gospels show how Jesus, through
his teaching and manner of life, revealed
God to humankind in human form.
Through his death and resurrection, he
broke the bondage of sin that separates
humans from God. He thereby opened
the kingdom (or reign) of God to all,
and so fulfilled the old Covenant (or
Testament) of Moses.

This is Good News indeed! The choice,
though, as always, is ours – to accept or
reject Jesus and his offer of freedom.

The Gospels are neither straightforward
history, nor straightforward biography.
Rather, because of the nature of
the central figure of Jesus, and his
achievement of free salvation for all,
they are a unique form of literature –
Gospel, Good News!

The Letters (or Epistles) were written
before the Gospels. Addressed to new
churches founded by leaders like Paul,
they deal with specific issues particular
to that church as it tries to apply the
Christian Gospel in belief and practice.

Later, as Christian leaders were killed in
persecution, the Gospels, proclaiming
the Good News of Jesus, were written.

The Acts of the Apostles has been shown
by scholars to be the sequel to St Luke's
Gospel. Sometimes called the Gospel of
the Holy Spirit, it describes the new life in
the power of the Spirit. It also traces the
various stages, under the guidance of the
Spirit, in the spread of Christianity from
the Jews to the Gentiles.

The book of Revelation describes in
graphic language scenes that depict
God's final victory over sin and death.

WHY ARE THE FIRST THREE GOSPELS SO ALIKE?

The "classical" view

A brief glance reveals that the first three
Gospels are very similar to each other
and very different in style and content
from St John's Gospel. For this reason,
Matthew, Mark and Luke are called the
"Synoptic" Gospels: "synoptic" means
"looked at together".

The word "criticism" comes from the
Greek word *krisis*, meaning judgement,
and in a biblical context has a different
emphasis from its ordinary everyday
use. Biblical scholars or "critics" are like
detectives: they scrutinise the internal
evidence of the Gospels (and relevant
external evidence) to "judge", and
evaluate or deduce, what we can tell
about how the Gospels came to be
written, and also the purpose of each
Gospel writer.

To answer the so-called "Synoptic
Problem", scholars ask:

(a) Why are large parts of the
    first three Gospels not only
    similar, but often identical
    word for word? This becomes
    very apparent in a synopsis of
    the Gospels, which prints the
    Gospels in parallel columns (see
    "Triumphal Entry" on page 52).

Old Testament Abraham Moses Liberator Teacher The Law David The Shepherd King The Covenant Solomon gnificent The New Testament St Luke's Gospel Salvation History The Roman Empire Galatians **part three** Ap he Gentiles The Prophets Amos Hosea **history embedded in literature** of Creation The Psalms The Wis rature Daniel The Passion Resurrection Jesus The Old Testament Abraham Moses Liberator Law David The Shep g The **new testament** The Roman Empire Acts of the Apostles Philippians Paul Apostle of the Gentiles Th :ament Abraham Moses Liberator Teacher The Law David The Shepherd King The Covenant Solomon the Magnif

(b) Why are there very real differences between the three Gospels?

The generally accepted solution is that there were various sources on which the evangelists drew.

Initially the early Church had thought it unnecessary to write down the story of Jesus, believing his second coming would happen during their lifetime. The story was told by eyewitnesses who had been with Jesus, and passed on orally. But in the first severe persecution of Christians by the Emperor Nero in Rome in AD 64, both Peter and Paul were martyred. Such a severe loss, both of leaders of the Church and of a leading eyewitness of Jesus, led the Church to realise its belief concerning a speedy second coming was misplaced and they must make provision for a longer-term future.

St Mark's Gospel is widely believed to have been written in Rome shortly after the persecution by Nero. The writers of Matthew and Luke both appear to have used Mark, since Matthew's Gospel contains about 600 of Mark's 661

verses, and Luke incorporates over half of Mark's account. Matthew and Luke share about 200 verses (mostly sayings of Jesus) which are not in Mark. The general view of scholars is that they come from another common source which they name "Q" (from *Quelle*, German for "source"). Material found

> Matthew is unlikely to be the author of Matthew's Gospel since, as a disciple and eyewitness of Jesus, he would be unlikely to draw on others' writings. It is suggested the Gospel claimed his name from a substratum he wrote that is incorporated in the **M** material, possibly a collection of Old Testament prophecies.

only in Matthew's Gospel they call "M" and that found only in Luke's Gospel is called "L".

Thus the "classical" solution to the Synoptic Problem states that the similarity between the three Gospels is because the authors of Matthew and Luke each drew on Mark's Gospel and Q. The distinctions are accounted for by Matthew's use of M and Luke's use of L. But there are many variations on this hypothesis: that Matthew came first, that there never was a Q, etc.

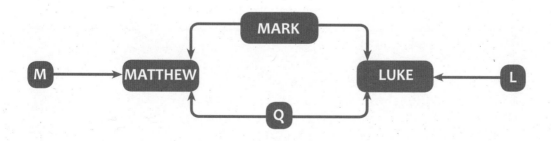

Old Testament Abraham Moses Liberator Teacher The Law David The Shepherd King The Covenant Solomon
nificent **part three** ament St Luke's Gospel Salvation History The Roman Empire Galatians Christian Paul Ap
e Gentiles The Prophets Amos Hose **history embedded in literature** of Creation The Psalms The Wis
rature Daniel The Passion Resurrection Jesus The Old Testament Abraham Moses Liberator Law David The Shep
The Covenant Galatians The Roman Empire Acts of the Apostles Philippians Paul Ap **new testament** The
ament Abraham Moses Liberator Teacher The Law David The Shepherd King The Covenant Solomon the Magnifi

THE TRIUMPHAL ENTRY INTO JERUSALEM

Matthew 21:1-9	Mark 11:1-10	Luke 19:28-38
1 When they had come near Jerusalem and had reached Bethphage, at the Mount of Olives, Jesus sent two disciples, 2 saying to them, "Go into the village ahead of you, and immediately you will find a donkey tied, and a colt with her; untie them and bring them to me. 3 If anyone says anything to you, just say this, 'The Lord needs them.' And he will send them immediately." 4 This took place to fulfil what had been spoken through the prophet, saying, 5 "Tell the daughter of Zion, Look, your king is coming to you, humble, and mounted on a donkey and on a colt, the foal of a donkey." 6 The disciples went	1 When they were approaching Jerusalem, at Bethphage and Bethany, near the Mount of Olives, he sent two of his disciples 2 and said to them, "Go into the village ahead of you, and immediately as you enter it, you will find tied there a colt that has never been ridden; untie it and bring it. 3 If anyone says to you, 'Why are you doing this?' just say this, 'The Lord needs it and will send it back here immediately.'"	28 After he had said this, he went on ahead, going up to Jerusalem. 29 When he had come near Bethphage and Bethany, at the place called the Mount of Olives, he sent two of the disciples, 30 saying, "Go into the village ahead of you, and as you enter it you will find tied there a colt that has never been ridden. Untie it and bring it here. 31 If anyone asks you, 'Why are you untying it?' just say this, 'The Lord needs it.'"
and did	4 They went away and found a colt tied near a door, outside in the street. As they were untying it, 5 some of the bystanders said to them, "What are you doing, untying the colt?"	32 So those who were sent departed and found it as he had told them. 33 As they were untying the colt, its owners asked them, "Why are you untying the colt?"
as Jesus had directed them; 7 they brought the donkey and the colt, and put their cloaks on them, and he sat on them. 8 A very large crowd spread their cloaks on the road, and others cut branches from the trees and spread them on the road.	6 They told them what Jesus had said; and they allowed them to take it. 7 Then they brought the colt to Jesus and threw their cloaks on it; and he sat on it. 8 Many people spread their cloaks on the road, and others spread leafy branches that they had cut in the fields.	34 They said, "The Lord needs it." 35 Then they brought it to Jesus; and after throwing their cloaks on the colt, they set Jesus on it. 36 As he rode along, people kept spreading their cloaks on the road.
		37 As he was now approaching, the path down from the Mount of Olives, the whole multitude of the disciples began to praise God joyfully with a loud voice for all the deeds of power that they had seen, 38 saying,
9 The crowds that went ahead of him and that followed were shouting, "Hosanna to the Son of David! Blessed is the one who comes in the name of the Lord! Hosanna in the highest heaven!"	9 Then those who went ahead and those who followed were shouting "Hosanna! Blessed is the one who comes in the name of the Lord! 10 Blessed is the coming kingdom of our ancestor David! Hosanna in the highest heaven!"	"Blessed is the King who comes in the name of the Lord! Peace in heaven, and glory in the highest heaven!"

Old Testament Abraham Moses Liberator Teacher The Law David The Shepherd King The Covenant Solomon gnificent The New Testament St Luke's Gospel Salvation History The Roman Empire Galatians **part three** Ap he Gentiles The Prophets Amos Hosea **history embedded in literature** of Creation The Psalms The Wis rature Daniel The Passion Resurrection Jesus The Old Testament Abraham Moses Liberator Law David The Shep g The **new testament** The Roman Empire Acts of the Apostles Philippians Paul Apostle of the Gentiles Th ament Abraham Moses Liberator Teacher The Law David The Shepherd King The Covenant Solomon the Magnif

A note on current scholarship

Until recently, biblical scholars concentrated on how the Gospels grew and were shaped. They therefore compared texts, and explored source criticism (sources used by the evangelists), form criticism (how and why the stories of Jesus were "shaped" by the early Christian communities that transmitted them), and redaction criticism (regarding the Gospel writer's intention in his particular selection of material).

The preceding pages present the "classical" account arrived at by biblical scholars. This shows that there is a real relationship between the first three Gospels, but also that the relationship is quite complicated.

However, a contemporary shift in emphasis now applies new literary methods borrowed from those used in studying English literature. This results in the starting point not being with the original intention of the author, as hitherto, but with the final text as we have received it, and with the individual reader of this text, whose understanding of it will be coloured by who he or she is and what his or her outlook, interests and experience are.

Thus a Gospel is regarded by scholars today as an entity or portrait in its own right. The question becomes, what is the evangelist saying to me now through the character(s) and events he depicts?

This brings two positive results:

(a) approaching a Gospel in this way enables it to become live to me in my situation;

(b) we don't need to trouble ourselves overmuch with critical details.

CAN WE KNOW THE HISTORICAL JESUS?

Following the Age of Reason in the eighteenth century, German scholars in the nineteenth century sought to find the historical Jesus in the Gospels. What they discovered was an ethical Jesus who reflected their own stance, so that it was said they looked down a well and saw their own reflection.

This stage ended with the publication in 1906 of Albert Schweitzer's *Quest of the Historical Jesus*. Instead of seeing Jesus as a liberal German Protestant as hitherto, Schweitzer saw Jesus as someone who was consumed with apocalyptic interests (i.e. revealing "what is hidden") and eschatology (prophecies concerning the "end" days).

Subsequent scholars initiated a New Quest, which centred on Jesus' teaching on the kingdom of God.

The current Third Quest asks, "What do you think Jesus was like?" There is a much stronger sense now of Jesus as a Jew in his first-century environment. Moreover, the fact that the Gospels were written *after* the resurrection (when the outcome of the story of Jesus was known) means they transfer a "resurrection interpretation" back into the teaching and ministry of Jesus. This enables the reader more easily to understand what, at the actual time of the events described, was initially confusing to the disciples.

A contemporary example might be if a man and woman, after years of marriage, were to compare *recollections* of their first meeting together, with what *actually* happened on that occasion. The results would be unlikely to tally! Similarly, the Gospel stories were not written at the time of the events described, but years later when a deeper understanding of Jesus had been gained.

Ultimately, we bring ourselves and our own experiences to our reading of the Gospels; no two people will therefore receive exactly the same picture of Jesus. If we are to relate to him at all, it is perhaps inevitable that to some extent we look down a well and see our own reflection.

Old Testament Abraham Moses Liberator Teacher The Law David The Shepherd King The Covenant Solomon
nificent **part three** ament St Luke's Gospel Salvation History The Roman Empire Galatians Christian Paul Apo
e Gentiles The Prophets Amos Hose **history embedded in literature** of Creation The Psalms The Wisd
ature Daniel The Passion Resurrection Jesus The Old Testament Abraham Moses Liberator Law David The Shepl
The Covenant Galatians The Roman Empire Acts of the Apostles Philippians Paul Ap **new testament** The
ament Abraham Moses Liberator Teacher The Law David The Shepherd King The Covenant Solomon the Magnifi

St Luke's Gospel: Salvation History

LUKE – AUTHOR OF "SALVATION HISTORY"

For many, Luke is the most popular theologian in the New Testament. The fourteenth-century poet Dante described Luke as "the evangelist of God's tenderness" and "a scribe of the gentleness of Christ", while the nineteenth-century French philosopher Renan regarded Luke's Gospel as "the most beautiful book in the world".

Luke is the only Gentile (i.e. non-Jewish) writer in the New Testament. His two volumes of the Gospel and the Acts of the Apostles, probably written in the 80s, are presented as researched treatises addressed in the opening verses of each volume to Theophilus (meaning "lover of God"), who is obviously an educated man of standing in the Roman Empire. Possibly Theophilus was known personally to Luke, but it is more likely that he represented any Gentile "lover of God" who, in a position of responsibility, had power to determine how Christians were to be treated in an age of uncertainty. Luke presents Christians as law-abiding citizens of the Empire.

From the second century AD, Luke has been regarded as author of Luke/Acts. He was a companion of Paul (2 Timothy 4:11; Philemon 24) and also a doctor (Colossians 4:14), and writes in elegant Greek. Possibly based in Syrian Antioch, the centre of the growing Gentile Church

(Acts 11:19-21; 13:1-3), his recurring theme is of universalism – the Gospel is for all peoples. So Luke's genealogy of Jesus goes back to Adam (Luke 3:38).

Luke presents us with "salvation history". He sees Jesus as the focal point in a three-part historical process which started with the Old Testament, is fulfilled in Jesus, and is continued (in the book of Acts) in the life of the Church, the era of the Holy Spirit.

Whereas Matthew uses Old Testament proof-texts to show how Jesus fulfils the Old Testament and is the Christ, Luke is more subtle. He sees the Old Testament as undergirding and giving meaning to all the events in the life of Jesus. Finally, the risen Lord shows the disciples, slow to understand his teaching, how all that had happened to him was foretold in the scriptures (24:27, 44-48).

Luke did not know the human Jesus. He had become a Christian through the witness of the Gentile churches, so the Lord he first came to know was already risen and exalted. This "end-of-story" knowledge colours his presentation of Jesus during his ministry.

God in his great love for estranged humanity has visited his people, sending his only Son to die for us, so that God might welcome us with his overflowing forgiveness (Luke 15:20-24). To convey this, each evangelist gives detailed accounts of Jesus' passion and crucifixion.

A good beginning would be to read the Gospel straight through as though it were a novel.

Old Testament Abraham Moses Liberator Teacher The Law David The Shepherd King The Covenant Solomon nificent The New Testament St Luke's Gospel Salvation History The Roman Empire Galatians **part three** Apo e Gentiles The Prophets Amos Hosea **history embedded in literature** of Creation The Psalms The Wis ature Daniel The Passion Resurrection Jesus The Old Testament Abraham Moses Liberator Law David The Shep The **new testament** The Roman Empire Acts of the Apostles Philippians Paul Apostle of the Gentiles The ament Abraham Moses Liberator Teacher The Law David The Shepherd King The Covenant Solomon the Magnifi

SUGGESTED READINGS AND POINTS TO CONSIDER AS YOU READ

Jesus' sermon at Nazareth proclaims his public ministry	Luke 4:14-44
Based on Isaiah 61:1-2 and 58:6, he outlines the nature of his mission under the guidance of the Holy Spirit – to the poor, oppressed and blind, all of whom are prominent in the Gospel.	
His mission includes Gentiles too (4:24-27); this precipitates fierce opposition.	
(The freedom and restoration to wholeness in Isaiah 61:1-2 reflect the year of Jubilee every fiftieth year, when theoretically debts were cancelled and slaves freed. See Leviticus 25:8-12.)	
"Today" (4:21), together with references at the beginning and end of the Gospel (2:11; 23:43), indicate how Jesus forms the pivotal point of history.	
The centrality of universalism (the Gospel is for all) in Luke	Luke 2:14, 32; 3:6; 13:29; 14:21-24; 24:47
Passages (only in Luke) referring to sinners, Samaritans and women show the compassion of Jesus and God's deep love for humankind	Luke 7:11-17, 36-50; 8:1-3; 9:51-56; 10:38-42; 13:10-17; 17:11-19; 19:1-10; 23:27-31,39-43
Note how people are constantly faced with choices. Luke wants his readers to share in the Gospel he has discovered.	
God's deep love for humankind is illustrated also by some of the best-known parables, found only in Luke	Luke 10:25-37; 15:1-32; 18:1-14
Other prominent features include references to joy	1:14; 2:10; 10:17; 15:7, 10; 24:41, 52
and to the Holy Spirit.	1:15, 35, 41, 67; 2:25-26; 4:1-2; 10:21; 24:49
Jesus' whole ministry is undergirded by prayer	Luke 3:21-22; 5:12-16; 6:12-13; 11:1-2
Note how many of the main points in Jesus' ministry take place in the context of prayer	22:31-32, 39-46; 23:34; 24:50-51
and his first and last recorded words are to his Father.	2:49; 23:46
Luke's Gospel is characterised also by sternness: disciples must be aware of the crucial decisions they make and of their implications.	9:57-62; 14:26 (see Matthew 10:37), 31-33

POSSIBLE ISSUES FOR DISCUSSION

1   At Nazareth, Jesus presents his mission as a fulfilment of Old
    Testament prophecies.

    Read Isaiah 61:1-2 and 58:6 and the account of the fiftieth year of
    Jubilee in Leviticus 25:8-12.

    Consider the costliness to Jesus himself (as early as Luke 4:29-30) of
    his programme of action.

    How does this relate to the challenge facing the rich nations to relieve
    the debts of the poorest nations?

    Is Jesus' teaching on universalism applicable here?

2   Women feature prominently in Luke's Gospel.

    Compare the position of women today in secular society and in the
    Church.

    Does their position in either sphere have any repercussions for men?

3   Is joy a characteristic you associate with Christians today?

    How do you account for your answer?

4   The disciples were so impressed with the priority and meaning prayer
    had for Jesus that they asked him to teach them to pray.

    He answered with the Lord's Prayer (Luke 11:2-4).

    What does this prayer mean for us and what are its implications?

5   "While there is life there is change."

    The thrust of Jesus' teaching is to encourage people to change their
    ways of perception and living.

    The importance of our choice regarding discipleship is crucial to Luke.

    Do we regard the importance of this choice as equally important to us
    today?

    Why are we so often resistant to such change?

Old Testament Abraham Moses Liberator Teacher The Law David The Shepherd King The Covenant Solomon
gnificent The New Testament St Luke's Gospel Salvation History The Roman Empire Galatians **part three**
he Gentiles The Prophets Amos Hosea **history embedded in literature** of Creation The Psalms The Wi
rature Daniel The Passion Resurrection Jesus The Old Testament Abraham Moses Liberator Law David The She
The **new testament** The Roman Empire Acts of the Apostles Philippians Paul Apostle of the Gentiles Th
ament Abraham Moses Liberator Teacher The Law David The Shepherd King The Covenant Solomon the Magni

SUGGESTED READINGS AND POINTS TO CONSIDER AS YOU READ

Jesus' prediction of his passion (suffering)	
(a) While praying, Jesus questions the disciples about their interpretation of him, and foretells his passion (suffering) on three occasions.	Luke 9:18-22, 43-45; 18:31-34
(b) While praying, Jesus' true glory is seen.	Luke 9:28-36
Jesus fulfils the Law and Prophets, represented by Moses and Elijah (believed not to have died, 2 Kings 2:9-12); they talk of Jesus' "departure" (i.e. death) in Jerusalem.	
How does this passage resonate with Jesus' baptism?	Luke 3:21-22
(c) 9:51 – 19:28 describes Jesus' ascent to Jerusalem – a journey he sees as inevitable, where he will die (see "must", "set his face").	Luke 9:22, 51; 12:50; 13:33
He is the Suffering Servant who will offer his life for others.	Luke 22:37 (see Isaiah 50:7; 53:12)

Jesus' passion and crucifixion	
(a) At the Last Supper, Jesus' actions with bread and wine signify the meaning of his death; he foretells Simon Peter's betrayal.	Luke 22:14-38
The women accompanying Jesus from Galilee (8:2-3; 23:55) may also have been present at the Last Supper, most probably sitting at upright tables in the same room, from which they served Jesus and his disciples, who would be reclining, Roman-fashion.	
(b) In the agony in the garden, Jesus struggles with himself and God, as his sweat flows like blood. Finally, he goes forward confidently to the cross, at one with himself and his Father, thinking only of others.	Luke 22:39-46
(c) The three trials of Jesus:	
After torture in the High Priest's house, Jesus is forwarded to the Jewish council. They base their charge of blasphemy (carrying the death sentence: see Leviticus 24:16) on Jesus' enigmatic response to their question. However, a death sentence requires Roman ratification.	Luke 22:54-71
The charge before Pilate is therefore changed to one of treason; Pilate three times protests Jesus' innocence (23:4, 14, 22).	Luke 23:1-5, 18-25
Pilate forwards Jesus for trial to Herod Antipas, tetrarch of Galilee, who hopes to see a sign performed by Jesus. Jesus' demeanour is that of the Suffering Servant.	Luke 23:6-17 (see 3:19-20; 9:7-9; 13:31-33; Isaiah 53:7)
Note how:	
(i) Herod finds Jesus innocent;	
(ii) Herod's soldiers, not Pilate's, mock Jesus;	
(iii) even as a prisoner, Jesus establishes reconciliation between enemies.	
Why do you suppose perhaps Pilate forwarded Jesus to Herod?	

In the Gospels of Luke and John, Pilate three times judges Jesus not guilty. Matthew also (following Mark) records Jesus' innocence three times, but in different contexts and with added details.

As Pilate sits on the judgement seat about to pronounce his verdict on Jesus, his wife sends him a message not to convict Jesus, who is innocent: she has suffered greatly in a dream concerning him. However, Pilate's subsequent efforts to "negotiate" Jesus' release founder and he succumbs to pressure (Matthew 27:19-23).

Both Judas and Pilate come to realise they have betrayed innocent blood; Pilate's washing of his hands after condemning Jesus is his attempted statement of both Jesus' – and his own – innocence (Matthew 27:3-5, 24).

SUGGESTED READINGS AND POINTS TO CONSIDER AS YOU READ
continued

The crucifixion	
Luke invites us to experience what it is to be the betraying and forgiven Peter (22:54-62); Simon of Cyrene bearing the cross; the women bewailing Jesus; the forgiven thief; to feel the forgiveness Jesus offers to his persecutors; to hear his final commendation of himself to God in the words of his night prayers (Psalm 31:5), prefixed by "Father"; and to hear the centurion's testimony.	Luke 23:26-56

The seven "words" from the cross as presented by each evangelist

My God, my God, why have you forsaken me? — Mark 15:34; Matthew 27:46 (Psalm 22:1)

Father, forgive them, for they do not know what they are doing. — Luke 23:34

Truly I tell you, today you will be with me in Paradise. — Luke 23:43

Father, into your hands I commend my spirit. — Luke 23:46 (Psalm 31:5)

Woman, here is your son; here is your mother. — John 19:26-27

I am thirsty. — John 19:28

It is finished. — John 19:30

(But note how the Church takes words from different Gospels and mixes them together [just as it mixes the birth narratives from Matthew and Luke].)

Old Testament Abraham Moses Liberator Teacher The Law David The Shepherd King The Covenant Solomon gnificent The New Testament St Luke's Gospel Salvation History The Roman Empire Galatians **part three** Ap he Gentiles The Prophets Amos Hosea **history embedded in literature** of Creation The Psalms The Wis rature Daniel The Passion Resurrection Jesus The Old Testament Abraham Moses Liberator Law David The Shep The **new testament** The Roman Empire Acts of the Apostles Philippians Paul Apostle of the Gentiles Th ament Abraham Moses Liberator Teacher The Law David The Shepherd King The Covenant Solomon the Magnif

SUGGESTED READINGS AND POINTS TO CONSIDER AS YOU READ
continued

The resurrection	
The empty tomb is discovered by the women.	Luke 24:1-12
The encounter by two disciples walking to Emmaus with the risen Jesus, who (though unrecognised) elucidates the scriptures foretelling the crucifixion and resurrection of the Messiah, Jesus of Nazareth. What was the effect on the disciples of Jesus talking with them? How did these disciples finally recognise the risen Lord? Note Jesus' special appearance to Simon Peter, following on his betrayal (24:34).	Luke 24:13-35
The risen Lord (no ghost, he is recognised through his wounds, and eats in their midst) elucidates the scriptures, and foretells the Gentile mission and descent of the Spirit. Jesus' exaltation and glorification result in the disciples joyfully waiting in the Temple for the coming of the Spirit.	Luke 24:36-49 24:50-53

Luke's is the only Gospel to restrict the resurrection appearances to Judea.

Mark's Gospel ended originally at 16:8. This was regarded by many as an abrupt ending, because apparently leaving the story "unfinished" when compared with the other three Gospels. A precis of resurrection stories from other Gospels was therefore appended to Mark. However, this is an unfair comparison, because Mark almost certainly wrote his Gospel before the other three. Mark feels he has ended the story, because his readers already know, and live daily in the power of, the risen Lord – so there is no need to say any more.

Matthew's Gospel includes the detail of the guard placed over the tomb; presumably Pilate intended the use of the Temple guard. The Gospel ends with Jesus' commission to the apostles on a mountain in Galilee to preach the Gospel to all nations, to baptise in the name of the Father, the Son and the Holy Spirit, and to pass on all Jesus' teachings.

Old Testament Abraham Moses Liberator Teacher The Law David The Shepherd King The Covenant Solomon
nificent **part three** ament St Luke's Gospel Salvation History The Roman Empire Galatians Christian Paul Ap
he Gentiles The Prophets Amos Hose **history embedded in literature** of Creation The Psalms The Wis
rature Daniel The Passion Resurrection Jesus The Old Testament Abraham Moses Liberator Law David The Shep
The Covenant Galatians The Roman Empire Acts of the Apostles Philippians Paul Ap **new testament** The
ament Abraham Moses Liberator Teacher The Law David The Shepherd King The Covenant Solomon the Magnifi

THE INFANCY NARRATIVES – LUKE CHAPTERS 1 AND 2

The infancy narratives introduce both Gospel and Acts by laying out theological themes; they appear to have an Aramaic background. If chapters 1 and 2 are read in a Bible with cross-references, the number of verses resonating with Old Testament passages (but without explicitly quoting them) is very striking.	Luke chapters 1 and 2
Jerusalem and the Temple are central.	Luke 1:8-9; 2:22, 41-50
Jesus is described as: Son of the Most High — Son of David Son of God — King Saviour — the Messiah the Lord a light for revelation to the Gentiles	Luke 1:32-35; 2:11, 32
Jesus comes for all peoples.	Luke 2:14, 32
The Holy Spirit initiates, guides, sanctifies.	Luke 1:15, 35, 41, 67; 2:25-26
The songs (which are prayers) spell out Jesus' mission.	Luke 1:46-55, 67-79; 2:29-32
Can you see any similarities between Mary's song of joy (1:46-55) and Jesus' sermon at Nazareth (4:14-30)?	
The shepherds, after witnessing the baby, go out to spread the message.	Luke 2:16-20
The presence of Jesus will demand a response, for or against him.	Luke 2:33-35
The climax of Jesus' childhood takes place in his Father's house.	Luke 2:41-50
As a historian, Luke gives careful cross-reference dates.	Luke 2:1-2; 3:1-2

Old Testament Abraham Moses Liberator Teacher The Law David The Shepherd King The Covenant Solomon
nificent The New Testament St Luke's Gospel Salvation History The Roman Empire Galatians **part three** Ap
he Gentiles The Prophets Amos Hosea **history embedded in literature** of Creation The Psalms The Wis
ature Daniel The Passion Resurrection Jesus The Old Testament Abraham Moses Liberator Law David The Shep
The **new testament** The Roman Empire Acts of the Apostles Philippians Paul Apostle of the Gentiles Th
ament Abraham Moses Liberator Teacher The Law David The Shepherd King The Covenant Solomon the Magnif

POSSIBLE ISSUES FOR DISCUSSION

1   Just as sick people need a doctor (Luke 5:31), Jesus shows how sinners desperately need the God whom he reveals as total love.

Since God the Father loves us more than we can ever love ourselves, and longs for us to know his love and forgiveness, he sent his Son to reveal his love, offer his life for us, and so woo us back from our selfishness, alienation and sin to his self-giving love.

Is this how you think of God the Father – as a God who longs for us and loves us more than we can imagine (and who therefore incidentally suffered fully alongside Jesus in his passion)? (See 15:11-32.)

If not, how do you think of him, and why?

2   In God's sending his Son to reveal his love, Jesus entered every aspect of human darkness and suffering with a total self-giving of his life – there is nowhere the love of God cannot penetrate.

We generally think of selfishness, alienation and sin in individual terms.

However, we are all involved also in corporate sin (i.e. sin committed by the groups to which we belong).

Can you see, for instance, the techniques used by any corporate group to bring about Jesus' death?

What power does the group give to its members?

Can you think of aspects of corporate sin in our day?

3   The story of the road to Emmaus (24:13-33) shows how the risen Lord accompanies us on our life's journey, engaging with our problems alongside us if we are open to him.

However, we often recognise his presence only with hindsight (24:31-32).

Can you recall any experiences in your own life where this was true?

4   Normally, saying goodbye to someone we love is accompanied by sadness.

How do you therefore account for the joy the disciples felt after Jesus' ascension (24:50-53)?

5   What do the poetic sections in the infancy narratives (chapters 1 and 2) tell us about the nature of Jesus' ministry?

Introduction to the Roman Empire in the First Century

Introduction to the Roman Empire in the First Century

In the first century, Christianity spread extremely rapidly throughout the Roman Empire.

This rapid spread was enormously aided by various factors:

(a) the "common" Greek language spoken throughout the Empire;

(b) the excellent network of military roads and seas free of pirates;

(c) peace throughout the Empire (the Pax Romana), together with Roman justice, which could usually be relied upon;

(d) the presence of Jews throughout the Empire, so that the synagogue provided the natural centre for initial preaching;

(e) the considerable disillusion among many pagans with their religions, which created a religious vacuum waiting to be filled.

Rome's religious policy required that all captive peoples add worship of the Emperor as divine to that of their own gods (so making any insurrection sacrilegious). This posed no problem to polytheists. But Jews, strict monotheists, refused this demand point-blank. Rome granted them exemption, for the sake of stability, and initially extended this to Christians, regarded as a sect of Judaism.

This tolerance towards Christians ended abruptly in AD 64 with the Emperor Nero's horrendous persecution in Rome of the Christians, whom he accused of setting the city on fire. Thereafter, persecution of Christians by Rome could break out at any time.

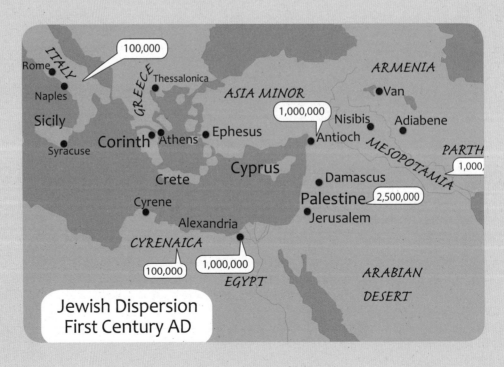

Jewish Dispersion First Century AD

Old Testament Abraham Moses Liberator Teacher The Law David The Shepherd King The Covenant Solomon gnificent The New Testament St Luke's Gospel Salvation History The Roman Empire Galatians **part three** A he Gentiles The Prophets Amos Hosea **history embedded in literature** of Creation The Psalms The Wi rature Daniel The Passion Resurrection Jesus The Old Testament Abraham Moses Liberator Law David The Sher g The **new testament** The Roman Empire Acts of the Apostles Philippians Paul Apostle of the Gentiles Th ament Abraham Moses Liberator Teacher The Law David The Shepherd King The Covenant Solomon the Magni

Galatians: Charter of Christian Freedom from Paul, Apostle to the Gentiles

This letter may be the earliest New Testament writing, though some argue that 1 Thessalonians is earlier. Galatians was written after Paul's first journey to the Roman province of Galatia in Asia Minor (Acts 13:1 – 14:28), and before the first General Council of the Church held in Jerusalem in about AD 49 (Acts 15:1-35). The Council was called to consider whether Gentiles could be Christians:

(a) on equal terms with Jews, but without keeping the Jewish Law, or

(b) only if they first became Jews (through male circumcision and adherence to the whole of the Law, including the food laws – the Jews ate apart from Gentiles). (This was the position of Paul's opponents.)

This issue was crucial for the future of the Church: what was now the status of the Law of Moses for Christians, whether Jew or Gentile? Was the Gospel for **all**, or only for Jews?

Were Christians still under the Law, or free in Christ?

Moreover, Paul has to defend his status as an apostle, which is under attack, or his teaching will not be accepted.

From Antioch (the first Gentile Church, Acts 11:19-26), Paul and Barnabas sailed to Galatia (Acts 13:1-3), where they converted and baptised many Gentiles without any insistence that they should

> Circumcision was abhorrent to most Gentiles. If it was to be required of all converts, Christianity would remain a Jewish sect which happened to believe the Messiah had come, rather than a universal faith for **all** peoples.

keep the Law. Now Paul's opponents have told these converts they aren't Christians at all, because they haven't become Jews first. They are confused… and reverting…

Paul describes God's free initiative of love in sending Jesus. His crucifixion at the hands of people not unlike us broke the power of the Law over us. All that is required now is our free response in love to God's initiative of love, and we will know true life and freedom, never obtainable under the Law (Galatians 2:21; 5:1).

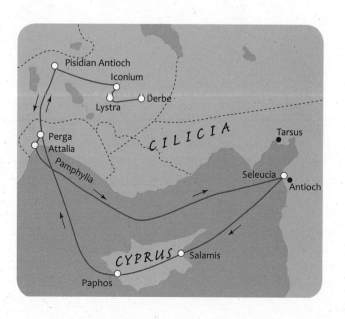

Old Testament Abraham Moses Liberator Teacher The Law David The Shepherd King The Covenant Solomon
ificent **part three** ament St Luke's Gospel Salvation History The Roman Empire Galatians Christian Paul Ap
e Gentiles The Prophets Amos Hose **history embedded in literature** of Creation The Psalms The Wis
ture Daniel The Passion Resurrection Jesus The Old Testament Abraham Moses Liberator Law David The Shep
The Covenant Galatians The Roman Empire Acts of the Apostles Philippians Paul Ap **new testament** The
ment Abraham Moses Liberator Teacher The Law David The Shepherd King The Covenant Solomon the Magnif

SUGGESTED READINGS AND POINTS TO CONSIDER AS YOU READ

*Cephas is **Peter** in Aramaic; **James**, related to Jesus, not one of the Twelve, was head of the Church in Jerusalem.*

Paul's converts are troubled by opponents of Paul who insist that Christians should keep the Jewish Law	Galatians 1:6-9; 3:1-5; 4:8-9, 19-20; 5:1-4
Paul defends his apostleship.	Galatians 1:1, 10-24 (compare Acts 9:1-19); 2:1-9
Personal experience of the risen Christ who has sent him to preach is the basis on which Paul defends his apostleship (these were the criteria used to choose the apostle who was chosen to fill Judas' place – Acts 1:21-22).	
How does Paul claim his apostleship is of equal status with Peter's?	
The showdown between Peter and Paul	Galatians 2:11-14
Salvation is by faith in Christ, not by Law	Galatians 2:15-21; 3:10, 13, 23-28; 4:6-7
Faith is our free acceptance of what God has done for us in Christ.	Galatians 5:11, 16-18, 25; 6:8b, 14-15
Christians are called to freedom in Christ	Galatians 5:1, 13, 18
All peoples (without distinction, 3:28) who accept Christ in faith and are baptised into him (3:27) are united with him and with each other in one family through his Spirit – and know him as our tender loving Father (4:6).	
Gentiles too are Abraham's descendants	Galatians 3:6-9, 14-18, 29
Abraham, the man of faith who received the promise, preceded (and therefore has precedence over) Moses, who gave the Law.	
The Law shows our need for Christ	Galatians 3:10-13, 19, 21; 4:1-5
The Law, good in itself, is a curse bringing death because no one can fulfil it completely. Jesus placed himself under the curse of the Law (Deuteronomy 21:23), so breaking its power over us.	
Love is the true fulfilment of the Law	Galatians 2:20c; 5:6b, 14, 22-23; 6:1-2

Old Testament Abraham Moses Liberator Teacher The Law David The Shepherd King The Covenant Solomon nificent The New Testament St Luke's Gospel Salvation History The Roman Empire Galatians **part three** Ap he Gentiles The Prophets Amos Hosea **history embedded in literature** of Creation The Psalms The Wis ature Daniel The Passion Resurrection Jesus The Old Testament Abraham Moses Liberator Law David The Shep The **new testament** The Roman Empire Acts of the Apostles Philippians Paul Apostle of the Gentiles The ament Abraham Moses Liberator Teacher The Law David The Shepherd King The Covenant Solomon the Magnifi

A suggestion for some practical work on the incident in Galatians 2:11-14

1 Peter (or Cephas) visits Antioch and happily joins in with the Jewish and Gentile Christians who are eating together. (See Peter's vision about Gentiles in Acts 10:1 – 11:18.)

2 Representatives arrive from James, head of the Church in Jerusalem. They complain that, since the Gentile Christians have not first become Jews through circumcision and adherence to the Law of Moses, they are not really Christians at all – thus challenging both Paul and his converts.

3 As a result, Peter, and even Barnabas (Paul's companion in converting the Galatians) withdraw from the Gentile Christians to eat with Jewish Christians only.

4 Paul tackles Peter in public, accusing him of inconsistency and of not practising what he believes.

An imaginative exercise

In an imaginative exercise we enter into another person's personality as far as possible and really feel what it is to be him/her. Thus it uses the *imagination* – and is different from *pretence*.

The various steps involved
(Steps 1 and 2 only may be used, if so desired.)

1 List all the characters in the story.

Peter; Paul; Barnabas; Gentile Christians; Jewish Christians accepting Paul's Gentile converts; opponents of Paul from Jerusalem.

2 If this is being done by a group, ask *all* the group members to consider *together* the following four questions, applying them to *each* of the salient characters/groups in the story in turn (if this book is being is being used for personal study, rather than group

work, this can still be done by an individual):

   a. **Who am I?**

   b. **What am I thinking?**

   c. **What am I doing?**

   d. **What am I saying?**

(NB Speech, which arises from what I'm thinking and doing, is not always necessary.)

These questions enable everyone to get into the skin of each character/ group, e.g.

   a. I'm Peter.

   b. I *thought* God had shown me Gentiles could be Christians without first becoming Jews (by circumcision and keeping the Law). But listening to these adherents of the Law from Jerusalem, I wonder if I'm right.

   c. So I'm getting up to eat with Jewish Christians – these Gentiles may not really be Christians after all; I'd better play safe...

   d. Suggest what he's saying (if *anything*).

3 Members are then selected for the various characters involved and present the situation to other group members.

4 Afterwards, let all members (first the characters, then the audience) share their various experiences and feelings.

5 *Debrief* all the characters. Be especially sure to let any who have entered deeply into particular characters talk things through in order to "become themselves" again. *This is most important*, as such an exercise can be very powerful, and no one should be left "in character".

If you wish you can repeat by recasting *and* debriefing.

POSSIBLE ISSUES FOR DISCUSSION

1 "The stumbling block of the cross" (Galatians 5:11b).

For Jews, how could one "cursed" under the Law be the Christ (Deuteronomy 21:22-23)?

For Gentiles, the concept of a crucified saviour was folly (see 1 Corinthians 1:18).

Is the cross still a stumbling block today?

> Graffiti from the period shows a man with the head of an ass on a cross, with the words "Alexamenos worships his god".

2 Note that Paul's opponents (enemies of his Gospel) are not "baddies".

They genuinely and fervently believe that to keep the Law is God's ordained way of serving him – a way that brings joy and blessing because of God's loving generosity in giving Jews the Law.

Therefore any Gentile wishing to serve God as a Christian must first become a Jew.

In contrast, Paul maintains God's grace is for all, through faith and baptism, irrespective of race or religion; therefore the Jewish Law is no longer essential.

(a) Are Paul's opponents attempting to force God's hand? Can human beings put pressure on God?

Can we "work our passage" into the kingdom?

(b) Listen in on the following conversation between two fifth-century Christians – Pelagius, from Britain, and St Augustine, Bishop of Hippo (in North Africa):

Pel: Human beings must make *some* moral effort of their own to be saved.

Aug: But we're saved by God's grace alone.

Pel: If that's true, then it's God alone who determines our salvation, and human beings have lost their freedom.

Aug: I say, "Love God, and do as you will." Our only *real* freedom is the freedom to do what *God* wills. And we will do this, provided we first love him.

Pel: That sounds to me rather like licence to do anything…

Aug: You've not heard what I said. It's not easy. But it's the only way…

Which of these two do you think is closest to the mind of Paul?

> The word **grace** refers to a gift from God that he *offers* – in pure generosity and love, and without any pressure for it to be received. It evokes from the recipient quite spontaneously a response of love, joy and deep gratitude.
>
> Based on W. H. Vanstone in *Fare Well in Christ*, DLT, 1997.

Old Testament Abraham Moses Liberator Teacher The Law David The Shepherd King The Covenant Solomon
gnificent The New Testament St Luke's Gospel Salvation History The Roman Empire Galatians **part three**
he Gentiles The Prophets Amos Hosea **history embedded in literature** of Creation The Psalms The Wi
rature Daniel The Passion Resurrection Jesus The Old Testament Abraham Moses Liberator Law David The She
g **new testament** The Roman Empire Acts of the Apostles Philippians Paul Apostle of the Gentiles Th
tament Abraham Moses Liberator Teacher The Law David The Shepherd King The Covenant Solomon the Magni

Acts of the Apostles: The Gospel Becomes Universal in the Age of the Holy Spirit

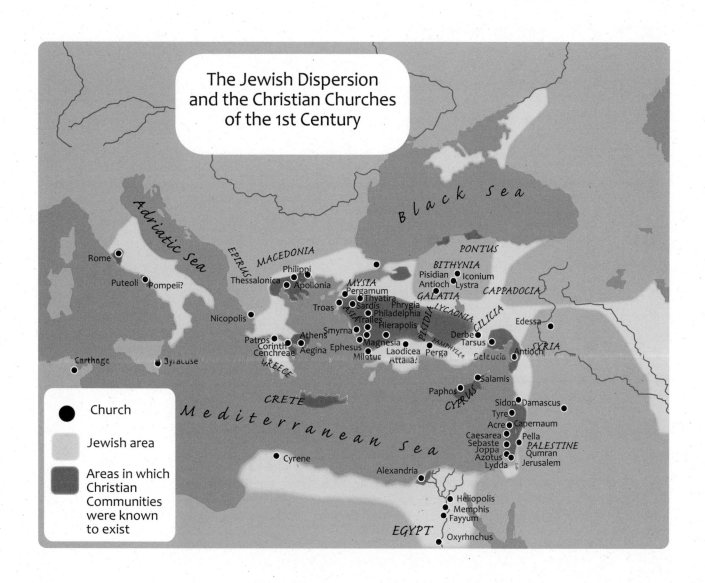

The Jewish Dispersion and the Christian Churches of the 1st Century

Church

Jewish area

Areas in which Christian Communities were known to exist

Old Testament Abraham Moses Liberator Teacher The Law David The Shepherd King The Covenant Solomon nificent **part three** ament St Luke's Gospel Salvation History The Roman Empire Galatians Christian Paul Apo e Gentiles The Prophets Amos Hose **history embedded in literature** of Creation The Psalms The Wis ature Daniel The Passion Resurrection Jesus The Old Testament Abraham Moses Liberator Law David The Shepl The Covenant Galatians The Roman Empire Acts of the Apostles Philippians Paul Ap **new testament** The ament Abraham Moses Liberator Teacher The Law David The Shepherd King The Covenant Solomon the Magnifi

ACTS OF THE APOSTLES

The Acts of the Apostles, written sometime in the 80s, is the companion to Luke's Gospel, continuing his account of "salvation history". (See "Luke – Author of Salvation History", page 54.) Full of adventure, Acts traces the rapid spread of Christianity (both geographically and racially) in the generation following Jesus from "Jerusalem… to the ends of the earth" (Acts 1:8), represented by Rome.

Certain passages in Acts describing Paul's journeys are written as "we" texts: this suggests Luke may possibly have been drawing on a diary he kept as he travelled with Paul (16:10-17; 20:5-8, 13-15; 21:1-18; 27:1 – 28:16). The speeches to Jews by Peter, Stephen and Paul (at Antioch of Pisidia), which concentrate largely on the Old Testament, reach their climax with its fulfilment in Jesus; however, the emphasis in Acts is on the third (present) stage of "salvation

Circumcision was abhorrent to most Gentiles.

history", the age of the Holy Spirit. The book of Acts continues where Luke's Gospel ends – that is, with the ascension of Jesus followed by the replacement of the twelfth apostle, as someone who could witness to the ministry and the resurrection of Jesus. Following the descent of the Holy Spirit at Pentecost (chapter 2), the rest of the book (sometimes described as "the Gospel of the Holy Spirit") shows how the apostles became changed and empowered through the presence of the Holy Spirit, under whose guidance the Gospel spread by stages from Jews to Gentiles. Each stage was, however, assessed by the central Church in Jerusalem.

Though Acts suggests that the Jerusalem Council ended the dispute over Gentiles, Paul's letters show the issue was vigorously disputed in local churches for some time.

The people converted in each stage were:

(a) Proselytes – Gentiles who had become Jews through baptism and circumcision;

(b) Samaritans – Jews of mixed race from intermarriage with Assyrians in 721 BC (2 Kings 17:5-6, 24; Acts 8:4-25). (See map and attached notes on page 85);

(c) Eunuchs – physical mutilation deprived them of full membership of Israel (Deuteronomy 23:1; Acts 8:26-39);

(d) God-fearers – Gentiles who attended the synagogue, without becoming Jews;

(e) Gentiles – which precipitated the conflict over the Jewish Law (see the section on Galatians). The Council of Jerusalem agreed to accept uncircumcised Gentiles equally as Christians (Acts 15:1-21).

The chief instrument in the Gentile mission was Saul of Tarsus, an educated Jew of the Dispersion and a Pharisee fanatically loyal to the Law (Philippians 3:5-6). While a persecutor of Christians, he was called by God to become the apostle to the Gentiles.

Old Testament Abraham Moses Liberator Teacher The Law David The Shepherd King The Covenant Solomon
gnificent The New Testament St Luke's Gospel Salvation History The Roman Empire Galatians **part three**
he Gentiles The Prophets Amos Hosea **history embedded in literature** of Creation The Psalms The Wi
rature Daniel The Passion Resurrection Jesus The Old Testament Abraham Moses Liberator Law David The She
g The **new testament** The Roman Empire Acts of the Apostles Philippians Paul Apostle of the Gentiles Th
tament Abraham Moses Liberator Teacher The Law David The Shepherd King The Covenant Solomon the Magni

Paul inherited the privileged status of Roman citizenship. This bestowed certain privileges: he could not be beaten, nor could he be crucified, and he had the right of ultimate appeal to the Emperor in person (22:22-29; 25:9-12). He used these privileges for the spread of the Gospel. His missionary policy wherever he went was, first, to preach in the synagogue to the Jews who were awaiting the Messiah and, only after that, to preach to the Gentiles.

The book of Acts ends with Paul, a prisoner in Rome, awaiting trial before the Emperor. He was, however, allowed visitors, so that, even from prison, the Gospel spread. Central, though, as Paul is in the second half of Acts, the book is not his biography. For Luke, the climax at the end of Acts is that the Gospel has now reached Rome. From this centre of the Empire it would now be carried by merchants and soldiers to the farthest corners of the Roman Empire.

Apostles had to have seen the risen Lord, and have been sent by him to preach (Acts 1:21-22), criteria fulfilled in Saul's conversion, after which he adopted the name Paul.

SUGGESTED READINGS AND POINTS TO CONSIDER AS YOU READ

The descent of the Holy Spirit (the birthday of the Church)	Acts 2:1-42
The Spirit, likened to "wind" (unseen power) and "fire" (which purifies), is a unifying power enabling understanding through "other languages" (2:4, 8, 11).	
The Gospel is spread by Jews of the Dispersion and proselytes (2:10).	
Peter's speech (to Jews) shows how Jesus and the Spirit fulfil Judaism.	
Membership of the Church is through repentance and baptism (2:37-38).	
Marks of the early Church.	Acts 2:42-47; 4:32-37
Attempts by Jewish authorities to stamp out Gospel after healing of lame man and teaching (chapter 3).	Acts 4:1-22; 5:12-42
First Christian martyrs: Stephen (first Christian martyr) stoned for blasphemy against Temple and Law; later, James, one of Twelve, killed	Acts 6:8-15; 7:1, 54 – 8:1; 12:1-3a
Gospel spreads following Jewish persecution of Church.	Acts 8:1-3
Conversion of Saul of Tarsus to be missionary to the Gentiles	Acts 9:1-30; 26:12-18
(See also his own account in Galatians 1:15-17.)	
Peter baptises Cornelius, a Roman God-fearer, and defends himself before the church in Jerusalem	Acts 10:1-48; 11:1-18
Gentile converts in Antioch accepted by Barnabas representing the church in Jerusalem. (First use of "Christians" – as term of abuse?)	Acts 11:19-26
Council of Jerusalem held to settle status of Gentile Christians, after widespread admission of Gentiles on Paul's first journey (chapters 13 and 14).	Acts 15:1-35
Note that unanimity is reached under guidance of Holy Spirit (15:28).	
Examples of Paul's preaching (a) To Jews in synagogue in Thessalonica, "proving" Jesus' messiahship from the scriptures.	Acts 17:1-4
(b) To Gentiles: in Lystra – an approach through natural religion; in Athens – relating to an educated intelligentsia.	Acts 14:8-19 Acts 17:16-34
Paul's appeal, as a prisoner, to be heard by the Emperor, and his imprisonment in Rome.	Acts 25:6-12 Acts 28:16-31

Old Testament Abraham Moses Liberator Teacher The Law David The Shepherd King The Covenant Solomon nificent The New Testament St Luke's Gospel Salvation History The Roman Empire Galatians **part three** Ap e Gentiles The Prophets Amos Hosea **history embedded in literature** of Creation The Psalms The Wis ature Daniel The Passion Resurrection Jesus The Old Testament Abraham Moses Liberator Law David The Shep The **new testament** The Roman Empire Acts of the Apostles Philippians Paul Apostle of the Gentiles The ament Abraham Moses Liberator Teacher The Law David The Shepherd King The Covenant Solomon the Magnifi

POSSIBLE ISSUES FOR DISCUSSION

1 Many slaves were among the first Christians, especially in Rome.

   Why do you think this was?

   How might it, perhaps, have affected the attitude of others to Christianity?

2 A strong Christian tradition believes that both Peter and Paul were martyred in Rome in AD 64.

   A saying arose in the early Church: "The blood of the martyrs is the seed of the Church."

   What does this mean?

   There were more Christian martyrs in the twentieth century than in any previous century.

   Do you think the saying of the early Church still applies today?

3 The evangelists in Acts adapted their approach in presenting the Gospel so that it related to the existing beliefs of their audience. (Compare preaching to Jews with that to Gentiles.)

   Do you think we today take enough notice of where others stand when we attempt to convey the Gospel to them?

   May this perhaps partly account for the success or failure of our approach?

4 Which do you consider more favourable to the growth of the Church –

   an age of persecution,

   or

   an attitude of indifference to Christian belief?

5 Members of the Council of Jerusalem hammered out their differences as to whether the Law was essential for all Christians till, under the guidance of the Holy Spirit, unity was achieved between them (Acts 15:28a).

   Are Christians too ready to agree to differ in their beliefs, rather than trying to persist in working out their differences till harmony is reached, open to and under the guidance of the Holy Spirit?

Joy to the Philippians from Paul, Apostle to the Gentiles

This letter, written when Paul was in prison, has traditionally been associated with his "house arrest" in Rome, where for two years he awaited the hearing of his case by Caesar (on the basis of his Roman citizenship, Acts 25:11). The fact that he surmises that the end of his life may be near supports this view.

seems harsher than would probably be the case if he was under house arrest in Rome.

Paul has a particular affection for the Philippian church, the only one he has allowed to send him money (via Epaphroditus, Philippians 2:25-30 and 4:15-19). It is a church which, through

Paul, as a Roman citizen, is believed to have been beheaded, and Peter crucified upside down, both in Rome, in the first persecution of Christians by Rome, under the Emperor Nero in AD 64.

However, an alternative view suggests the letter was written during Paul's stay of two years in Ephesus during his third journey (Acts 19:1 – 20:1). Although Acts contains no specific record of imprisonment there, Paul tells us he "fought with wild animals at Ephesus" (1 Corinthians 15:30-32; 2 Corinthians 1:8-10), and the imprisonment described in Philippians

experiencing suffering (1:29b), seems most clearly to have grasped the nature of Christian living. In spite of Paul's imprisonment, the letter resonates with joy and tranquillity.

Old Testament Abraham Moses Liberator Teacher The Law David The Shepherd King The Covenant Solomon
gnificent The New Testament St Luke's Gospel Salvation History The Roman Empire Galatians **part three** Ap
he Gentiles The Prophets Amos Hosea **history embedded in literature** of Creation The Psalms The Wi
rature Daniel The Passion Resurrection Jesus The Old Testament Abraham Moses Liberator Law David The Shep
g The **new testament** The Roman Empire Acts of the Apostles Philippians Paul Apostle of the Gentiles Th
cament Abraham Moses Liberator Teacher The Law David The Shepherd King The Covenant Solomon the Magnif

SUGGESTED READINGS AND POINTS TO CONSIDER AS YOU READ

Paul's love for the Philippians	Philippians 1:3-11
(1:1) Bishops, priests and deacons as we know them today probably did not emerge until the end of the third century.	
Paul's imprisonment enables evangelism.	Philippians 1:12-18
Paul's attitude to imminent death	Philippians 1:19-26; 2:17-18; 3:20-21
Paul seems to vacillate over whether Christ's second coming will happen before he dies (compare 1:23; 2:17 with 3:20).	
Christ's humility and obedience ... (Paul is quoting a hymn already in use in the Church.)	Philippians 2:5-11 (see Isaiah 53:3, 11-12)
... is the pattern for Christians in God's strength	Philippians 1:27 – 2:4, 14-16; 4:1-3
Warning against those who insist on observance of the Law.	Philippians 3:1-3
Paul's Christian testimony, continuing growth up into Christ, and attitude to life's vagaries	Philippians 3:4-16, 20-21; 4:11-13
3:6: "blameless" as a Pharisee, but only outwardly so. (See Romans 7:15-17, 19-20.)	
Characteristics of Christian life in Christ's power	Philippians 4:4-8, 12-13
Note the frequency of the words *joy* and *rejoice* throughout this letter.	

Old Testament Abraham Moses Liberator Teacher The Law David The Shepherd King The Covenant Solomon nificent **part three** ament St Luke's Gospel Salvation History The Roman Empire Galatians Christian Paul Ap he Gentiles The Prophets Amos Hose **history embedded in literature** of Creation The Psalms The Wis ature Daniel The Passion Resurrection Jesus The Old Testament Abraham Moses Liberator Law David The Shep The Covenant Galatians The Roman Empire Acts of the Apostles Philippians Paul Ap **new testament** The ament Abraham Moses Liberator Teacher The Law David The Shepherd King The Covenant Solomon the Magnifi

POSSIBLE ISSUES FOR DISCUSSION

1 How do our attitudes to death compare with Paul's attitude to death?

   What reasons can you suggest for possible discrepancies?

2 Paul's Christian testimony is utterly frank to his friends.

   What in it appeals to you most?

3 Is joy the same as happiness?

   Paul regards joy as a hallmark of the Christian (see also Galatians 5:22a).

   Where does it come from?

   How prominent is it in the Church today?

You might like to read the extract from a talk in 1946 by Leonard Wilson, Bishop of Singapore, about his imprisonment. (He later became Bishop of Birmingham.)

Old Testament Abraham Moses Liberator Teacher The Law David The Shepherd King The Covenant Solomon
nificent The New Testament St Luke's Gospel Salvation History The Roman Empire Galatians **part three** Apo
e Gentiles The Prophets Amos Hosea **history embedded in literature** of Creation The Psalms The Wisc
ature Daniel The Passion Resurrection Jesus The Old Testament Abraham Moses Liberator Law David The Sheph
new testament The Roman Empire Acts of the Apostles Philippians Paul Apostle of the Gentiles The
ment Abraham Moses Liberator Teacher The Law David The Shepherd King The Covenant Solomon the Magnific

A BISHOP'S BROADCAST ACCOUNT OF GRACE UNDER JAPANESE TORTURE

Sustained by glory glimpsed

In 1946, Leonard Wilson spoke on the BBC Home Service about his imprisonment by the Japanese when he was Bishop of Singapore. This is an extract from that talk.

When the Japanese captured Singapore in 1942, they gave permission for me and two other clergy to remain on parole. In Rangoon the cathedral became a distillery, but in Singapore services were held every day. This was largely because a Japanese Christian, Captain Ogawa, was made Director of Education and Religion. He was quite courageous in claiming for the Church the religious liberty the Japanese had promised, and he himself got into difficulties with his own military police because of his friendliness to the Christian Church.

But suspicion of us as a source of danger increased; and in 1943 I was interned and sent to Changi gaol.

Though the conditions were appallingly crowded, life was not too difficult until October, when the military police – that is, the Japanese Gestapo – raided the prison, searched all our luggage, and arrested some fifty of us. It is not my purpose to relate the tortures they inflicted upon us, but rather to tell you of some of the spiritual experiences of that ordeal. I knew that this was to be a challenge to my courage, my faith and my love.

I remember Archbishop Temple, in one of his books, writing that if we pray for any particular virtue, whether it be patience or courage or love, one of the answers that God gives to us is an opportunity for exercising that virtue. After my first beating I was almost afraid to pray for courage, lest I should have another opportunity for exercising it; but my unspoken prayer was there, and without God's help I doubt whether I should have come through.

Long hours of ignoble pain were a severe test. In the middle of that torture they asked me if I still believed in God. When by God's help I said "I do", they asked me why God did not save me; and by the help of his Holy Spirit I said, "God does save me. He does not save me by freeing me from pain or punishment, but he saves me by giving me the spirit to bear it." And when they asked me why I did not curse them I told them it was because I was a follower of Jesus Christ, who taught us that we were all brethren.

I did not like to use the words, "Father, forgive them." It seemed too blasphemous to use our Lord's words, but I felt them, and I said, "Father, I know these men are doing their duty. Help them to see that I am innocent." And when I muttered "Forgive them", I wondered how far I was being dramatic, and if I really meant it, because I looked at their faces as they stood round and took it in turn to flog, and their faces were hard and cruel, and some of them were evidently enjoying their cruelty.

But by the grace of God I saw those men not as they were, but as they had been. Once they were little children playing with their brothers and sisters, and happy in their parents' love, in those far-off days before they had been conditioned by their false nationalistic ideals; and it is hard to hate little children. But even that was not enough. There came into my mind as I lay on the table the words of that communion hymn;

> *Look, Father, look on his anointed face*
> *And only look on us as found in him.*

And so I saw them not as they were, not as they had been, but as they were capable of becoming, redeemed by the

Old Testament Abraham Moses Liberator Teacher The Law David The Shepherd King The Covenant Solomon
gnificent **part three** ament St Luke's Gospel Salvation History The Roman Empire Galatians Christian Paul Ap
he Gentiles The Prophets Amos Hose **history embedded in literature** of Creation The Psalms The Wi
rature Daniel The Passion Resurrection Jesus The Old Testament Abraham Moses Liberator Law David The Shep
g The Covenant Galatians The Roman Empire Acts of the Apostles Philippians Paul Ap **new testament** Th
ament Abraham Moses Liberator Teacher The Law David The Shepherd King The Covenant Solomon the Magnit

power of Christ; and I knew that it was only common sense to say "Forgive".

It is true, of course, that there were many dreary and desolate moments, especially in the early morning. I was in a crowded, filthy cell with hardly any power to move because of my wounds, but here again I was helped tremendously by God. There was a tiny window at the back of the cell, and through the bars I could hear the song of the golden oriole. I could see the glorious red of the flame of the forest tree, and something of God's indestructible beauty was conveyed to my tortured mind.

Behind the flame trees I glimpsed the top of Wesley's church, and was so grateful that the Church had preserved so many of Wesley's hymns. One that I said every morning was "Christ, whose glory fills the skies". Do you remember the second verse?

> *Dark and cheerless is the morn*
> *Unaccompanied by thee,*
> *Joyless is the day's return*
> *Till thy mercy's beams I see.*

So I went on to pray; "Visit then this soul of mine, Pierce the gloom of sin and grief." And gradually the burden of this world was lifted, and I was carried into the presence of God, and received from him the strength and peace which were enough to live by, day by day.
This joy of prayer was used by God to help others. Many non-Christians came to ask me to teach them to pray, because prayer evidently meant so much to those of us who were Christians. We were not supposed to talk to each other, but when the guards were not looking I told them some of the elementary things of prayer; thanking him, being sorry for things done wrong, and praying for others. And so we formed a wider fellowship than any I had known before, a fellowship of suffering humanity; and people knew that when they were taken out of the

cell for questioning or torture there were others of us behind praying for them, praying that if it be God's will they should not suffer, but if they suffered they would be given the spirit to bear it and not involve others.

One Chinese, after many weeks of teaching during the silent hours of the night, asked to be baptised; and I baptised him in the only water available, a lavatory basin at the back of the cell which had to be used for all purposes. Later, I had the joy of confirming him before I left Singapore.

But there were other battles to be fought. I do not know how many of you know what real hunger is, but the temptation to greed is almost overwhelming. Here again we were helped. There was a young Roman Catholic in the cell. He was a privileged prisoner; he was allowed food from the outside. He could have eaten all of it and more than all of it but never a day passed without his sharing it with some people in the cell. It was a small amount we got, but what an enormous difference it made. It raised the whole tone of our life and made it possible for others to follow his noble example and to learn to share with one another.

After eight months I was released, and for the first time got into the sunlight. I have never known such joy. It seemed like a foretaste of the resurrection. For months afterwards I felt at peace with the universe, although I was still interned; and I had to learn the lesson or the discipline of joy. How easy it is to forget God and all his benefits. I had known him in a deeper way than I could ever have imagined; but God is to be found in the resurrection as well as in the cross, and it is the resurrection that has the final word.

This article is reprinted from the *Church Times*, 11th August 1995, used with permission.

Old Testament Abraham Moses Liberator Teacher The Law David The Shepherd King The Covenant Solomon nificent The New Testament St Luke's Gospel Salvation History The Roman Empire Galatians **part three** Apo e Gentiles The Prophets Amos Hosea **history embedded in literature** of Creation The Psalms The Wis ature Daniel The Passion Resurrection Jesus The Old Testament Abraham Moses Liberator Law David The Sheph The **new testament** The Roman Empire Acts of the Apostles Philippians Paul Apostle of the Gentiles The ament Abraham Moses Liberator Teacher The Law David The Shepherd King The Covenant Solomon the Magnific

A Challenge to Philemon from Paul, Apostle to the Gentiles

This letter was also written when Paul was in prison (verse 1). Traditionally, this imprisonment has been identified with his "house arrest" in Rome from AD 61 to 63 (Acts 28:16,30-31).

However, another possibility is that Paul wrote the letter during his two-year imprisonment in Caesarea from AD 58 to 60 (Acts 24:27). More recently, Ephesus has also been suggested (AD 56–57; see note at beginning of Philippians, page 72). Ephesus was within easy reach of Colossae, where Philemon lived.

Philemon is a personal letter (the only one in the New Testament) from Paul to his friend Philemon.

Philemon lived in Colossae and was wealthy. He had been converted by Paul (v. 19b) and the local church met in his house (v. 2c).

A young slave, Onesimus (the name means "useful"), also lived in Colossae (Colossians 4:7-9). He had stolen his master Philemon's money, then fled to Rome. When his fortunes slumped, he sought out Paul, his old master's friend (see Acts 28:30), and became a Christian and "useful" to Paul. Paul challenged him that as a Christian he must make amends for his theft, and so offer to

> Both names, Philemon and Onesimus, have the emphasis on the second syllable, pronounced as a long "e". (The "i" in Philemon is also long.)

return as a slave. But Paul "covers" Onesimus with a character reference to Philemon, pleading mercy, witnessing to Onesimus' new character (v. 11) and reminding Philemon of the debt he owes Paul because of his conversion. Paul appeals to Philemon in love (but doesn't command him) to forgive Onesimus, release him from slavery and return him to Paul as a helper.

Presumably, as the letter is preserved, this is exactly what Philemon did.

POINTS TO CONSIDER AS YOU READ PHILEMON

a. Note how Paul makes a pun on Onesimus' name (vv. 10 and 11).

b. What line does Paul take to ensure the outcome he wants? (This includes also his hope that Philemon will return Onesimus to him: vv. 13, 20 and 21.)

   Does Paul's approach illustrate Jesus' teaching to "be wise as serpents and innocent as doves"? (Matthew 10:16b)

c. Paul challenged Onesimus deeply on the full meaning of Christian discipleship.

   What do you feel were Onesimus' feelings as he entered Philemon's front gate?

   What made him see it through?

Old Testament Abraham Moses Liberator Teacher The Law David The Shepherd King The Covenant Solomon
gnificent **part three** ament St Luke's Gospel Salvation History The Roman Empire Galatians Christian Paul A
he Gentiles The Prophets Amos Hose **history embedded in literature** of Creation The Psalms The W
rature Daniel The Passion Resurrection Jesus The Old Testament Abraham Moses Liberator Law David The She
g The Covenant Galatians The Roman Empire Acts of the Apostles Philippians Paul Ap **new testament** T
tament Abraham Moses Liberator Teacher The Law David The Shepherd King The Covenant Solomon the Magni

POSSIBLE ISSUES FOR DISCUSSION

1   On what basis can an imprisoned ex-rabbi (Paul), a Gentile patrician
    (Philemon) and a runaway slave meet as equals? (see Galatians 3:28.)

2   Jesus taught us to pray:

    "Forgive us our trespasses, **as we** forgive those who trespass against us."

    (Common version of Lord's Prayer: compare Matthew 6:12; Luke 11:4.)

    He makes God's forgiveness of us dependent upon our having forgiven
    others (and so possessing the open attitude of love which can receive God's
    forgiveness).

    This was a challenge to both Onesimus and Philemon, and remains a
    challenge to each of us today.

    If forgiveness is a human (rather than purely Christian) necessity, do you feel
    (for our overall health and well-being) we need more of it in our personal,
    social and international relationships?

    Where does it begin?

    Why do we find it so hard?

3   Do you consider this letter has a unique value in the New Testament?

    Is it still relevant today?

4   In the eighteenth century, Christians argued from the Epistle to Philemon to
    support the institution of slavery.

    Though this may be shocking to us, they felt they were taking biblical
    teaching literally.

    How do we learn from this about the use of the Bible in moral debate?

Old Testament Abraham Moses Liberator Teacher The Law David The Shepherd King The Covenant Solomon
gnificent The New Testament St Luke's Gospel Salvation History The Roman Empire Galatians **part three** A
he Gentiles The Prophets Amos Hosea **history embedded in literature** of Creation The Psalms The Wi
rature Daniel The Passion Resurrection Jesus The Old Testament Abraham Moses Liberator Law David The Shep
g The **new testament** The Roman Empire Acts of the Apostles Philippians Paul Apostle of the Gentiles Th
ament Abraham Moses Liberator Teacher The Law David The Shepherd King The Covenant Solomon the Magnif

ATONEMENT

Lieutenant Eric Lomax of the Royal Signals, aged 20 and 6 feet tall, was imprisoned by the Japanese when Singapore fell in 1942, and with other prisoners of war (POWs) put to work on building the Burma–Siam Railway (where it is said a POW died for each sleeper laid). When a map of the railway was discovered in Lomax's hat he was imprisoned in a hutch-like cage (five feet long, two feet across and four feet high), and brought out for constant interrogation and savage torture. The voice and person of the young Japanese interpreter began to jar on him and cause him nightmares. After a court martial, he was sentenced to five years' imprisonment in unspeakable conditions of squalor and famine.

At home, after the war, Lomax suffered terrible nightmares and was frequently unable to function normally. The war still dominated his life. He longed to take revenge, especially on the Japanese interpreter – and this became an obsession after his retirement in 1982 – but he did not know his name, or if he was still living. His second marriage to Patti came under increasing strain.

A former army chaplain told him of a Japanese, Nagase Takashi, who had performed various acts of reparation (atonement) for his war excesses but this left Lomax cold. Instead, he sought help from The Care of Victims of Torture in Ely. Then in 1989, he read an article about Nagase – and immediately recognised him from the picture as his Japanese interpreter. He'd found his man. As well as acts of reparation, the article described how Nagase too had ghastly nightmares about the torture of a POW accused of possessing a map. Nagase now had heart trouble and the nightmares got worse whenever he had a cardiac attack.

For two more years, Lomax found out more about Nagase – could his sorrow possibly be genuine? Finally, a letter to Nagase from Patti resulted in Eric Lomax and Patti meeting Nagase at the railway bridge over the River Kwai – where Nagase had built a Buddhist temple in reparation. For three weeks they were Nagase's guests in Thailand and at his home in Japan, and Lomax tested how genuine Nagase's sorrow and repentance were. Finally convinced, Lomax presented Nagase with a letter of forgiveness, also acknowledging his courageous stand against militarism and his work for reconciliation. The past fell away from each of them and, sharing many common cultural and literary interests, they felt like blood brothers. Now they were truly at peace with themselves and each other, and the nightmares have disappeared.

Eric Lomax writes of leaving Osaka after his visit to Nagase:

"As the plane tilted us over the Bay of Osaka, I held my wife's hand. I felt that I had accomplished more than I could ever have dreamed of. Meeting Nagase has turned him from a hated enemy, with whom friendship would have been unthinkable, into a blood brother. If I had never been able to put a name to the face of one of the men who had harmed me, and never discovered that behind that face there was also a damaged life, the nightmares would always have come from a past without meaning. And I had proved for myself that remembering is not enough, if it simply hardens hate. Sometime the hating has to stop."

Based on articles in *The Sunday Times* (13th August 1995) and *Radio Times* (12th-18th August 1995)

Old Testament Abraham Moses Liberator Teacher The Law David The Shepherd King The Covenant Solomon
nificent **part three** ament St Luke's Gospel Salvation History The Roman Empire Galatians Christian Paul Ap
e Gentiles The Prophets Amos Hose **history embedded in literature** of Creation The Psalms The Wi
ature Daniel The Passion Resurrection Jesus The Old Testament Abraham Moses Liberator Law David The Shep
The Covenant Galatians The Roman Empire Acts of the Apostles Philippians Paul Ap **new testament** Th
ment Abraham Moses Liberator Teacher The Law David The Shepherd King The Covenant Solomon the Magnif

NEW TESTAMENT CHRONOLOGY (approximate dates)

	The Early Church	The New Testament	Rulers of Palestine	Rulers of the Empire
BC			Herod the Great (37 BC – 4 BC)	Augustus Caesar (31 BC – AD 14)
			Archelaus (4 BC – AD6) { Judea Samaria Idumaea	
6-5	Birth of Christ			
			Antipas (4 BC – AD 39) Galilee Philip (4 BC – AD 34) Ituraea	
AD			Roman Procurators Judea (from AD 6)	Tiberius Caesar (14–37)
	Ministry of Jesus			
29	Crucifixion and resurrection		Pontius Pilate (AD 26–36)	
31/32	Stoning of Stephen			
32/33	Conversion of Saul			
34/35	Paul's first visit to Jerusalem		Agrippa I (39–44)	Caligula (37–41)
45	Famine in Jerusalem		Judea under Rome (44)	Claudius (41–54)
	Paul's second visit to Jerusalem			
47/49	First missionary journey	Galatians (48/49 or 52)		
49	Council of Jerusalem			
	Paul's third visit to Jerusalem		Agrippa II (50–100)	
49–52	Second missionary journey	Thessalonians (51/52)		
52	Paul's fourth visit to Jerusalem		Felix (52–58)	
53–56	Third missionary journey	Corinthians (55)		Nero (54–68)
56	Paul's fifth visit to Jerusalem	Romans (56)		
56–58	Paul in Caesarea		Festus (58)	
58–59	Journey to Rome	Colossians Ephesians Philippians Philemon } (59–66)		
59–61	Paul imprisoned in Rome			
61	Probable release of Paul			
	Preaching in Asia Minor			
64	Fire of Rome			
	Persecution of Christians	Timothy 1,2 Titus (64/55)		
	Peter and Paul martyred	Mark (64/65) 1 Peter ?		
70	Fall of Jerusalem			Civil Wars (68–69)
	Persecution of Jews			Vespasian (67–79)
80		Luke (80)		Titus (79–81)
82		Acts (82) Hebrews ?		Domitian (81–96)
85		Matthew (85)		
95		Revelation (95)		
100		John (100)		Trajan (98–117)
		Other books at turn of century – 1, 2, 3 John, James, Jude, 2 Peter)		

NB   This list places Peter and Paul's martyrdom around AD 66.

Old Testament Abraham Moses Liberator Teacher The Law David The Shepherd King The Covenant Solomon nificent The New Testament St Luke's Gospel Salvation History The Roman Empire Galatians **part three** Apo e Gentiles The Prophets Amos Hosea **history embedded in literature** of Creation The Psalms The Wisc ature Daniel The Passion Resurrection Jesus The Old Testament Abraham Moses Liberator Law David The Sheph The **new testament** The Roman Empire Acts of the Apostles Philippians Paul Apostle of the Gentiles The ment Abraham Moses Liberator Teacher The Law David The Shepherd King The Covenant Solomon the Magnific

Review

ATTITUDES TO THE BIBLE RECONSIDERED

1   In this section you will review your attitudes to the Bible now, compared
    with when you started this book.

    Have your attitudes changed?

    If so, how?

2   You might also like to consider how people's understanding of God
    developed over the periods studied.

    Does the Bible speak with one voice, or must we consider historical period
    and context?

    (For example, can you imagine finding the story of the sacrifice of Isaac in
    the New Testament?)

3   Which of the biblical passages have you appreciated the most?

    Do you know why?

4   What are some of the chief things you have learnt so far?

5   Has your study so far led to further questions you would like to explore?

Old Testament Abraham Moses Liberator Teacher The Law David The Shepherd King The Covenant Solomon
gnificent **part four** stament St Luke's Gospel Salvation History The Roman Empire Galatians Christian Paul A
the Gentiles The Prophets Amos Hosea **literature spun from history** s of Creation The Psalms The W
erature Daniel The Passion Resurrection Jesus The Old Testament Abraham Moses Liberator Law David The She
g The Covenant Galatians The Roman Empire Acts of the Apostles Philippians Paul Apo **old testament** T
tament Abraham Moses Liberator Teacher The Law David The Shepherd King The Covenant Solomon the Magni

Introduction to the Prophets

A prophet is one who proclaims God's words to the people, often with the introductory phrase, "Thus says the Lord". Prophets are forthtellers rather than foretellers; that is, they tell forth God's requirements of and demands on his people under the Covenant relationship, rather than foretell events in a distant future. However, because they read the signs of the times, they can often foresee probable outcomes in the near future if the people continue to persist in their ways.

Since the Covenant relationship (summarised in the Ten Commandments, Exodus 20:1-17) covers the whole of life's relationships (with God, others and self), the prophets are concerned with worship, and also with social and political relationships. They proclaim new insights into God's character based on revelations they have received from God. In order to promote the "spirit" or "inwardness" of the Covenant relationship, they challenge people to understand more deeply what God is like, and so what is demanded of them.

The prophets used every available means of communication in order to convey their message. This included the spoken word, various actions, and could even involve their families by naming their children (as did Hosea and Isaiah) with names that proclaimed their message.

Samuel is regarded as the first of the prophets. The early prophets, such as Elijah (1 Kings 16:29 – 2 Kings 2:12) and Elisha (1 Kings 19:16 – 2 Kings 13:21), did not write down their messages. From the eighth century BC onwards, however, the message of the prophets is written down, either by themselves or by their disciples, presumably because of the hard-heartedness of their listeners. Since listeners did not automatically believe the prophets, the prophets and their disciples kept a record so that they could point it out when prophecies were fulfilled.

The prophets' teaching from the eighth to the sixth century BC reaches unsurpassed heights in the unfolding of the Jewish religion. Although their insights are true for all time (since God's nature does not change), they initially emerged from the immediate context of the religious, social and political situations in which the prophets lived.

Old Testament Abraham Moses Liberator Teacher The Law David The Shepherd King The Covenant Solomon
gnificent The New Testament St Luke's Gospel Salvation History The Roman Empire Galatians **part four** A
he Gentiles The Prophets Amos Hosea **literature spun from history** of Creation The Psalms The Wi
rature Daniel The Passion Resurrection Jesus The Old Testament Abraham Moses Liberator Law David The Shep
g The **old testament** The Roman Empire Acts of the Apostles Philippians Paul Apostle of the Gentiles Th
ament Abraham Moses Liberator Teacher The Law David The Shepherd King The Covenant Solomon the Magnit

The Prophets (dates are approximate)
(Elijah, Elisha and the main writing prophets)

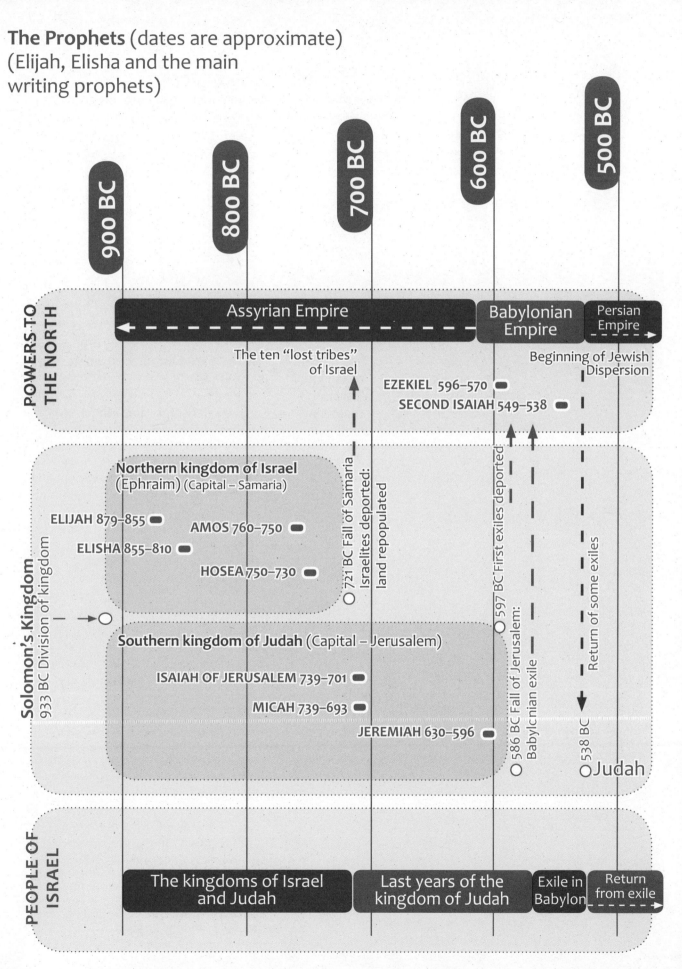

Old Testament Abraham Moses Liberator Teacher The Law David The Shepherd King The Covenant Solomon nificent **part four** stament St Luke's Gospel Salvation History The Roman Empire Galatians Christian Paul Apc he Gentiles The Prophets Amos Hosea **literature spun from history** s of Creation The Psalms The Wis ature Daniel The Passion Resurrection Jesus The Old Testament Abraham Moses Liberator Law David The Shep The Covenant Galatians The Roman Empire Acts of the Apostles Philippians Paul Apo **old testament** The ament Abraham Moses Liberator Teacher The Law David The Shepherd King The Covenant Solomon the Magnifi

LEADING INSIGHTS OF THE MAIN WRITING PROPHETS

1. Verse references are not given for prophets studied in more detail in the course.
2. The time chart of the prophets on page 83 gives the historical context of each prophet's message.

Active BC	Location	Prophet	Message
mid 8th century	Northern kingdom (Israel / Ephraim)	Amos	God's perfect holiness and justice must condemn and destroy this unjust society.
750–730	Northern kingdom (Israel / Ephraim)	Hosea	God's holiness requires judgement; God's love implies mercy.
730s–700	Southern kingdom (Judah)	Isaiah of Jerusalem (Isaiah chapters 1–39)	A holy God requires a holy people (see Isaiah 6:1-8). Oracles of judgement and of hope ("a virgin shall conceive", Isaiah 7:14)
730s–700	Southern kingdom (Judah)	Micah	"What does the Lord require of you but to do justice, and to love kindness, and to walk humbly with your God?" (Micah 6:6-8)
late 7th to early 6th century	Jerusalem	Jeremiah	Why resist the Babylonian invaders? Judah is being punished justly for her sins. See how God works through the life and suffering of his servant Jeremiah. "The days are surely coming, says the Lord, when I will make a new covenant with my people Israel… and I will write it on their hearts; and I will be their God and they shall be my people." (Jeremiah 31:31-34)
596–570s	Babylon? (in exile)	Ezekiel	The overwhelming glory of God, who can be worshipped even in Babylon (Ezekiel 1). Defeat in war is punishment for our own sins, not those of the generation before us (Ezekiel 18).
540s–530s	Babylon? (in exile)	"Second Isaiah" (Isaiah chapters 40–55)	The one and only God, Creator and Redeemer, will shortly remake and redeem his people and bring them home to Jerusalem. His love is expressed in the redemptive suffering of his Servant.

The book of Daniel is treated as a Wisdom book.

Old Testament Abraham Moses Liberator Teacher The Law David The Shepherd King The Covenant Solomo
gnificent The New Testament St Luke's Gospel Salvation History The Roman Empire Galatians **part four** A
he Gentiles The Prophets Amos Hosea **literature spun from history** of Creation The Psalms The Wi
rature Daniel The Passion Resurrection Jesus The Old Testament Abraham Moses Liberator Law David The Shep
g The **old testament** The Roman Empire Acts of the Apostles Philippians Paul Apostle of the Gentiles Th
tament Abraham Moses Liberator Teacher The Law David The Shepherd King The Covenant Solomon the Magni

Amos and Hosea

Introductory note

Amos, followed soon after by Hosea, prophesied in the northern kingdom of Israel shortly before its fall in 721 BC to Assyria.

Their messages complement each other and should be taken together:

Amos God is just; an unjust society will inevitably be swept away by his holiness.

Hosea God is just; so he must sweep away an unjust society. But he is also merciful and loving – so he must spare his people; there is unbearable tension in God's heart.

If, however, you have time to consider only one of the prophets, it is important to be aware of the message preached by the other one also.

SOCIAL AND RELIGIOUS CONDITIONS IN EIGHTH-CENTURY ISRAEL

One hundred and fifty years after Solomon's death, the northern kingdom of Israel (Ephraim) under Jeroboam II (787–741 BC) had expanded, developed agriculture and become prosperous through international trade. But there was great social inequality; the extreme wealth and luxury of the few were at the expense of vast poverty of the many, who could, through their debts, easily find themselves sold into slavery for the price of a pair of shoes. The rich women were no better, revelling in idleness and excesses.

When the kingdom of Israel was formed, shrines with golden calves had been set up at Dan and Bethel for the worship of God (to prevent Israelites journeying to the kingdom of Judah for worship at the Temple). By Jeroboam II's reign, religious practices at these shrines were hollow and insincere. People awaited the Day of the Lord, anticipating God's vindication of his people against their enemies.

The two kingdoms

The northern kingdom of Israel (or Ephraim), with Samaria as its capital, consisted of ten tribes, and was on the international trade routes. The royal line was not descended from David. The southern kingdom of Judah, with Jerusalem as its capital, consisted of two tribes (Judah and Benjamin). Kings were descended from David.

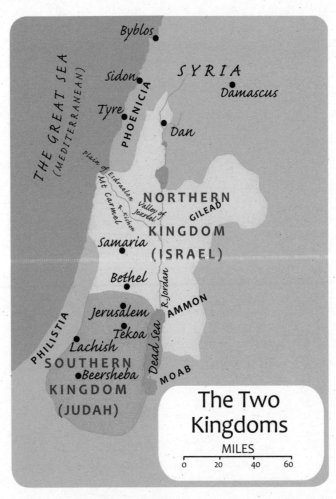

The Two Kingdoms

MILES
0   20   40   60

85

part four   stament St Luke's Gospel Salvation History The Roman Empire Galatians Christian Paul Apo
e Gentiles The Prophets Amos Hosea **literature spun from history** s of Creation The Psalms The Wisc
ature Daniel The Passion Resurrection Jesus The Old Testament Abraham Moses Liberator Law David The Sheph
The Covenant Galatians The Roman Empire Acts of the Apostles Philippians Paul Apo **old testament** The
ment Abraham Moses Liberator Teacher The Law David The Shepherd King The Covenant Solomon the Magnific

The end of the northern kingdom, 721 BC
after Amos (760–750 BC) and Hosea (750–730 BC)

In 721 BC, Israel fell to Assyria, and the ten tribes were carried into bondage. There they lost their identity and became absorbed by their captors. Assyrians were sent to settle in the land of Israel to prevent further uprising and subdue its religion (2 Kings 17:5-6, 24-28). The Assyrians intermarried with the remaining Israelites and became ancestors of the New Testament Samaritans, a people of mixed race with mixed religion.

AMOS
Amos (active sometime during 760–750 BC) was a shepherd from Tekoa on the edge of the Judean wilderness in the southern kingdom of Judah and a dresser of "fig" trees. He tended his flock, and visited the more lucrative markets in Israel to sell his high quality wool. Observing the situation there, he preached his message that God is righteous and just, and demands justice and righteousness in the dealings of his people.

Justice   has been described as love in its social context.

Righteousness   involves integrity and keeping the commandments.

Amos saw that unless the Israelites changed their ways, they would be conquered by Assyria, and he saw this as God's coming punishment. Gathering an approving audience, he castigates the surrounding nations (1:3 – 2:3) – but the climax is God's judgement on Israel (2:6-16). Most of the book is a tirade of judgement by God against Israel for their insincerity in worship, their cheating and malpractices in transactions, and the huge gulf between rich and poor. The "day of the Lord", to which they looked forward for vindication by God against their enemies, would instead be one of awful judgement.

Old Testament Abraham Moses Liberator Teacher The Law David The Shepherd King The Covenant Solomon
nificent The New Testament St Luke's Gospel Salvation History The Roman Empire Galatians **part four** Apo
e Gentiles The Prophets Amos Hosea **literature spun from history** of Creation The Psalms The Wis
ature Daniel The Passion Resurrection Jesus The Old Testament Abraham Moses Liberator Law David The Shep
The **old testament** The Roman Empire Acts of the Apostles Philippians Paul Apostle of the Gentiles The
ament Abraham Moses Liberator Teacher The Law David The Shepherd King The Covenant Solomon the Magnifi

SUGGESTED READINGS AND POINTS TO CONSIDER AS YOU READ

Amos, called to be a prophet	Amos 1:1; 7:14-15; 3:7-8
Social malpractices and conditions (Bashan produced particularly lush pasture for cattle.)	Amos 2:6b-8; 3:10, 15; 5:10-12; 6:4-7; 8:4-6
Religious malpractices	Amos 4:4-5; 5:21-24
Amos challenges Amaziah, priest at shrine of Bethel	Amos 7:10-17
Israel called to special relationship with God who has tried to call her back.	Amos 3:1-2a; 5:14-15
Kernel of Amos' message	Amos 5:24
God who is just and righteous demands the same from his people.	
God will use the builder's plumb-line to measure righteousness in Israel	Amos 7:7-9
God's judgement on Israel (8:1-3: "Summer fruit" and "end" are puns in Hebrew.)	Amos 2:6; 3:13-15; 8:1-3; 9:1
Punishment will come from neighbouring powers.	Amos 3:9-12; 5:27
The "day of the Lord" (also called "that day") will be doom.	Amos 5:18-20; 8:9-11

The "happy ending" epilogue in 9:8b-15 is thought by scholars to have been added by a later author.

part four stament St Luke's Gospel Salvation History The Roman Empire Galatians Christian Paul A
he Gentiles The Prophets Amos Hosea **literature spun from history** s of Creation The Psalms The W
rature Daniel The Passion Resurrection Jesus The Old Testament Abraham Moses Liberator Law David The She
g The Covenant Galatians The Roman Empire Acts of the Apostles Philippians Paul Apo **old testament** Th
tament Abraham Moses Liberator Teacher The Law David The Shepherd King The Covenant Solomon the Magni

HOSEA

Hosea's prophecy (active between 750–730 BC) covers the closing years of prosperity of Jeroboam II's reign (chapters 1–3) followed by civil unrest from 741 BC when six kings followed in quick succession, often in panic making overtures first to Assyria, then Egypt (7:7-11).

Unlike Amos, who visited Israel from Judah, Hosea was a native of Israel and so prophesied to his own people – one reason why his message (delivered shortly after Amos') is much less harsh than that of Amos.

Hosea married Gomer, who had been a prostitute (probably with the priests of Baal, to instil agricultural fertility). Hosea was distraught when she left him; searching everywhere for her, he finally found her in a slave market. Seared with love and pity for her, he bought her back. For a while they lived happily; then again she left him and his distress returned.

The social ills of Amos' day had worsened, but Israel's heresy in worshipping Baal, the Canaanite god of agriculture, concerns Hosea most. He came to recognise his marriage experience as God's call to him to prophesy. Calling Israel to repent to avoid God's punishment, he emphasises God's love, pity and mercy for a people he has chosen and can never ever stop loving, no matter how they behave – just as Hosea could never stop loving Gomer.

Old Testament Abraham Moses Liberator Teacher The Law David The Shepherd King The Covenant Solomon gnificent The New Testament St Luke's Gospel Salvation History The Roman Empire Galatians **part four** A he Gentiles The Prophets Amos Hosea **literature spun from history** of Creation The Psalms The Wi erature Daniel The Passion Resurrection Jesus The Old Testament Abraham Moses Liberator Law David The Shep g The **old testament** The Roman Empire Acts of the Apostles Philippians Paul Apostle of the Gentiles Th tament Abraham Moses Liberator Teacher The Law David The Shepherd King The Covenant Solomon the Magni

SUGGESTED READINGS AND POINTS TO CONSIDER AS YOU READ

Hosea's marriage and family The names of the children (the last two possibly not Hosea's own) make them a living prophecy of God's coming punishment (especially 1:2 and 1:6 and 9).	Hosea 1:1-8; 3:1-5
Hosea's experience reflects God's relationship with Israel Israel, covenanted to God in the wilderness, has become God's harlot, turning to Baal worship. But God will eventually lure her back to her first love in the wilderness and the children's names will be reversed to blessings.	Hosea 2:1-23 (God is speaking); 1:10-11
Criticism of the cult of Baal, and of golden calves at Dan and Bethel	Hosea 4:1-3, 12-14; 8:4b-6; 11:2; 13:2
Constitutional treason with kings ousting each other	Hosea 8:4a, 10
Political alliances offer no security	Hosea 7:11; 8:9-10
God cannot be manipulated by superficial repentance 6:6 summarises Hosea's message, and is quoted by Jesus twice in Matthew 9:13 and 12:7.	Hosea 6:4-6
Destruction is near	Hosea 9:6; 10:7-8
But God's love and mercy persist	Hosea 11:1-4, 8-9

Old Testament Abraham Moses Liberator Teacher The Law David The Shepherd King The Covenant Solomon
nificent **part four** stament St Luke's Gospel Salvation History The Roman Empire Galatians Christian Paul Apc
e Gentiles The Prophets Amos Hosea **literature spun from history** :s of Creation The Psalms The Wisc
ature Daniel The Passion Resurrection Jesus The Old Testament Abraham Moses Liberator Law David The Sheph
The Covenant Galatians The Roman Empire Acts of the Apostles Philippians Paul Apo **old testament** The
ment Abraham Moses Liberator Teacher The Law David The Shepherd King The Covenant Solomon the Magnific

POSSIBLE ISSUES FOR DISCUSSION

On Amos

1   Do you agree that justice can be described as "love in its social context or dimension"?

   If not, how would you describe it?

2   How do we evade "justice" today – individually, corporately, internationally?

3   Courageously, Amos criticises Amaziah, priest of Bethel (7:14-17).

   How courageous are we in defending justice

   (a)   with friends?

   (b)   in public (e.g. workplace etc.)?

On Hosea

4   How may we abuse religious practices, and so God, today?

   Repentance means to "turn around" and face towards God.

   What makes this so costly?

5   Hosea's insight into God was derived from his personal experience of life.

   Can the same apply to us today?

On Amos and Hosea

6   How can justice and mercy be held together:

   (a)   in bringing up children?

   (b)   in the penal system?

   (c)   in our dealings with Government services?

7   The Hebrews believed that God is the Lord of history.

   But after settling in Canaan, they turned to the Canaanite god of agriculture, Baal, for their daily livelihood and needs.

   Do we turn to modern "Baals" for our economic necessities today?

Old Testament Abraham Moses Liberator Teacher The Law David The Shepherd King The Covenant Solomon
nificent The New Testament St Luke's Gospel Salvation History The Roman Empire Galatians **part four** Apo
e Gentiles The Prophets Amos Hosea **literature spun from history** of Creation The Psalms The Wis
ature Daniel The Passion Resurrection Jesus The Old Testament Abraham Moses Liberator Law David The Sheph
old testament The Roman Empire Acts of the Apostles Philippians Paul Apostle of the Gentiles The
ment Abraham Moses Liberator Teacher The Law David The Shepherd King The Covenant Solomon the Magnifi

The Exile and the Great Unknown Prophet of the Exile

Judah now showed similar social and religious characteristics to those of Israel under Jeroboam II, against which the statesman, Isaiah of Jerusalem, prophesied (Isaiah 1–39; 739–701 BC).

A hundred years later, King Josiah recalled Judah from apostasy and failure to keep the Law. In the Temple spring clean (622 BC), a scroll of the Law was found (probably a version of our Deuteronomy or "second" Law), on which Josiah acted, prohibiting sacrifice anywhere except in Jerusalem.

In 612 BC Nineveh, capital of Assyria, fell to Babylon. As Judah courted first Babylon, then Egypt, the prophet Jeremiah saw clearly the impending catastrophe. In 597 BC Jerusalem surrendered to King Nebuchadnezzar of Babylon; the Jewish King Jehoiachin, leaders, craftsmen and the priest-prophet, Ezekiel, were taken captive to Babylon. In a letter Jeremiah urged them to settle in Babylon and prosper (Jeremiah 29:1-23).

But in 586 BC Jerusalem revolted and was completely destroyed by Babylon. Temple, palace and city walls were razed to the ground; the successor king, Zedekiah, was blinded and taken in chains to Babylon, after first seeing his sons killed. (The horrendous account is described in 2 Kings 24:8 –25:26.) The Davidic dynasty was ended. The elite were taken into exile; Judah was left leaderless. God, it seemed, had finally deserted his people.

> Up to the exile, God's chosen people are conventionally called "the Hebrews" or "the Israelites/people of Israel".

The grandeur and beauty of Babylon stunned the exiles. A square city with a hundred gates, its wide walls supported roads for chariots. Nebuchadnezzar's hanging gardens on the Euphrates were one of the seven wonders of the ancient world. Such splendour and power were attributed to the Babylonian gods – Marduk, Bel and Nebo.

The Jewish captives were well treated, allowed to practise their religion and trade, and to rise socially. But they were despondent in this alien land. God appeared to have deserted them finally; sacrifice (restricted to Jerusalem) was impossible, nor did they believe they could worship God outside Judah.

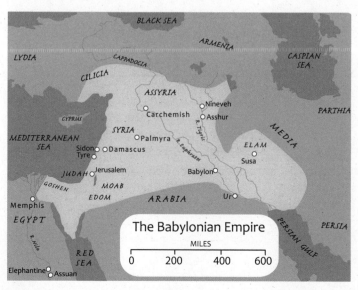

The Babylonian Empire

MILES
0   200   400   600

91

Old Testament Abraham Moses Liberator Teacher The Law David The Shepherd King The Covenant Solomon
part four stament St Luke's Gospel Salvation History The Roman Empire Galatians Christian Paul A
he Gentiles The Prophets Amos Hosea **literature spun from history** s of Creation The Psalms The W
rature Daniel The Passion Resurrection Jesus The Old Testament Abraham Moses Liberator Law David The She
g The Covenant Galatians The Roman Empire Acts of the Apostles Philippians Paul Apo **old testament** Th
tament Abraham Moses Liberator Teacher The Law David The Shepherd King The Covenant Solomon the Magni

Their reflection on what had caused such affliction resulted in the writing of the "deuteronomic history", i.e. the books of Joshua, Judges, 1 and 2 Samuel and 1 and 2 Kings. These give a single connected history of Israel and Judah from the conquest of Canaan to the fall of Jerusalem. The history draws on much older sources and stories, but the final version was not completed until after 560 BC (2 Kings 25:27-30 describes King Jehoiachin's release from prison in Babylon that year).

This history (unlike Genesis, Exodus and Numbers) attributes disaster to disobedience by earlier generations to the Covenant laws. The kings are therefore assessed as good or (mostly) bad rulers, according to whether they did good or evil in the sight of the Lord.

Ezekiel, however, disagreed: if the catastrophe of 586 BC was a punishment for sin, it was for the sins of the *present* generation (Ezekiel chapter 18, especially verses 2-3 and 20). But God could be worshipped even in Babylon, for it was by the River Chebar in Babylon that in 593 BC Ezekiel had his mysterious vision of God (Ezekiel 1:1-3). Moreover, God would eventually restore his people (Ezekiel 37) for "the sake of his great name" (36:22-28; 39:25-29).

Gradually the Jews recovered their religion, emphasising circumcision and Sabbath observance. Sacrifice was replaced by a corporate form of worship based on the scriptures, the precursor of synagogue worship. Priests and scribes re-edited the scriptures, producing the final version of Genesis to Chronicles, called the Priestly version.

Two generations later (c. 540 BC), a great unknown prophet appeared on the scene, and we reach the peak of Old Testament prophecy. As his prophecies in Isaiah 40–55 are appended to those

> After the exile, they began to be called "the Jews".

of Isaiah of Jerusalem (Isaiah 1–39) he is called "Second" ("Deutero" in Greek) Isaiah. His message is of hope, deliverance and return to Judah, because the policy of Cyrus, the King of Persia, whom he perceived would shortly capture Babylon, was to allow captives to return home.

Second Isaiah pronounces the Jews' God, Yahweh, to be the Creator and God of the whole world and all peoples. Four passages, called the Servant Songs, describe the mysterious Suffering Servant of God.

In 538 BC the Exile ended. Jews were allowed to return to Judah, and many did so; other groups returned subsequently. But some remained in Persia, so forming the beginning of the Jewish "Dispersion" (Diaspora) or "scattering".

The Persian Empire
MILES
0   200   400   600

Old Testament Abraham Moses Liberator Teacher The Law David The Shepherd King The Covenant Solomon
nificent The New Testament St Luke's Gospel Salvation History The Roman Empire Galatians **part four** Ap
he Gentiles The Prophets Amos Hosea **literature spun from history** of Creation The Psalms The Wis
ature Daniel The Passion Resurrection Jesus The Old Testament Abraham Moses Liberator Law David The Sheph
The **old testament** The Roman Empire Acts of the Apostles Philippians Paul Apostle of the Gentiles The
ament Abraham Moses Liberator Teacher The Law David The Shepherd King The Covenant Solomon the Magnifi

SUGGESTED READINGS AND POINTS TO CONSIDER AS YOU READ

The fall and destruction of Jerusalem	2 Kings 24:8 – 25:12
The initial total rejection by God felt by the exiles	Psalm 137
Second Isaiah's message of comfort, hope and deliverance from exile	Isaiah 40; 43:1-7; 52:7-12
This poses a challenge to the now settled and prosperous exiles, as Judah is lying waste. The prophet therefore offers them much encouragement.	
The God of the Jews, Yahweh, is Creator and Lord of the whole world.	
God's agent in deliverance will be Cyrus, King of Persia, described as "my [= God's] shepherd" and the Lord's "anointed" (i.e. Messiah).	Isaiah 44:24, 28; 45:1-4
The Jews are called to witness to the Gentiles, who will come to acknowledge the Jewish God, Yahweh, as Lord.	Isaiah 42:5-7 and 49:5a, 6
The Babylonians' man-made idols are objects of scathing scorn	Isaiah 44:9-20; 46:5-7
The Songs of the Suffering Servant describe the Servant's call to be a light to the Gentiles; his failure, trust and faithfulness through suffering	Isaiah 42:1-7; 49:1-6; 50:4-9 and especially 52:13 – 53:12
Who was the Servant? An individual? The nation in exile? Those courageous enough to consider returning to Judah? We can't say.	
The Jews considered suffering a mark of God's displeasure, and the passages lay dormant – till used by Jesus and his disciples as foretelling his sacrificial death and triumph through (not in spite of) suffering (e.g. Mark 8:31; Luke 24:25-27; 1 Corinthians 15:3-5).	

Old Testament Abraham Moses Liberator Teacher The Law David The Shepherd King The Covenant Solomo gnificent **part four** stament St Luke's Gospel Salvation History The Roman Empire Galatians Christian Paul A he Gentiles The Prophets Amos Hosea **literature spun from history** s of Creation The Psalms The W rature Daniel The Passion Resurrection Jesus The Old Testament Abraham Moses Liberator Law David The She g The Covenant Galatians The Roman Empire Acts of the Apostles Philippians Paul Apo **old testament** T tament Abraham Moses Liberator Teacher The Law David The Shepherd King The Covenant Solomon the Magni

POSSIBLE ISSUES FOR DISCUSSION

1 Do we ever feel God lets us down?

2 What man-made idols does our culture worship?

   Are Christians implicated too?

3 Second Isaiah sees God working through Cyrus (Isaiah 44:28 and 45:1).

   Does God work through non-Christians (people of other faiths and of no faith) today?

4 A painful and costly death to the familiar was the necessary prelude to new truth almost beyond understanding.

   Does "dying" always precede being "raised to new life"?

5 It is sometimes said that Christians today live in an alien, post-Christian culture.

   Do you agree?

   If so, how is this experienced?

   Can our understanding of the exile and Second Isaiah offer any understanding and hope?

6 Does our experience of life affect our faith and our understanding of God?

The Rise of Belief in the One and Only God of the Whole Universe

The Rise of Belief in the One and Only God of the Whole Universe

Initially it was believed that each tribe and nation had their own god whose responsibility was to care for that people. So, the God of Abraham, Isaac and Jacob, after saving the Hebrews from slavery in Egypt, invited the whole tribe to become his special people (Exodus 19:3-6) and said he would then be their God. This invitation they accepted and ratified with the sealing of the Covenant at Mount Sinai (Exodus 24:3-8).

> The belief that there is only one God of the whole world is "monotheism" meaning "one God".

On entering the Promised Land, the challenge to the Hebrews was to remain loyal to their God. Surrounded by the Canaanites who worshipped Baal (a god of fertility and agriculture), and settling down from a nomadic to an agricultural existence themselves, the temptation was to switch to the worship of the local god of agriculture. Moreover, each god was believed to hold sway over the territory his people occupied, and this presented another seductive temptation to the Hebrews to worship Baal.

When David therefore is exiled by Saul, he says it is equivalent to being told to "Go, serve other gods" (1 Samuel 26:19). Later, Naaman, the Syrian general, when healed of his leprosy through Elisha, takes back to Syria some Israelite soil so that, back home, he can stand on it, and worship the God of Israel who has healed him (2 Kings 5:17-19).

With the prophets, we can trace the gradual development of the belief that the God of the Hebews is the one and only true God of the whole world. For instance, in 1 Kings 19:15, Elijah is told to go and anoint the new king of Syria (i.e. outside Israel), and Amos claims God's jurisdiction over the surrounding tribes (Amos 1:3, 6, 9, 11, 13 and 2:1). The belief becomes fully explicit during the exile, when the Jews learn from Ezekiel that they can worship God in foreign lands, and from Second Isaiah that their God is the one and only God of all peoples and Creator of the whole universe.

Old Testament Abraham Moses Liberator Teacher The Law David The Shepherd King The Covenant Solomon
nificent **part four** stament St Luke's Gospel Salvation History The Roman Empire Galatians Christian Paul Ap
e Gentiles The Prophets Amos Hosea **literature spun from history** s of Creation The Psalms The Wis
ature Daniel The Passion Resurrection Jesus The Old Testament Abraham Moses Liberator Law David The Shep
The Covenant Galatians The Roman Empire Acts of the Apostles Philippians Paul Apo **old testament** The
ament Abraham Moses Liberator Teacher The Law David The Shepherd King The Covenant Solomon the Magnifi

Stories of Creation

The word "myth", as commonly used, suggests something is untrue, a fantasy – "That's a myth!" But in a religious context, the word has a different and very important positive meaning. It describes a story that is not literally true, but which contains truth, in the same way as do Aesop's Fables (e.g. the race of the hare and the tortoise), and the parables of Jesus (i.e. stories Jesus told).

The stories in Genesis chapters 1–11 are myths, denoting the prehistoric (even eternal) background against which the historical story of Abraham in chapter 12 emerges. The stories deal with the perennial topics human beings ask about: e.g.

Chapters 1–2
Who made the world?
What sort of world is it?
Are human beings distinctive?

Chapter 3
How do we account for evil in the world?

Chapters 6–8
God's justice must punish evil (the Flood),
but he has mercy too: his armour (the rainbow) is laid aside for ever.

Chapter 11
Why are there so many languages, resulting in so much confusion between peoples?
(Answer: Human pride makes us strive to be "like" God.)

The division between the two creation stories in Genesis chapters 1–2 comes halfway through verse 4 of chapter 2. The "first" story (1:1 – 2:4a) is the later Priestly account reflecting Second Isaiah's teaching of God as the transcendent Creator of all, whose word is powerfully effective. Written in Babylon around the middle of the fifth century BC and resonating with the Babylonian creation legend, it differs from it in the supreme position it gives to God as Lord of creation. The "second", more primitive, story (2:4b-25), which presents God in the form of a man, is an earlier version by the JE editors from around 800 BC (see pages 24-26).

Hebrew Conception of the Universe
When the windows in the firmament are opened, it rains.

Sheol (also called the Pit) is the place of a shadowy existence of the departed, who are generally believed to be cut off from God.

Old Testament Abraham Moses Liberator Teacher The Law David The Shepherd King The Covenant Solomon
nificent The New Testament St Luke's Gospel Salvation History The Roman Empire Galatians **part four** Apo
e Gentiles The Prophets Amos Hosea **literature spun from history** of Creation The Psalms The Wis
ature Daniel The Passion Resurrection Jesus The Old Testament Abraham Moses Liberator Law David The Sheph
The **old testament** The Roman Empire Acts of the Apostles Philippians Paul Apostle of the Gentiles The
ment Abraham Moses Liberator Teacher The Law David The Shepherd King The Covenant Solomon the Magnifi

SUGGESTED READINGS AND POINTS TO CONSIDER AS YOU READ

The creation of the world (P)	Genesis 1:1 – 2:4a
The creation of the world (JE)	Genesis 2:4b-25

Points to note concerning these stories:

(a) Science asks the question "How?", religion the question "Why?"

These stories are not concerned, as we might be, with the origin of the material universe and the creation of matter from nothing. Their concern is with producing order out of chaos – part of God's continuing work in creation.

(b) How do the two stories contradict each other in detail?

(Consider order of creation, amount of water etc.)

If they are not scientific accounts, does it matter?

(c) Though different, the two accounts agree remarkably in the religious truths they affirm.

What are these?

(d) *Adam* is Hebrew for man. Genesis chapters 2 and 3 claim to be about the common experiences of Mr and Mrs Everyman.

Do you agree?

Other important passages on God and his creation:

Proverbs 8:22-31	Wisdom is speaking (see 8:12). The Wisdom of God is older than creation.
Job chapters 38 and 39 and 40:15 – 41:34	In 40:15 Behemoth is the hippopotamus. In 41:1 Leviathan is the crocodile.
Second Isaiah 40:12-14, 21-28a; 42:5	
Psalms 104 and 8	

Old Testament Abraham Moses Liberator Teacher The Law David The Shepherd King The Covenant Solomo gnificent **part four** stament St Luke's Gospel Salvation History The Roman Empire Galatians Christian Paul A the Gentiles The Prophets Amos Hosea **literature spun from history** s of Creation The Psalms The W erature Daniel The Passion Resurrection Jesus The Old Testament Abraham Moses Liberator Law David The She g The Covenant Galatians The Roman Empire Acts of the Apostles Philippians Paul Apo **old testament** T tament Abraham Moses Liberator Teacher The Law David The Shepherd King The Covenant Solomon the Magni

POSSIBLE ISSUES FOR DISCUSSION

1   How satisfactory are Genesis 1–2 to you in exploring:

   (i)   who we are?

   (ii) how we came to be?

   (iii) the nature of the universe?

(The stories in Genesis 1 and 2 declare: [a] God is Creator of everything; [b] everything he has made is good; [c] human beings are in some sense akin to him – made in his image, 1:27; and filled with his breath/Spirit, 2:7.)

2   Where do you find answers in our culture to the questions listed above and to God's part in creation?

   (In the scientific story of creation? Music? Art? Poetry?)

3   In Genesis 1:26 and 28, God gives human beings "dominion over" the creation, with the command to be "fruitful and multiply, and fill the earth and subdue it..."

Whereas in 2:15, Adam is given the garden (creation) "to till it and keep it".

How have human beings responded to each of these commands?

Which one do you consider needs greatest emphasis today?

4   A friend of yours says of Genesis 1 and 2: "Those stories can't be true – science contradicts them – and anyway, they contradict each other!"

How would you reply?

5   A five-year-old child was heard to say: "God made the world for joyness!"

Do you agree?

Hebrew Poetry

Hebrew poetry is concrete rather than abstract, and depends on rhythm rather than rhyme.

The commonest form of rhythm adopted is **parallelism**. In this form, there are two lines about equal in length, in which the second line runs roughly parallel to the first in one of three ways:

either   by **repeating** the concept of the first line in different words:

> e.g. Psalm 15:1

> O Lord, who may abide in your tent?
> Who may dwell on your holy hill?

or   by **developing** the idea in the first line:

> e.g. Psalm 42:1

> As a deer longs for flowing streams,
> so my soul longs for you, O God.

or   by **contrasting** with the idea in the first line:

> e.g. Proverbs 10:1

> A wise child makes a glad father,
> but a foolish child is a mother's grief.

The book of Psalms is the primary example of Hebrew poetry, consisting of a collection of hymns and prayers from 1000 to 200 BC. After the exile, they were used in worship in the rebuilt Temple, and sung to music with orchestral accompaniment.

Modern translations of the Bible indicate many other passages which were written in poetic form, such as Job, Proverbs and much of Second Isaiah.

Old Testament Abraham Moses Liberator Teacher The Law David The Shepherd King The Covenant Solomon
nificent **part four** stament St Luke's Gospel Salvation History The Roman Empire Galatians Christian Paul Ap
e Gentiles The Prophets Amos Hosea **literature spun from history** s of Creation The Psalms The Wi
ature Daniel The Passion Resurrection Jesus The Old Testament Abraham Moses Liberator Law David The She
The Covenant Galatians The Roman Empire Acts of the Apostles Philippians Paul Apo **old testament** Th
ment Abraham Moses Liberator Teacher The Law David The Shepherd King The Covenant Solomon the Magni

The Psalms

After the exile, religious practice became institutionalised by the priests. Judah was impoverished and politically weak; the heyday of prophecy was over. The devout found expression of their religion through devotional meditation expressed in the Psalms, and in reflection on daily life, illustrated in the Wisdom literature.

Both these bodies of literature, while containing pre-exilic material, reached their final form after the exile. They are excellent examples of Hebrew poetry.

The Psalms are the greatest example of Hebrew poetry. Used in both public and private worship, they are a frank expression of human relationships with God. Primarily a collection of hymns of praise to God, they also express the whole range of human emotions: joy, sorrow, fear, confidence, hope, anxiety, frustration, anger, rejection, sinfulness, peace. The individual and corporate heart of Israel can be so frankly revealed before God because of knowing and believing his promise to them:

> "You are precious in my sight,
> and honoured, and I love you."
> Isaiah 43:4

Named after David, who as a shepherd boy possibly might have compiled Psalm 23, the Psalms have been added to and worked over to suit changing conditions. Their timeless and universal quality has led to their use devotionally in worship for 3,000 years. Psalm 150 lists many of the instruments used in musical accompaniment.

The Psalms were central to Jesus' prayer, and formed his dying words:

"My God, my God, why have you forsaken me?" Mark 15:34 and Matthew 27:46 from Psalm 22:1

and

"Into your hands I commit my spirit" Luke 23:46 from Psalm 31:5

(Note how here Jesus has prefixed the phrase with "Father", making the prayer peculiarly his own.)

You may possibly have your "special" Psalms, which you have made your own. Those listed for reading are a sample only.

Old Testament Abraham Moses Liberator Teacher The Law David The Shepherd King The Covenant Solomon
gnificent The New Testament St Luke's Gospel Salvation History The Roman Empire Galatians **part four** A
he Gentiles The Prophets Amos Hosea **literature spun from history** of Creation The Psalms The Wi
rature Daniel The Passion Resurrection Jesus The Old Testament Abraham Moses Liberator Law David The Shep
g The **old testament** The Roman Empire Acts of the Apostles Philippians Paul Apostle of the Gentiles Th
tament Abraham Moses Liberator Teacher The Law David The Shepherd King The Covenant Solomon the Magni

SUGGESTED READINGS AND POINTS TO CONSIDER AS YOU READ

The Psalms of Ascent	Psalms 120–134
(a) These Psalms were sung by pilgrims climbing up to Jerusalem for the annual festivals. The pilgrims re-enacted and made present now, in the life of each individual, God's past redemption of his people. (It is you and I who are saved from Egypt.)	
(b) Note the varied imagery of both the Jewish history of salvation and everyday life which speaks of God.	
(c) Choose a verse from one of these Psalms, and be prepared to say in the group how it speaks to you and why you chose it.	
The God of Creation	Psalm 8
Note:	
(a) This Psalm was written at night-time (verse 3);	
(b) The double status accorded to humans who are "too lowly" for God's consideration in all his majestic creation (verse 4), but also "a little lower than God" (verse 5);	
(c) God entrusts human beings with the care of his creation (verses 6-8).	
Behold! I am fearfully and wonderfully made!	Psalm 139:1-18
(a) What does this Psalm proclaim about God?	
(b) Note the unusual Old Testament view in verse 8 that even Sheol (see diagram on page 96) cannot cause separation from God, when compared with the generally held belief expressed in Psalm 6:5.	

Further Reading (if time)

God's faithful servant	Psalm 15
Thanksgiving for rescue	Psalm 40:1-10
A Psalm of longing for God	Psalm 42:1-5
God is our eternal protection	Psalm 46 (and Psalm 91)
A Psalm of penitence	Psalm 51
God's tender love, concern and mercy	Psalm 103
A Psalm written in the Babylonian exile	Psalm 137
A final paeon of praise from the whole created order	Psalms 145–150

nificent **part four** stament St Luke's Gospel Salvation History The Roman Empire Galatians Christian Paul Apo
e Gentiles The Prophets Amos Hosea **literature spun from history** s of Creation The Psalms The Wis
ature Daniel The Passion Resurrection Jesus The Old Testament Abraham Moses Liberator Law David The Shepl
The Covenant Galatians The Roman Empire Acts of the Apostles Philippians Paul Apo **old testament** The
ament Abraham Moses Liberator Teacher The Law David The Shepherd King The Covenant Solomon the Magnifi

POSSIBLE ISSUES FOR DISCUSSION

1   Identify and, if using this book in a group, share with the group, the
    verse you chose from the Psalms of Ascent or a favourite verse of yours
    from any of the Psalms.

    Why does your chosen verse speak to you?

2   The prayer of simply being oneself

> "No one is nearer to God than the person who has a hunger, a
> want – however tiny and inarticulate. And that is where prayer
> can begin, the prayer of simply being oneself in utter sincerity.
>
> One can pray like this:
>
> 'O my God, I want you, help me to want you more.'
> 'O my God, I love you so little, help me to love you as you love
> me.'
> 'O my God, I scarcely believe in you, increase my tiny faith.'
> 'O my God, I do not really feel sorry for my sin: but I want to,
> give me a true sorrow for it.'
>
> We don't find God by trying to be more religious than we are or
> can be.
>
> No, we are near God by being true to ourselves, and then God
> can begin to find us, to fill our emptiness, and some of the old
> phrases of religion can be near to what is in the heart."

Michael Ramsey, Archbishop of Canterbury 1961–74

How easy or hard do we find it to be really frank and honest in
expressing our emotions to God?

Do we present ourselves to God in a sanitised way, or as we really are?

Does our approach depend on whether our prayer is in public or private?

Is it appropriate to express anger and cursing in worship?

3   Try praying one of the Psalms of Ascent (Psalms 120– 134).

    Sit comfortably; a focal point like a candle or flowers can be a help.

    First, read the Psalm aloud; then read it silently, perhaps several times
    over, and really savour it, concluding with praying it. Then focus on a
    verse which has specially stood out – this may be different for each
    person, if the book is being used by a group. Then try rephrasing the
    verse in your own words.

Testament Abraham Moses Liberator Teacher The Law David The Shepherd King The Covenant Solomon
ficent The New Testament St Luke's Gospel Salvation History The Roman Empire Galatians **part four** Ap
Gentiles The Prophets Amos Hosea **literature spun from history** of Creation The Psalms The Wis
ture Daniel The Passion Resurrection Jesus The Old Testament Abraham Moses Liberator Law David The Shep
he **old testament** The Roman Empire Acts of the Apostles Philippians Paul Apostle of the Gentiles The
nent Abraham Moses Liberator Teacher The Law David The Shepherd King The Covenant Solomon the Magnifi

4   In *Common Worship*, Psalm 8:5-7 is translated in two different ways:

Literal interpretation	Using inclusive language
4. *(for context)* When I consider your heavens, the work of your fingers, the moon and the stars that you have ordained,	

5.
What is man, that you should be
    mindful of him;
the son of man, that you should seek
    him out?
	5.
	What are mortals, that you should be
	mindful of them;
	mere human beings, that you should
	    seek them out?

6.
You have made him little lower than
    the angels
and crown him with glory and honour.
	6.
	You have made them little lower than
	    the angels
	and crown them with glory and
	    honour.

7.
You have given him dominion over the
    works of your hands
and put all things under his feet.
	7.
	You have given them dominion over
	    the works of your hands
	and put all things under their feet.

(a)   The phrase "son of man" can also mean just "man".

However, "Son of Man" was a favourite title Jesus took up and used to
convey, and also to hide, the nature of his messiahship as the Christ.

Do you feel that you can "perceive" Christ in this Psalm? If so, how?

(b)   Human beings have a special relationship with God and special task entrusted
by him.

What is needed from us today to fulfil this special relationship and task?

Have we the will to carry this through?

The Wisdom Literature

Most of the Bible is about God taking the initiative to reveal himself. In the Wisdom literature, however, the starting point is ordinary human experience of life which, when reflected upon, can result in insight into two forms of wisdom. Firstly, it illustrates the application of general moral rules in the Law to specific situations in life (e.g. "Do not dally with a singing girl, or you will be caught by her tricks", Sirach 9:4). But it can also lead to the discernment of truths about God.

> The book of Daniel may be regarded as a Wisdom book; it is treated separately (see pages 107-111).

In Hebrew, "Wisdom" is a feminine noun. After the exile, divine Wisdom, though one with God, becomes personified as a divine attribute or aspect of God, but with a personality of her own. She is recognised as the source of all human wisdom, and may be observed at work in creation. Ultimately, however, she is beyond understanding.

Named after Solomon, and in his tradition of wisdom (e.g. 1 Kings 3:16-28; 10:1-7), the Wisdom literature consists of the books of Job, Proverbs and Ecclesiastes (meaning "the Preacher") in the Old Testament, and the books of Ecclesiasticus (also called the Wisdom of Jesus, son of Sirach, or just "Sirach") and Wisdom (or the Wisdom of Solomon) in the Apocrypha (see page 11).

JOB (fifth–fourth century BC) wrestles with the questions of the undeserved suffering of the righteous. He protests vigorously against his three friends, who try to persuade him he must have sinned to deserve his misfortunes. Job is finally silenced by his awesome vision of God (Job 38:1 – 42:6). The editor adds a prologue and epilogue, pronouncing the traditional doctrine of reward for virtue (chapters 1 and 2 and 42:7-17).

PROVERBS (around 250 BC) consists primarily of instruction to young men, often warning them of the excesses of wine and women. Its message is that good is rewarded and evil is punished.

ECCLESIASTES (around 200 BC) has been said to contain "faith, without hope or love". It describes realistically and with resignation a disillusionment with much of human experience.

SIRACH (around 190 BC) identifies reverence for the Law with wisdom (24:23, where Wisdom has been speaking). It describes the devotion of the "pious ones", soon to be put to the test (see page 110 on Daniel).

WISDOM (around 50 BC), written in Greek by a Hellenised Jew in Alexandria (see "Hellenisation" on page 107), seeks to safeguard Jewish faith in a Greek setting.

Old Testament Abraham Moses Liberator Teacher The Law David The Shepherd King The Covenant Solomon gnificent The New Testament St Luke's Gospel Salvation History The Roman Empire Galatians **part four** A the Gentiles The Prophets Amos Hosea **literature spun from history** of Creation The Psalms The Wi erature Daniel The Passion Resurrection Jesus The Old Testament Abraham Moses Liberator Law David The She g The **old testament** The Roman Empire Acts of the Apostles Philippians Paul Apostle of the Gentiles Th tament Abraham Moses Liberator Teacher The Law David The Shepherd King The Covenant Solomon the Magni

SUGGESTED READINGS AND POINTS TO CONSIDER AS YOU READ

Reflections on Experiences of Daily Life

(a) Wisdom bestows quietness of mind and generosity of attitude.	Proverbs 3:13-35
(b) Lessons learnt from observing the ant.	Proverbs 6:6-11
(c) Seven things abhorrent to God.	Proverbs 6:16-19
(d) Beware the seductive woman.	Proverbs 7:4-19
(e) Each aspect of life has its own time.	Ecclesiastes 3:1-8
(f) Daily work faithfully performed is prayer (38:34b Revised English Bible: "the practice of their craft is their prayer").	Sirach 38:24-34 (especially 38:31-34)

Passages on the Personification of Divine Wisdom

(a) Wisdom is known fully to God alone.	Job 28:20-28
(b) Divine Wisdom speaks as a person present with God from eternity and active in creation. (In verse 30 alternative readings are "master worker" or "little child".)	Proverbs 8:22-31 (Wisdom is speaking throughout)
(c) Divine Wisdom is an outpouring of God's glory renewing the world and human beings.	Wisdom 7:21 – 8:1

Attitudes to Death

(a) Death comes to all.	Ecclesiastes 12:1-8
(b) Immortality of the soul. The Alexandrian Jewish author of Wisdom has imbibed Greek Platonic philosophy, which sees a distinction between body and soul. Therefore, at death, the transitory body returns to dust and the immortal soul returns to God. In contrast, the traditional Palestinian Jewish view was that human nature is a unity demanding both soul and body, the soul expressing itself through the body. This led to belief in resurrection of the body in the book of Daniel.	Wisdom 3:1-9

POSSIBLE ISSUES FOR DISCUSSION

1   In Israel, "the wise" were the elderly, full of experience of life.
    Whom do we, in our society today, regard as wise?

2   Does reflection on the experiences of daily life today help in our
    understanding of the meaning of things?

3   God's activity in our lives is often most easily perceived through
    hindsight.

    Do you agree?

4   Belief is born out of experience.

    The early Church's experience of new life through Jesus quickly led to
    their belief that Jesus too is one with God the Father, yet distinct from
    him.

    Do you think the concept of divine Wisdom might have helped the
    Christians in developing their belief?

    See for example: 1 Corinthians 1:24 and 30
                                Colossians 2:2-3 and 1:15
                                Hebrews 1:1-3a

Old Testament Abraham Moses Liberator Teacher The Law David The Shepherd King The Covenant Solomon nificent The New Testament St Luke's Gospel Salvation History The Roman Empire Galatians **part four** Ap e Gentiles The Prophets Amos Hosea **literature spun from history** of Creation The Psalms The Wis ature Daniel The Passion Resurrection Jesus The Old Testament Abraham Moses Liberator Law David The Sheph The **old testament** The Roman Empire Acts of the Apostles Philippians Paul Apostle of the Gentiles The ament Abraham Moses Liberator Teacher The Law David The Shepherd King The Covenant Solomon the Magnifi

Daniel

HELLENISATION

After 538 BC Cyrus, King of Persia, having conquered Babylon, allowed the Jews to return to Judea. Under subsequent "returns", the Temple (520–516 BC) and walls (444 BC) were rebuilt, while the updated Priestly Law, introduced in 398 BC, emphasised the exclusiveness of the Jews.

Alexander the Great (356–323 BC), King of Macedon (north of Greece), had as his tutor Aristotle, the Greek philosopher. Through him he imbibed a love of all things Greek (Hellenic) – physical fitness, theatre, architectural beauty.

In 333 BC Alexander defeated Persia; in the next ten years his conquests included Greece, Egypt, Libya and Mesopotamia, right through to India. Greek language, customs and culture accompanied his conquests, and the world became Hellenised. He died of a fever, aged 33.

Jonah, a parable from around 300 BC, was written in protest against the increasing exclusivity of Judaism in this period. It reminded the Jews of their mission to the whole world.

On Alexander's death his territories were divided between four generals. Once again Judea was sandwiched between two centres of power: the Ptolemies in Egypt and the Seleucids, who ruled from Syria. In 198 BC Judea passed from the Ptolemies to Seleucid rule.

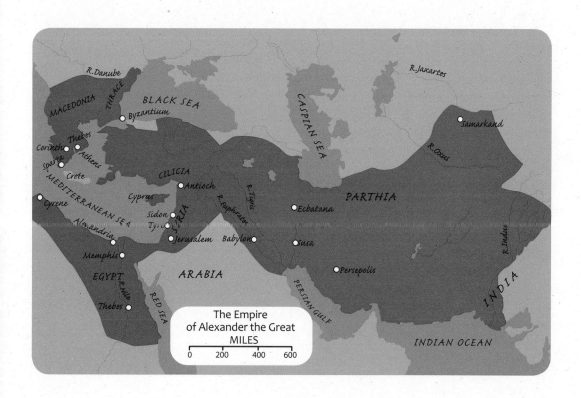

The Empire of Alexander the Great
MILES
0   200   400   600

Old Testament Abraham Moses Liberator Teacher The Law David The Shepherd King The Covenant Solomon
gnificent **part four** stament St Luke's Gospel Salvation History The Roman Empire Galatians Christian Paul Ap
he Gentiles The Prophets Amos Hosea **literature spun from history** s of Creation The Psalms The Wi
rature Daniel The Passion Resurrection Jesus The Old Testament Abraham Moses Liberator Law David The Shep
g The Covenant Galatians The Roman Empire Acts of the Apostles Philippians Paul Apo **old testament** Th
tament Abraham Moses Liberator Teacher The Law David The Shepherd King The Covenant Solomon the Magni

BACKGROUND TO THE BOOK OF DANIEL

The Seleucid ruler Antiochus IV (175–163 BC) named his capital, Antioch, after himself, and surnamed himself "Epiphanes", claiming to be god "manifest".

Meanwhile in Judea, certain Jews led by Jason (a Greek name replacing the Hebrew Joshua), who had bought the office of High Priesthood, and Menelaus (originally Menahem), who succeeded Jason, began to force people to abandon traditional Jewish practices (like circumcision) in favour of Hellenistic practices (like athletic exercises in the nude, see 1 Maccabees 1:11-15). So in effect people were forced to deny God and the Law. These "modernisers" found ready support from Antiochus IV. (This illustrates a recurrent tension for Jews down the ages: to what extent should they accommodate to the culture around them? Should they assimilate, or remain loyal to the Law, and so separate?)

With political unrest in Judea, and the support of Jewish modernisers, from 168 to 164 BC, Antiochus systematically set about imposing Hellenisation on the Jews and eliminating their characteristic Jewish practices. The Temple was desecrated and devastated; an image of Zeus (king of the Greek gods) was set up in the Temple (but bearing Antiochus' features), and the Jews were ordered to sacrifice to it. Circumcision was forbidden on pain of death. Scrolls of the Law were confiscated and burnt, and the Jews were ordered to eat pork and work on the Sabbath. Many Jews died rather than acquiesce; others became slaves. It was the first time they had been martyred for their religious beliefs.

The modernising Jewish aristocracy, including the priests, later became the New Testament party of the Sadducees. Those who remained true to the Law led the opposition of guerrilla warfare under the leadership of Mattathias, and later his son, Judas "Maccabeus", the "hammerer". Seeing a group of radical Law-keepers massacred when they would not fight on the Sabbath, Judas' forces realised they must defend themselves if they were to survive. They were joined by a company of Hasidim, or "Pious Ones" – perhaps the ancestors of the Pharisees in the New Testament.

THE BOOK OF DANIEL

The book of Daniel is believed to have been written and circulated between 168 and 164 BC to provide encouragement to the resistance. The hero is Daniel, who was a faithful Jew in the Babylonian exile (Ezekiel 14:14, 20; 28:3). The book therefore purports to have been written during the exile, so would not be recognised as dangerous if read by their Greek enemies. However, the chronology is worked out from 164 BC, and parts of the text are in Aramaic (a later form of Hebrew), confirming this later date.

Chapters 1–6 recount stories to illustrate how Jews in the past have remained loyal under intense persecution and have been vindicated by God. The four empires of the Babylonians, Medes, Persians and Greeks (including the Seleucids) are frequently referred to under imagery, and in each case are succeeded by God's final victory. Chapters 7–12 contain visions showing God as Lord of history.

This style of literature, in which the stories and visions consist of allegories, is known as apocalyptic, meaning to "reveal". It reveals God's ultimate victory, hidden in times of persecution.

Old Testament Abraham Moses Liberator Teacher The Law David The Shepherd King The Covenant Solomon
nificent The New Testament St Luke's Gospel Salvation History The Roman Empire Galatians **part four** Ap
he Gentiles The Prophets Amos Hosea **literature spun from history** of Creation The Psalms The Wis
ature Daniel The Passion Resurrection Jesus The Old Testament Abraham Moses Liberator Law David The Shepl
The **old testament** The Roman Empire Acts of the Apostles Philippians Paul Apostle of the Gentiles The
ament Abraham Moses Liberator Teacher The Law David The Shepherd King The Covenant Solomon the Magnifi

But Daniel is also a Wisdom book. Because Daniel is faithful to God's Law, God gives him wisdom – wisdom to be the king's minister, wisdom to interpret dreams, wisdom to read the signs of the times.

The Jewish rebellion succeeded, and the Temple was rededicated on the 25th day of the lunar month Chislev, 164 BC. Jews still celebrate this event at Chanukkah, the Feast of Lights.

An allegory contains a parallel meaning throughout, e.g. *Pilgrim's Progress.*

SUGGESTED READINGS AND POINTS TO CONSIDER AS YOU READ

(NB The persecution is described in 1 Maccabees which is in the Apocrypha.)

The persecution by Antiochus IV	1 Maccabees 1:1 – 3:2
The Temple is rededicated on the third anniversary of the first sacrifice to Zeus (1 Maccabees 1:59 and 4:52). This annual Festival of Dedication (Chanukkah in Hebrew) is also called the Feast of Lights. It is still kept by Jews when, over the eight days, an extra light is lit (from the central candle) in the window each night. The date is near 25 December, but varies each year as the Jews use a lunar calendar.	1 Maccabees 4:36-61

Two stories from Daniel chapters 1–6

Shadrach, Meshach and Abednego ridicule idol worship and survive the fiery furnace	Daniel 3
The four Jewish youths with Jewish names (including Daniel) are given Babylonian names in 1:6-7.

A cubit is measured from the tip of the finger to the elbow (about 18 inches or 46 cm). | |
| **Daniel is thrown into the lions' den for refusing to worship the king – who comes to acknowledge the Lord God** | Daniel 6 |

Old Testament Abraham Moses Liberator Teacher The Law David The Shepherd King The Covenant Solomor gnificent **part four** stament St Luke's Gospel Salvation History The Roman Empire Galatians Christian Paul A the Gentiles The Prophets Amos Hosea **literature spun from history** s of Creation The Psalms The Wi rature Daniel The Passion Resurrection Jesus The Old Testament Abraham Moses Liberator Law David The She g The Covenant Galatians The Roman Empire Acts of the Apostles Philippians Paul Apo **old testament** T tament Abraham Moses Liberator Teacher The Law David The Shepherd King The Covenant Solomon the Magni

Two visions from Daniel 7–12

(Remember the need for code language in case the book falls into enemy hands. The language is purposely mysterious.)

In the vision, the four beasts represent the sequence of the four kingdoms, the horn on the fourth beast being Antiochus. They lose their authority to the venerable "son of man" (7:13), who acquits the "holy ones of the Most High" (7:27) before the Ancient of Days (God). "Son of man" is an elusive phrase meaning "man" (or "human being"). But here he also has supernatural powers, and is both an individual and a corporate being (compare 7:13-14 and 7:27). The enigmatic phrase was taken up by Jesus, and expressed his understanding of messiahship, so different from that of his contemporaries. Daniel's last vision (chapters 10–12) depicts the persecution by Antiochus (king of the north) in the context of a supernatural war between the angels of evil and Michael, the archangel (12:1); it will last 3½ years (a "time" is a year, 12:7). At the end (11:35, 45; 12:13), God and his people will triumph. The "contemptible person" in 11:21 is Antiochus, and the "abomination that makes desolate" (11:31; 12:11) is the statue of Zeus he set up in the Temple.	Daniel 7 Daniel 10:1-6, 11, 20-21; 11:1-4, 20-23, 36-45; 12:1-13
Note the encouragement to the Pious Ones (12:1-13). For the first time, belief in a partial resurrection – of the very good and the very bad – is stated; a belief necessitated by the fact that God is just, but his faithful servants receive not justice, only martyrdom, in this life. The Pious Ones were forerunners of the New Testament Pharisees who, unlike the Sadducees, believed in the resurrection of the dead.	Daniel 12:1-4

Old Testament Abraham Moses Liberator Teacher The Law David The Shepherd King The Covenant Solomon
gnificent The New Testament St Luke's Gospel Salvation History The Roman Empire Galatians **part four** A
the Gentiles The Prophets Amos Hosea **literature spun from history** of Creation The Psalms The Wi
rature Daniel The Passion Resurrection Jesus The Old Testament Abraham Moses Liberator Law David The She
g The **old testament** The Roman Empire Acts of the Apostles Philippians Paul Apostle of the Gentiles Th
tament Abraham Moses Liberator Teacher The Law David The Shepherd King The Covenant Solomon the Magni

POSSIBLE ISSUES FOR DISCUSSION

1   Why do good stories make good theology?

    (e.g. Daniel 1–6; Jonah; the parables of Jesus)

2   Are there modern stories that are parallels to the book of Daniel?

3   Can suffering affect our understanding of God?

4   Daniel 12:1-3 describes for the first time a belief in a resurrection,
    though at this stage not yet for all.

    What is the distinction between belief in immortality of the soul and
    the resurrection of the body? (See Attitudes to Death, page 105.)

5   "The Church that marries the spirit of the age will be a widow in the
    next." *Dean Inge (Dean of St Paul's 1911–1934)*

    The book of Daniel describes an acute struggle between the demands
    of God and the spirit of the age.

    Is a tension between the demands of God and the spirit of the age
    always present, even if low key?

The Period between the Testaments

The Period between the Testaments

From 142 BC, the Jews were independent and were ruled by priest-kings as a theocracy, that is, according to the Law of God.

In 63 BC, Pompey, the Roman general, conquered Jerusalem. Wishing to discover the statue of the deity that the Jews worshipped, he entered the Holy of Holies and was baffled to find it completely empty.

Under Caesar Augustus, the first emperor (27 BC – AD 14), the Romans allowed subject territories to continue to worship their own gods, as long as they also added to this the worship of Caesar as divine. Thus the Roman Empire was sanctified, and insurrection became not just treason but sacrilege also. Other peoples were quite happy to add yet another god to those they already worshipped. But the Jews as monotheists steadfastly refused to worship Caesar, and since the Diaspora was now spread throughout the countries of the Roman Empire, the Romans (rather than suffer widespread unrest) granted the Jews a religious dispensation from worshipping Caesar.

Though the Romans now wielded political and military power, they adopted Hellenistic culture, and Greek became the common language throughout the empire.

From 40 BC, Herod, an Edomite Jew, called the Great because of his power and talents, gradually assumed power as a puppet king under Rome over the territories of Judea, Samaria, Galilee and lands to the east and north-east of the Jordan River.

This culture of Hellenisation and assimilation under Rome was a fertile period in the production of Jewish literature, including contributions by Jews of the Dispersion. This literature, much of which relates to judgement and resurrection, bridges the gap between the Old and New Testaments, and provides a crucial background to the New Testament. Much of it is contained in the Apocrypha.

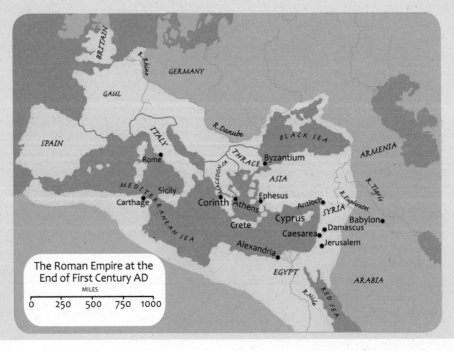

The Roman Empire at the End of First Century AD

MILES

0   250   500   750   1000

Old Testament Abraham Moses Liberator Teacher The Law David The Shepherd King The Covenant Solomon
nificent The New Testament St Luke's Gospel Salvation History The Roman Empire Galatians **part five** Apc
e Gentiles The Prophets Amos Hosea **literature spun from history** of Creation The Psalms The Wise
ature Daniel The Passion Resurrection Jesus The Old Testament Abraham Moses Liberator Law David The Sheph
The **new testament** The Roman Empire Acts of the Apostles Philippians Paul Apostle of the Gentiles The
ment Abraham Moses Liberator Teacher The Law David The Shepherd King The Covenant Solomon the Magnifi

St John's Gospel

BACKGROUND TO ST JOHN'S GOSPEL

We have noted how each evangelist presents his own portrait of Jesus, and have observed a family likeness between the first three Gospels (see pages 50-51). John, writing after the Synoptics and so able to assume that most of his readers already know the story of Jesus, is able to concentrate on the profound depth of meaning of that story, and we are offered the fruits of some sixty or so years' meditation on the experience of having been close to Jesus in the flesh.

But there are surprising omissions in his account: e.g. the baptism of Jesus is referred to (1:32-34) but not actually described, nor is there an account of blessing bread and wine at the Last Supper. John, however, adds important details too: whereas the Synoptic Gospels describe just one final Passover in Jerusalem, John's Gospel tells of Jesus visiting Jerusalem for three different Passovers, so presenting a more realistic length of his ministry.

Certain words and themes are central and keep recurring: e.g. life, death, love, light, sight, glory, belief, joy, peace, the hour, sign, witness, above/below (up/down), I am, the Son of Man and the Son of God. John's Gospel is to be meditated upon, especially as it often operates at more than one level. A speaker's word may mean one thing, but John, famous for his irony, sees the words as also possessing a deeper significance (e.g. 11:49-52). This is a clue that there may be multiple meanings in the Gospel.

John writes from the experience of knowing what it is to be fully accepted by Jesus. He knows that eternal life lies not in some distant future, but that God's life through the Spirit is fully present and available now to all who believe in Jesus. John has come to recognise Jesus not only as the Son of God, but also as God the Son.

The one who was active in creating the universe laid aside his Godhead voluntarily; he restricted himself to becoming totally human, not holding on to any special divine privileges. Experiencing to the full the human lot, Jesus nevertheless maintained, as a human being, a completely open union with and knowledge of God the Father. In his person, he therefore unites God with human nature and human nature with God; to express this union, he uses the phrase "I AM". The words "I AM" when used by Jesus indicate the name of God (Exodus 3:14).

The Father is the centre of Jesus' mission and ministry: Jesus came from the Father and returns to the Father; he does the will and work of the Father; he says nothing of his own but only what he has learnt of the Father. Completely human and completely free, his union with the Father is nevertheless total, and he reveals to us the secrets he has learnt from his Father.

The apostle John, traditionally associated with the Church in Ephesus, is concerned to bridge the gulf between the Jewish roots of the Christian faith and the

Old Testament Abraham Moses Liberator Teacher The Law David The Shepherd King The Covenant Solomon
gnificent **part five** stament St Luke's Gospel Salvation History The Roman Empire Galatians Christian Paul A
he Gentiles The Prophets Amos Hosea **literature spun from history** s of Creation The Psalms The W
rature Daniel The Passion Resurrection Jesus The Old Testament Abraham Moses Liberator Law David The She
. The Covenant Galatians The Roman Empire Acts of the Apostles Philippians Paul Apo**new testament**T
ament Abraham Moses Liberator Teacher The Law David The Shepherd King The Covenant Solomon the Magn

Greek culture in which he now lives. One way he attempts this is by using (in the Prologue) the Greek word, "Logos": to Jews, this would mean God's "Word", and to Gentiles, the "Reason" that orders the universe.

John also counters the docetic heresy, which claimed that Jesus only **seemed** to be human, and only **seemed** to die. John frequently points out Jesus' full humanity: he hungers, thirsts, is tired and mourns. Similarly, John confirms Jesus' death. His Gospel alone says there was no need to break the legs of Jesus, as he was already dead, and that "blood and water" (the components of blood after death) issued from his side after the spear wound (19:31-35).

At the same time, however, John also presents Jesus with perfect foreknowledge, especially concerning the significance of his death. May this perhaps be the result of hindsight inserted by John into Jesus' ministry as a result of years of meditation on these events and their significance for us?

"Docetic" comes from the Greek word "doceo", which means "I seem".

Authorship

The Gospel is traditionally attributed to John the apostle, writing in Ephesus in his old age. However, it may well be that an elder of the Church at Ephesus was the actual writer of the Gospel, presenting John's own teaching, which impregnates the book.

The apostle John is not named in the Gospel, but is often identified with "the disciple whom Jesus loved", who is referred to in the passion and resurrection narratives. The community which first read and used this text seems to have cherished a special memory of this "beloved disciple". His purpose in so describing himself may be intentional if, as seems probable, he is inviting each one of us also to become "the disciple whom Jesus loves", and so to enter into the intimate relationship with Jesus that he himself has experienced.

THE PROLOGUE

John's purpose in writing is given right at the end in 20:30-31. (Chapter 21 is regarded as an appendix added later on.) His purpose is "that you may come to believe that Jesus is the Messiah, the Son of God, and that through believing you may have life in his name".

In the Prologue (1:1-18), John unfolds the mystery of the Incarnation (God's "enfleshment" in human form).

In a detective novel, the mystery is solved at the end of the story. John, however, gives us the vital clue in the Prologue: the Prologue proclaims the relationship between Jesus Christ and the creation and salvation of the world.

In a religious context, the word "mystery" refers to truths beyond our total comprehension, because the human mind is inferior to the mind of God; we can never therefore fully understand the truths propounded in the Prologue, as they lead us beyond the limits of our intellect. It is by continuing to ponder upon them throughout our life that we come to discern their truth.

The Prologue has been likened to the overture to an opera. Semi-poetic, it contains the main themes that will be enlarged upon later on, notably: life, light, witness, believing, children of God, truth, glory, grace.

Old Testament Abraham Moses Liberator Teacher The Law David The Shepherd King The Covenant Solomon
gnificent The New Testament St Luke's Gospel Salvation History The Roman Empire Galatians **part five**
he Gentiles The Prophets Amos Hosea **literature spun from history** of Creation The Psalms The Wi
rature Daniel The Passion Resurrection Jesus The Old Testament Abraham Moses Liberator Law David The She
g The **new testament** The Roman Empire Acts of the Apostles Philippians Paul Apostle of the Gentiles Th
ament Abraham Moses Liberator Teacher The Law David The Shepherd King The Covenant Solomon the Magni

A note on the use of
I AM and "I am"

When printed in capital letters, I AM
denotes the name of God given to Moses
(Exodus 3:14). However, the Hebrew may
equally validly be translated I WILL BE;
this is important, as it shows that God
is not static but dynamic, continually
moving ahead of us and leading us on.

In John's Gospel, Jesus' use of I AM
proclaims how, through his full and open
union as a human being with the Father,
he reveals God to us. This open union
means also that Jesus is a fully integrated
human being, since he expresses human
nature as God intends it to be. In Jesus is
accomplished the total union of God with
human nature and of human nature with
God – a dynamic two-way relationship.

"I am" (printed in this study in ordinary
letters) denotes the goal towards which
John is pointing us, through divine grace.
Ordinary humans ("I am") dynamically
move on to the "I will be" of becoming
fulfilled as children of God, fully open to
the divine life – that is the kind of human
beings God intends us to be/become.

SUGGESTED READINGS AND POINTS TO CONSIDER AS YOU READ

Look again at John's reason for writing his Gospel, and consider the Prologue in this context	John 20:30-31

The Prologue		
(NB This is a challenging passage. Do not worry if you find it hard going – you can always return to it later on! If necessary, pass straight on to page 127.)		
vv. 1-4, 9	Prior to time, the divine Word is eternal with God in an endless dialogue of love. Verse 1 resonates with Genesis 1:1; throughout Genesis 1, God creates through his spoken Word ("and God said…"); his Word is the agent both in creation and in sustaining creation. The creation bears his character of organic, active, evolving life, which in humans results in a capacity for knowing God as they reflect on his natural creation.	John 1:1-18
vv. 5, 9-11	The darkness of self-centredness, blindness and death cannot recognise, cohabit with or overcome light, life and love. God's own nation and people failed to receive the true light.	
vv. 12-13	But all who do receive him and trust in his name (i.e. his being, character) are empowered, through the divine life imparted to them, to become children of God.	
v. 14	The Word became flesh, subject to the full pains and limitations of human flesh: "flesh" emphasises how totally complete was the Incarnation. "Lived among us" means more literally "tabernacled" (i.e. pitched his tent) among us. In his human being, we beheld the glory of the eternal Word/Son of the Father (just as the tabernacle in the wilderness housed the glory of God).	
	Fully incarnate flesh becomes the means for revealing the glory of the incarnate Son.	
vv. 6-8,15	The revelation of who the light is first made through the witness of John the Baptist: "He was before me", i.e. the eternal I AM.	
vv. 16-18	The writer adds his testimony to the ongoing grace available to the children of God, leading them to become ever more fully "I am" – to be and become what God intended, through the Son in the person of Jesus Christ. The process which was started through Moses is completed through Jesus Christ.	

Old Testament Abraham Moses Liberator Teacher The Law David The Shepherd King The Covenant Solomon
gnificent The New Testament St Luke's Gospel Salvation History The Roman Empire Galatians **part five** A
he Gentiles The Prophets Amos Hosea **literature spun from history** of Creation The Psalms The Wi
rature Daniel The Passion Resurrection Jesus The Old Testament Abraham Moses Liberator Law David The She
g The **new testament** The Roman Empire Acts of the Apostles Philippians Paul Apostle of the Gentiles Th
tament Abraham Moses Liberator Teacher The Law David The Shepherd King The Covenant Solomon the Magni

After reading the Prologue with the notes, reread it straight through, almost like listening to a piece of music.

Recognise in it a profound and awe-inspiring proclamation and hymn of worship, praising the wonder, humility and love of God in creation and in the Incarnation.

John shows how, in the Incarnation, God uses the material and physical to reveal himself.

Compare the sweep and symbolism of the Prologue with the four embroideries shown below, used by kind permission of St Albans Cathedral. John likes to emphasise how material aspects of our world can be channels for God's revelation.

WATER
The Spirit of God moving over the waters. The ark riding the flood. Moses strikes water from the rock. The people of God go through the Red Sea. Ezekiel's vision. Christ the source of living water. His baptism in the Jordan sanctifies water. Water and blood flow from the crucified. St John's vision.

EARTH
Creation of the world. Fruits of the earth and pasture. Man tills the soil. Grain dies and bears fruit. Man made from dust and will return to it. The first and the second man.

FIRE
God appears in the burning bush. Column of cloud and fire leading God's people. God hidden in the fire and smoke on Sinai. Three young men in the burning fiery furnace. The new fire at Easter. The fire of the Holy Spirit at Pentecost.

WIND and SPIRIT
The wind over the surface of the waters. God breathes into man's nostrils the breath of life. Wind brings rain. The Lord was in the sound of a gentle breeze. Breath brings the dead bones to life. Jesus and Nicodemus. The rush of a mighty wind blows where it wills.

part five stament St Luke's Gospel Salvation History The Roman Empire Galatians Christian Paul Apo
literature spun from history :s of Creation The Psalms The Wisc
new testament

Early witnesses and their infectious response

John 1:19-51 and 4:1-42 illustrate Jesus' dealings with people. To those who are genuine and honest, he invariably shows respect. Moreover, he perceives what they have it in them to become – their potential "I am" – and modifies his approach to each individual to promote this goal in their lives.

The good news is for sharing. As individuals begin to discover in Jesus someone unique, their infectious enthusiasm spreads to others: "Come and see!"

The story of the Samaritan woman is important for the following reasons:

(a) The unorthodoxy of Jesus, a Jewish man, recognised by his disciples as a rabbi (4:31), speaking at all to a woman and a Samaritan, astounds the disciples. Jesus regards her as a human being rather than, with prejudice, as a stereotype – and, in so doing, shows that the Gospel is for **all** people.

(b) Jesus' approach to the woman is not from superiority or power, but through vulnerability: "Give me a drink." He places himself at her mercy and, in so doing, is able to affirm and free her. Declaring his own need, he enables her to face her own vulnerability and need.

(c) The story may be taken to illustrate the relationship between the Gospel and sexual relationships; it shows how two of the most powerful forces in human life, religion and sex, can be united and so redeemed. The woman's relationships with men have been in disarray; she

is alienated from the life-giving contribution sexuality might play in her life. Jesus, in challenging her to face up to this, leads her on to the possibility of new life through the Spirit, and to a new wholesomeness in relationships where there is respect, honesty, equality and love.

(d) This resonates with Genesis 1:26-27: since God in his very being (as Trinity) is a relationship, it is men and women **in relationship with each other** who **together** reflect the image of God. Made together in his image, they are called in relationship together to grow into/ become his likeness.

(e) The story shows Jesus' affirmation of sex as God's free creative gift to us. By reaching out to others in friendship, intimacy and loving companionship, our whole beings are nourished. Just as Jesus showed God to us through his bodily incarnation, so we, as physical beings, grow towards knowing God who is incarnate within each of us and among us. Love for self, for each other and for God becomes integrally united.

(f) This and other stories also show how Jesus (as we would expect in a fully incarnate life) enjoyed and needed the company and companionship of women as well as men.

Old Testament Abraham Moses Liberator Teacher The Law David The Shepherd King The Covenant Solomon
nificent The New Testament St Luke's Gospel Salvation History The Roman Empire Galatians **part five** Apo
e Gentiles The Prophets Amos Hosea **literature spun from history** of Creation The Psalms The Wis
ature Daniel The Passion Resurrection Jesus The Old Testament Abraham Moses Liberator Law David The Shep
The **new testament** The Roman Empire Acts of the Apostles Philippians Paul Apostle of the Gentiles The
ament Abraham Moses Liberator Teacher The Law David The Shepherd King The Covenant Solomon the Magnifi

SUGGESTED READINGS AND POINTS TO CONSIDER AS YOU READ

John the Baptist's further witness (presumably after Jesus' baptism and temptation)		John 1:19-34
The witness of the first disciples		John 1:35-51
(a) What do you consider leads these people to respond to Jesus?		
(b) Simon's new name, Peter (meaning "rock"), is a foretaste of what Jesus sees he is capable of becoming.		
(c) "Come and see" (1:39, 46) illustrates the importance of experience, then and now.		
Jesus and the Samaritan woman		
v. 5	Samaritans, of mixed race, also had foreign elements in their religion (see page 86). Their scriptures were just the first five books of the Old Testament (the Law). Sychar was situated on the slopes of Mt Gerizim, where Samaritans had built their rival Temple.	John 4:1-42
v. 6	Noon, the hottest part of the day, is not the usual time for drawing water. Why perhaps was this woman coming then?	
v. 10	"Living water" (i.e. flowing, "live" water) frequently refers to the Holy Spirit in John's Gospel (see 7:37-39). The fountain of water Jesus will give those who believe will convey eternal life here and now. The woman thinks Jesus is referring to the live spring beneath the well, but Jesus, with no bucket, offers only himself.	
vv. 16-18	Jesus respects without condemnation the woman's honest reply, "I have no husband"; but for the healing of her relationships, the "husband" is also needed.	
vv. 22-24	Jews know God through the prophets (whom the Samaritans do not recognise) – but eternal life for all, through the Spirit, is imminent.	
v. 26	Jesus' reply in Greek is "I AM [talking with you]".	
v. 29	The woman rushes off to proclaim, "Come and see" – with amazing results.	
Through these events, John is showing us that a further missionary boundary has been broken.		

Names, which denote character, are important for Jews.

POSSIBLE ISSUES FOR DISCUSSION

1   A person's spirit is expressed through the body.

    What would you describe as a wholesome attitude to our bodies?

2   What do you consider from these stories that Jesus suggests should be the true ideal for Christian living, both individually and in personal relationships?

3   To those who were sincere and knew their need, Jesus' approach, in not condemning but affirming them, helped them to grow as individuals.

    How good are we today at affirming people?

4   Jesus "named" Peter, and rescued the Samaritan woman (it appears) from the way others had "labelled" her.

    What is the difference between "naming" and "labelling"?

    What do our prejudices do to others?

Old Testament Abraham Moses Liberator Teacher The Law David The Shepherd King The Covenant Solomon
gnificent The New Testament St Luke's Gospel Salvation History The Roman Empire Galatians **part five** Ap
he Gentiles The Prophets Amos Hosea **literature spun from history** of Creation The Psalms The Wis
rature Daniel The Passion Resurrection Jesus The Old Testament Abraham Moses Liberator Law David The Shep
g The **new testament** The Roman Empire Acts of the Apostles Philippians Paul Apostle of the Gentiles Th
ament Abraham Moses Liberator Teacher The Law David The Shepherd King The Covenant Solomon the Magnif

THE SIGNS OF JESUS

John's Gospel contains only seven miracles of Jesus (excluding the one in the Appendix, chapter 21): three "nature" miracles (2:1-11; 6:1-15, 16-21); three healing miracles (4:46-54; 5:1-15; 9:1-12); and one raising from the dead (11:1-44).

In John's Gospel, miracles are called "signs". In the Synoptic Gospels, "sign" is a "bad" word: it is a deed demanded of Jesus by the Pharisees to prove conclusively who he is (Mark 8:11-12). Jesus emphatically refuses such requests. In John's Gospel, however, "sign" is a "good" word, indicating that the miracles point to something (or someone) beyond themselves. They reveal the "glory" of Jesus, provoke thought and may lead to faith (John 2:11). The discourses which follow them enlarge on their significance.

All the "signs" show that Jesus never acted alone without the desire of the one helped, or another on that person's behalf (see Mark 6:1-6). Jesus' question to the sick man (John 5:6b) especially emphasises this; the man's reply hints at a previous lack of desire, which Jesus now quickens into life.

Since the last enemy is death, the last sign in John is the sign that points to life. Restoration of Lazarus' physical life is a sign pointing to the fullness and continuity of eternal life, here and now, and beyond physical death, to be released by Jesus' own death.

SUGGESTED READINGS AND POINTS TO CONSIDER AS YOU READ

The healing of the lame man at the Pool of Bethesda (Bethzatha)		
vv. 6-7	Jesus questions the lame man on his will to live and grow as a person. The man appears to have become used to his situation – even accepted it – and so to have lost the desire for and belief in the possibility of changing or improving things.	John 5:1-18 (and 19-24)
v. 8	Jesus reawakens a deep desire long dormant in him for wholeness and healing – so enabling the man to spring up in response to Jesus' command.	
	Compare the sick man's life by the pool for 38 years with Jesus' promise: "I came that they may have life, and have it abundantly." (John 10:10)	
vv. 19-24	The relationship between Father and Son is expounded.	

The healing of the man born blind

v. 1	The Greek word translated "man" here means more literally a human being. John seems to treat him both as an individual and as Everyman.	John 9:1-41
vv. 2-3	Jesus roundly condemns the commonly held belief of his day that suffering is a punishment for wrongdoing or sin.	
	How does this compare with commonly held attitudes today to illness and misfortunes?	
vv. 6-7	Saliva was regarded as an eye salve. The man's own contribution in his healing is required by washing in the Pool of Siloam (which means "sent").	
v. 9b	The Greek literally means "[The blind man] kept saying, 'I am'." As the Father sent the Son, so the Son has sent the man now filled with new life. He first witnesses among the Pharisees and refuses to be browbeaten (v. 25b).	
v. 5 and	"I AM the light of the world": the whole episode is about light and darkness.	
vv. 35-41	The man receives not just physical sight, but insight, while the Pharisees who claim to see remain blind. Jesus sees the Sabbath as pre-eminently the day in which to do God's work: in this case, of healing.	
v. 39	In John's Gospel, Jesus does not judge. His very presence, however, precipitates responses by which people judge themselves (see 3:19; 8:15; 12:47). The Pharisees' self-centred assurance that they are right prohibits their own salvation and is an obstacle to others whom they claim to guide.	

The raising of Lazarus

vv. 3, 5	Jesus' love for the two sisters and Lazarus is of the quality of God's love (*agape* in Greek) for us. Knowing Jesus is in great danger (10:31, 39-40), the sisters simply inform him of Lazarus' illness, perhaps hoping for healing from a distance (as in 4:46-54)?	John 11:1-53
	Does Jesus reject this option because:	
	(a) to heal from a distance would put his own safety before his friends' need?	
	(b) he does not panic as though death were the final disaster?	
	(c) he is preparing for his own death (which he knows is the consequence of returning to Bethany) – and so is struggling to bring his will in line with the Father's, and so be true to and live with himself?	
vv. 7-8, 15-16	The disciples are fearful, knowing they too are marked men; their faith needs strengthening.	
vv. 6, 11-14	Lazarus is now totally and legally dead; the spirit (which the Jews believed remained near the corpse for three days) has fully departed.	

Testament Abraham Moses Liberator Teacher The Law David The Shepherd King The Covenant Solomon
icent The New Testament St Luke's Gospel Salvation History The Roman Empire Galatians **part five** Apc
Gentiles The Prophets Amos Hosea **literature spun from history** of Creation The Psalms The Wisc
ure Daniel The Passion Resurrection Jesus The Old Testament Abraham Moses Liberator Law David The Sheph
new testament The Roman Empire Acts of the Apostles Philippians Paul Apostle of the Gentiles The
ent Abraham Moses Liberator Teacher The Law David The Shepherd King The Covenant Solomon the Magnific

		John 11:1-53
vv. 21-22	Martha meets Jesus privately outside the village. Is there anger, rebuke, guilt (common components of bereavement) in her greeting? Or just affection and sadness that Jesus is "too late"? And, either way, faith in him still…	
vv. 23-24	Jesus' words do not specify if Lazarus will rise now – or in the future (which is how Martha takes them, offering her little comfort).	
vv. 25-27	"I AM the resurrection and the life…" challenges Martha: how can Jesus "be" a future event? Jesus is claiming those in union with him **already now** have the quality of resurrection life, which physical death can never destroy. This truth, to be revealed when Lazarus is raised and, even more, through Jesus' own resurrection, is not yet fully understood by Martha, who, however, states her profound belief in Jesus as Messiah.	
vv. 28-32	Mary is denied the privacy with Jesus that Martha had. Her greeting, reflecting Martha's, perhaps expresses what the sisters had said so often before Jesus' arrival.	
vv. 33, 35-36, 38	Jesus' great physical and spiritual agitation appears to express: (a) his own grief in bereavement; (b) indignation at the power of death over people; (c) his own preparation for the great sign he is about to perform. (**All** Jesus' miracles were very costly to him, physically and spiritually, because of the self-giving and personal draining involved. See Mark 5:30.)	
vv. 39-42	For John, the stone to be removed also signifies that which imprisons each human spirit in its own tomb of anxiety, worry, resentment, rigidity of habit: Jesus' life-giving voice demands its removal (something Jesus cannot do without cooperation) for the release of new life. Jesus, looking into the open tomb, perceives the glory of God. His prayer indicates that: (a) throughout the whole incident he has been praying and been sustained by prayer; (b) he works only through his openness to the power of the Father, to whom he returns the glory – and he wants the onlookers to understand this.	

Old Testament Abraham Moses Liberator Teacher The Law David The Shepherd King The Covenant Solomon
gnificent **part five** stament St Luke's Gospel Salvation History The Roman Empire Galatians Christian Paul A
the Gentiles The Prophets Amos Hosea **literature spun from history** s of Creation The Psalms The W
rature Daniel The Passion Resurrection Jesus The Old Testament Abraham Moses Liberator Law David The She
g The Covenant Galatians The Roman Empire Acts of the Apostles Philippians Paul Apo**new testament** T
tament Abraham Moses Liberator Teacher The Law David The Shepherd King The Covenant Solomon the Magni

v. 43	Jesus shouts aloud, "Lazarus, come out!"	John 11:1-53
	Lazarus! the life-giving voice of the friend who believes in Lazarus, calls him by name and quickens him with power to respond; the dead are encompassed by God's love.	
	Come out! to Jesus and the Father; become what you are – alive! ("I am"!) from the self-inflicted tomb we create, to a new risen life and all it entails in discipleship. Jesus' call is to each one of us. Our dead areas, when confronted, can become the womb of new life.	
v. 44	The "dead man" comes out, now alive. "Unbind him, and let him go!" Old habits may still bind the returning life; the completion of the miracle requires human assistance. "Let go" is the same Greek word used for forgiveness of sin. It implies relaxation after tension, release from prison, racing horses released at the starting line, turning around from being "off target" to "on target". It has a much more lively meaning than is implied by "forgiveness of sin".	
	"Let him go [home]" – to Martha and Mary, but also to the goal of his and everyone's destiny (home with God), once individuals are released from the death of sin, the grave of convention and the trappings of habit.	
	Jesus calls each of us to join in rolling away the stone, and in releasing individuals to go where God leads them.	
vv. 45-46	The sign results in faith for those who are open to God; others reject Jesus. Ultimately, the truth of the story can only be discerned in the heart, soul and life of the believer.	
vv. 47-53	In John, Jesus' giving of life to Lazarus becomes the immediate cause of his own death, engineered by the Jewish council (Sanhedrin), led by the High Priest.	
	Why do you think the Sanhedrin was so rattled by this episode?	

In the Synoptic Gospels, Jesus' death is precipitated by the cleansing of the Temple; this event, in John, occurs at the beginning of the ministry (2:13-22).

Old Testament Abraham Moses Liberator Teacher The Law David The Shepherd King The Covenant Solomon
nificent The New Testament St Luke's Gospel Salvation History The Roman Empire Galatians **part five** Apo
e Gentiles The Prophets Amos Hosea **literature spun from history** of Creation The Psalms The Wiso
ature Daniel The Passion Resurrection Jesus The Old Testament Abraham Moses Liberator Law David The Sheph
The **new testament** The Roman Empire Acts of the Apostles Philippians Paul Apostle of the Gentiles The
ment Abraham Moses Liberator Teacher The Law David The Shepherd King The Covenant Solomon the Magnific

POSSIBLE ISSUES FOR DISCUSSION

1   A human contribution (which as a minimum meant asking Jesus for help) was always required before Jesus performed a miracle.

    Why do you think this was so?

    Does it have implications for the way we see God at work today (e.g. how we perceive prayer)?

2   Some disabled and powerless people have a profound serenity about them and seem to be specially close and precious to God.

    Are they perhaps more able to receive what we still seek?

    In our frenetic world which demands "being in control", can they teach us something important?

> Teilhard de Chardin (1881–1955, a French Jesuit, theologian and geologist) believed the next stage in human evolution would be in the spiritual dimension, and would be measured by the way disabled people and those who suffer are treated.

3   What "stones" do you think can wall us in from life?

    How can we help each other to "roll back the stone"?

4   Jesus needed human cooperation in the raising of Lazarus.

    "Unbind him, and let him go."

    In what "little ways" can we daily give or withhold life from others?

    For instance, how important can a smile be, a friendly word, or the readiness to give time to listen?

5   Jesus said, "Everyone who lives... in me will never die" (John 11:26).
    (a)   One aspect of this truth may be experienced when a deeply loved one dies; his or her life has become part of us and changed us in a deeply personal way, drawing us into a fuller life of love which never dies.

          Does this thought connect with our own experience of bereavement?

    (b)   Occasionally people experience deeply significant moments in life when they are aware they are part of a whole far greater than themselves.

          Have you experienced any such moments?

Old Testament Abraham Moses Liberator Teacher The Law David The Shepherd King The Covenant Solomon
gnificent **part five** stament St Luke's Gospel Salvation History The Roman Empire Galatians Christian Paul A
he Gentiles The Prophets Amos Hosea **literature spun from history** s of Creation The Psalms The W
rature Daniel The Passion Resurrection Jesus The Old Testament Abraham Moses Liberator Law David The She
g The Covenant Galatians The Roman Empire Acts of the Apostles Philippians Paul Apo**new testament**
tament Abraham Moses Liberator Teacher The Law David The Shepherd King The Covenant Solomon the Magn

The Passion, Death and Resurrection of Jesus

THE LAST SUPPER: JOHN 13–17

The prelude

12:23-24, 27-28, 32: these verses show that "the hour" and the "glory" are focused on Jesus' death on the cross, which will release eternal life for others.

Jesus, having fought with his own vulnerability (and horror at what lies ahead), again brings his will into union with the Father's (12:27). United with the Father in complete self-giving love, he is not imprisoned by any of the events that follow.

John's dating of the Last Supper and crucifixion

The Jewish day starts at sunset (around 6.00 pm). In the Synoptic Gospels, Jesus' Last Supper with his disciples is the Passover meal itself. In John, however, the night of Passover is the night between Friday and Saturday; Saturday is therefore both the Sabbath and the Feast of the Passover.

Jesus' death is at the exact moment (Friday, 3 pm) that the Passover lambs are being killed in the Temple Court for Passover meals that evening. In both datings, the symbolism of the Passover (celebrating deliverance from slavery in Egypt) is central to understanding the meaning of the death and resurrection of Jesus.

The Last Supper

John omits the blessing of bread and wine, probably because:

(a) the "breaking of bread" was already being practised in Christian churches;

(b) Jesus' claim, "I AM the bread of life", is expanded in chapter 6, after the feeding of the 5,000. This makes the whole Gospel, in a sense, Eucharistic.

The Last Supper discourses (13:31 – 16:33)

The artificial ending at 14:31 suggests that these discourses (rather than necessarily all being delivered at the Last Supper) are a collection of Jesus' teaching given on various occasions. Chosen because specially precious to his disciples, they were treasured as his "last words".

Old Testament Abraham Moses Liberator Teacher The Law David The Shepherd King The Covenant Solomon
gnificent The New Testament St Luke's Gospel Salvation History The Roman Empire Galatians **part five** Ap
he Gentiles The Prophets Amos Hosea **literature spun from history** of Creation The Psalms The Wis
rature Daniel The Passion Resurrection Jesus The Old Testament Abraham Moses Liberator Law David The Shep
g The **new testament** The Roman Empire Acts of the Apostles Philippians Paul Apostle of the Gentiles Th
ament Abraham Moses Liberator Teacher The Law David The Shepherd King The Covenant Solomon the Magnif

SUGGESTED READINGS AND POINTS TO CONSIDER AS YOU READ

The washing of the disciples' feet		John 13:1-20
vv. 1-5	The "hour" refers to Jesus' return to the Father, his total self-giving completed in death. His self-giving love for his friends is demonstrated in washing their feet as a servant – an act of service and of belonging together. They are to follow this example, serving and accepting service (v. 15).	
v. 7	When events have run their course, Peter will understand the significance of Jesus' act.	
	Why did Peter react as he did? Did he feel unworthy?	
	Or was it that he could not possibly allow Jesus to love him to this extent?	
	Would you too rather give service than accept it? If so, do you know why?	
	Is it necessary to have accepted service before one is truly able to give it? (In John 12:1-8, Jesus had accepted Mary's anointing of his feet.)	
v. 19	On the cross, Jesus will reveal the love of I AM.	
Judas goes out "and it was night" (v. 30)		John 13:21-31
	Judas, informant and betrayer, is unable to accept all that Jesus has to offer – simply his love. Jesus, confronted by the evil in which Judas is involved, is deeply shaken (v. 21); but Judas' free choice is respected after he rejects Jesus' last appeal in giving him the choicest morsel for the favoured guest (v. 26). In not opposing (nor even publicising) Judas' act, Jesus signs his own death warrant.	
vv. 30-31	The battle is now joined between light and darkness. The glory of the Son's love will be revealed as he encounters evil head-on, and transforms it through love.	

Old Testament Abraham Moses Liberator Teacher The Law David The Shepherd King The Covenant Solomon
nificent **part five** stament St Luke's Gospel Salvation History The Roman Empire Galatians Christian Paul Apc
e Gentiles The Prophets Amos Hosea **literature spun from history** s of Creation The Psalms The Wis
ature Daniel The Passion Resurrection Jesus The Old Testament Abraham Moses Liberator Law David The Shep
The Covenant Galatians The Roman Empire Acts of the Apostles Philippians Paul Apo**new testament**The
ament Abraham Moses Liberator Teacher The Law David The Shepherd King The Covenant Solomon the Magnifi

The Last Supper discourses: selected passages		John 13:31 – 16:33
	a) The new commandment, to love: 13:34-35; 14:15; 15:9-10, 12-13, 17.	
	(b) Joy: 15:11; 16:20-24.	
	(c) "Peace I leave with you": 14:27; 16:33.	
	(d) The complete union of Jesus with the Father: 14:8-11.	
	(e) The vine illustrates the depth of mutual union and shared life between the Father, Jesus and his disciples: 15:1-11.	
	(f) No longer servants, but friends of Jesus: 15:12-17.	
	(g) Prayer in the name of Jesus: 14:13-14; 15:7, 16b; 16:23-24.	
	(h) Jesus goes to prepare a place in the life beyond the grave: 13:36; 14:1-7.	
	(i) The Holy Spirit will continue Jesus' work with the disciples: 14:16-17, 26; 15:26; 16:7-15.	
	(j) "But take courage; I have conquered the world": 16:33b.	
The prayer of Jesus		Chapter 17
vv. 1-5	The love between Father and Son. "The hour has come" for the glory of the full mutual love of Father and Son to shine forth. The cross is the culmination of Jesus' life of self-giving love (v. 4).	
vv. 6-19	Prayer for the disciples who have responded to Jesus' revelation of God's character (or "name", v. 6).	
vv. 17-19	Jesus prays that they may be made holy in becoming "I am", in the same way that he consecrates himself to reveal to us God through human flesh.	
vv. 20-26	Prayer for all those who will believe through them – especially that their unity may reflect the openness of the union between Father and Son – "that the world may believe".	

Old Testament Abraham Moses Liberator Teacher The Law David The Shepherd King The Covenant Solomon
nificent The New Testament St Luke's Gospel Salvation History The Roman Empire Galatians **part five** Apc
e Gentiles The Prophets Amos Hosea **literature spun from history** of Creation The Psalms The Wis
ature Daniel The Passion Resurrection Jesus The Old Testament Abraham Moses Liberator Law David The Shepl
The **new testament** The Roman Empire Acts of the Apostles Philippians Paul Apostle of the Gentiles The
ment Abraham Moses Liberator Teacher The Law David The Shepherd King The Covenant Solomon the Magnifi

POSSIBLE ISSUES FOR DISCUSSION

1   Peter and Judas were both men of action.
    What do you think accounts for their contrasting behaviour in this
    narrative?

    We readily judge each of them, but can you think of anything to be
    said on behalf of either of them?

2   What do you think prayer "in the name of Jesus" means?

    (John 14:13-14; 15:7, 16b; 16:23-24)

3   Jesus prays that unity amongst Christians might reflect the openness
    of the union between Father and Son, "that the world may believe"
    (John 17:20-23).

    Why do representatives of different styles of Christianity sometimes
    find it so hard to get on together?

    How much do we really try to understand and respect people whose
    worship and witness are expressed in a different way from our own?

    Can you think of any special examples?

4   The Last Supper discourses (John 13:31 – 16:33) contain Jesus' most
    precious sayings, remembered by his friends.

    If you were choosing Jesus' most precious saying for you, what
    would it be?

    What might be the collection of sayings (i.e. Gospel/good news) of
    your group?

Old Testament Abraham Moses Liberator Teacher The Law David The Shepherd King The Covenant Solomon
gnificent **part five** stament St Luke's Gospel Salvation History The Roman Empire Galatians Christian Paul Ap
he Gentiles The Prophets Amos Hosea **literature spun from history** s of Creation The Psalms The Wi
rature Daniel The Passion Resurrection Jesus The Old Testament Abraham Moses Liberator Law David The Shep
g The Covenant Galatians The Roman Empire Acts of the Apostles Philippians Paul Apo**new testament**Th
ament Abraham Moses Liberator Teacher The Law David The Shepherd King The Covenant Solomon the Magnif

THE ARREST, THE TRIALS AND THE CRUCIFIXION: JOHN 18 AND 19

Throughout this Gospel, the term "the Jews" refers to the Jewish leaders or members of the Jewish council (Sanhedrin). This consisted of aristocratic priests, who were Sadducees, and well-to-do Pharisees, who were laymen.

Through all the following events, the strength and composure of Jesus are displayed, as he reveals the glory of self-effacing love. The other characters bring judgement upon themselves by their motives and their actions. Jesus, the prisoner and the one who is supposedly being judged, is really the only one who is free (because of his inner freedom): "No one takes [my life] from me, but I lay it down of my own accord" (John 10:18). The truth "speaks" through him, mostly through silence.

Gethsemane
John does not record Jesus praying in an agony in Gethsemane (John does not name the garden).

Jesus is continually offering his will to be aligned with the Father's.

The Jewish trials
These were held at night, which was illegal in Jewish law.

Jesus is first taken for an informal trial before Annas, who had been deposed by Rome in favour of his son-in-law, Caiaphas, but who was still regarded by many Jews as the real High Priest. Afterwards, the Sanhedrin meets under the chairmanship of Caiaphas to ratify a charge of blasphemy, for which the penalty was stoning (Leviticus 24:16). But only Rome could authorise a death sentence.

The Roman trial
The Roman Governor, normally resident in the Roman garrison town of Caesarea (on the Mediterranean coast), moved to Jerusalem for major festivals, to forestall any disturbances. A Roman sentence of death was carried out by crucifixion.

The crucifixion
John's account of the crucifixion is brief; it is the culmination of self-giving love (like God's love, *agape* in Greek). Jesus reigns from the cross and triumphs on the cross; there is no cry of dereliction ("My God, my God, why have you forsaken me?"), nor darkness over the land (as in Mark 15:33-34 and Matthew 27:45-46). John is portraying the cross as if it were a throne of glory.

John emphasises that it is Jesus, the human being, who really dies: he carries his own cross, and "blood and water" (the components of blood after death) flow from his side when pierced. John is here combating docetism, which suggested that perhaps Simon of Cyrene had died instead of Jesus, or that Jesus did not really die, but swooned on the cross and later recovered.

The burial
Romans left corpses on crosses as a deterrent, but Jewish law required their burial before sunset (Deuteronomy 21:22-23). Pilate's permission for burial is therefore required.

Old Testament Abraham Moses Liberator Teacher The Law David The Shepherd King The Covenant Solomon
gnificent The New Testament St Luke's Gospel Salvation History The Roman Empire Galatians **part five** A
he Gentiles The Prophets Amos Hosea **literature spun from history** of Creation The Psalms The Wi
rature Daniel The Passion Resurrection Jesus The Old Testament Abraham Moses Liberator Law David The Shep
g The **new testament** The Roman Empire Acts of the Apostles Philippians Paul Apostle of the Gentiles Th
:ament Abraham Moses Liberator Teacher The Law David The Shepherd King The Covenant Solomon the Magni

SUGGESTED READINGS AND POINTS TO CONSIDER AS YOU READ

The garden (of Gethsemane)		John 18:1-11
v. 1	The garden (not named in this Gospel) lay on the way to Bethany, where Jesus possibly lodged with Martha, Mary and Lazarus.	
vv. 5, 6, 8	Why are the soldiers from the Temple guard awestruck at Jesus' reply, "I AM"?	
vv. 4, 8b	Why do you think Jesus voluntarily surrenders himself?	
The Jewish trials and Peter's threefold denial		John 18:12-27
	The trial before Annas establishes a charge which is then ratified by the Sanhedrin.	
v. 14	Caiaphas' prophecy (11:49-52) is coming true: Jesus will die to bring in a new order for all peoples.	
v. 15	"another disciple" refers to John. The narratives throughout bear the stamp of an eyewitness.	
vv. 17, 25, 27	Do Peter's denials, "I am not" (contrasting with "I am"): (a) reveal his fear of mockery or possible arrest? (b) show his complete lack of understanding of Jesus' acceptance of events (see v. 10), and his desire to "rescue" Jesus? (He has a sword, hidden.)	
v. 24	The Sanhedrin is chaired by Caiaphas, the High Priest, who was close to the Roman governing power.	
The Roman trial		John 18:28 – 9:16
18:28	The Sanhedrin takes Jesus to Pilate as early as possible, hoping for a sentence of crucifixion to be completed before Passover (i.e. sunset). Already ritually prepared for the Passover, its members refuse to enter a Gentile's residence; Pilate therefore comes out to them.	
18:31-33	Jesus, constant in his commitment to the Father, had long foreseen that inevitably the Sanhedrin would press for his crucifixion by Rome (3:14; 12:32). Rome would ignore a charge of blasphemy, so the charge that emerges is one of treason.	
18:38	Pilate, a hard-headed Roman governor, faced with the difficult intransigence of the Jewish leaders (which made Judea such an unacceptable posting for Roman governors), expresses disdain for the priests, and cynicism, "What is truth?" – yet is unnerved by Jesus' self-composure and lack of belligerence. Recognising the prisoner's innocence, he tries in vain to uphold the renowned standards of Roman justice.	
19:1	A Roman scourging was a terrifying ordeal; here it is accompanied by racial disdain.	

Old Testament Abraham Moses Liberator Teacher The Law David The Shepherd King The Covenant Solomon **part five** stament St Luke's Gospel Salvation History The Roman Empire Galatians Christian Paul Apo e Gentiles The Prophets Amos Hosea **literature spun from history** s of Creation The Psalms The Wis ature Daniel The Passion Resurrection Jesus The Old Testament Abraham Moses Liberator Law David The Shepl The Covenant Galatians The Roman Empire Acts of the Apostles Philippians Paul Apo**new testament** The ament Abraham Moses Liberator Teacher The Law David The Shepherd King The Covenant Solomon the Magnifi

19:7-11	The Sanhedrin finally reveal their real charge against Jesus, which shakes Pilate's superstitious dread of the supernatural; he and Jesus are on totally different wavelengths.	John 18:28 – 19:16
19:12-16	Pilate, threatened with disloyalty to Caesar, humiliates the priests by obtaining their profession of loyalty to Caesar, before pronouncing judgement.	
	How does Pilate try to release Jesus? Are his methods legal?	
	Why do you think Pilate finally gives in?	
	Compare Pilate's external authority over others, imposed by force, with Jesus' internal authority expressed in love and truth through powerlessness.	

The crucifixion — John 19:17-37

v. 22	Pilate remains firm over the superscription ("Jesus of Nazareth, the King of the Jews"), so humiliating the chief priests again.	
v. 23	The soldiers take their perks for crucifixion duty.	
vv. 25-27	Jesus provides for his mother. John and Mary become the nucleus of the new community, the Church, living the new life released through Jesus' death.	
v. 30	"It is finished" is a cry of triumph, possibly heard far off (Mark 15:37; Matthew 27:50; Luke 23:46). Jesus' task is fulfilled: self-giving love has gone beyond the limits of death. Jesus has embraced the full onslaught of evil with love: the victory is complete.	
vv. 24, 28, 33	John sees: (a) scripture being fulfilled: see Psalms 22:15, 18; 69:21; (b) in Jesus' death, the Passover lamb, with no bones broken, being offered in sacrifice (Exodus 12:46).	
v. 34	Water and blood may be seen as symbolising death and life. The moment of the death of Jesus is also the moment releasing new life to humanity through the New Covenant and the two life-giving sacraments of baptism and communion which Jesus instituted.	

The burial — John 19:38-42

v. 38	Joseph of Arimathea and Nicodemus, both members of the Sanhedrin (John 7:50; Mark 15:43), finally come out openly as disciples of Jesus.	
vv. 39-40	One hundred pounds' weight of spices (75 imperial pounds or 32.7 kilos) are wrapped in the burial cloth.	
v. 41	Tombs were regularly recycled, and the dried bones placed in ossuaries.	
	Why does John see special significance in the "new" tomb?	

Old Testament Abraham Moses Liberator Teacher The Law David The Shepherd King The Covenant Solomon
gnificent The New Testament St Luke's Gospel Salvation History The Roman Empire Galatians **part five** Ap
he Gentiles The Prophets Amos Hosea **literature spun from history** of Creation The Psalms The Wi
rature Daniel The Passion Resurrection Jesus The Old Testament Abraham Moses Liberator Law David The Shep
g The **new testament** The Roman Empire Acts of the Apostles Philippians Paul Apostle of the Gentiles Th
ament Abraham Moses Liberator Teacher The Law David The Shepherd King The Covenant Solomon the Magnif

POSSIBLE ISSUES FOR DISCUSSION

1 What drives Pilate and the chief priests in these events?

   Are similar patterns at work in State and Church today?

2 Christian shorthand can be misleading – e.g. "God sent his Son to die for us" might seem to suggest that God the Father is cruel.

   How do you think of God the Father?

   If God is a God of love, and Jesus and the Father are in such intimate union, does it mean the Father shares equally with his Son in all the suffering (see John 3:16)?

   How does this relate to us when our loved ones suffer in any way?

3 Why do you think that Christians chose the cross as their logo and sign?

   What does the cross mean for you?

   Here is Vanstone's meditation on the cross:

   4. Love that gives gives ever more,
      Gives with zeal, with eager hands,
      Spares not, keeps not, all outpours,
      Ventures all, its all expends.

   5. Drained is love in making full;
      Bound in setting others free;
      Poor in making many rich;
      Weak in giving power to be.

   6. Therefore he who thee reveals
      Hangs, O Father, on that Tree
      Helpless; and the nails and thorns
      Tell of what thy love must be.

   7. Thou art God; no monarch thou
      Thron'd in easy state to reign;
      Thou art God, whose arms of love
      Aching, spent, the world sustain.

   Taken from *Love's Endeavour, Love's Expense*, by W.H. Vanstone, published and copyright 1977 by Darton Longman and Todd Ltd., London, and used by permission of the publishers.

   What do you think that John means by the "glory" of the cross?

   What is your favourite Passiontide hymn, and why?

4 Are there occasions when we know crucifixion in our own lives (e.g. a car accident, broken relationships, a bitter disappointment, a bereavement, etc.)?

   Can the example of Jesus, as he goes to his death, help us at such a time?

THE RESURRECTION OF JESUS: JOHN 20 AND 21

The resurrection is the miracle by which God the Father raised up Jesus from the dead (Jesus did not raise himself). Unlike the raising of Lazarus, which was a return to this life, to be followed by death one day, the resurrection of Jesus is into a totally new order of life beyond death. With us and for us, a human life has been lived throughout in full union with God in the way intended for all human beings. With us and for us, death itself has been conquered once and for all.

In John, the resurrection takes place quietly, in the tranquillity of the garden before dawn, as a new creation begins on the first day of the week. Although the victory was won on Friday, it would be unrecognised without the resurrection on Sunday, when the distraught disciples experience the victorious love which reaches them from beyond the grave. The tremendous release of this spiritual energy of love revitalises them as they come to recognise the presence of the risen Lord with them now and **always**, not dependent on sight. They are on the threshold of perceiving its full implications for all humanity.

So John selects stories and appearances of the risen Lord to those who had believed in him. Each individual has to learn to let go of the earthly Jesus they had known; then the release of his Spirit can invigorate and vitalise them always and everywhere. Sight, touch and physical presence have to make way for faith, which will fulfil Jesus' words, "Abide in me as I abide in you" (15:4a).

The body of the risen Lord still bears the wounds of the cross, his glorious identification marks, with him now for all eternity. He is often not recognised immediately, yet he makes himself known through characteristic gestures, words and tone of voice. He is the same, yet different, for the normal constraints of time and space do not restrict his glorious risen body, and his presence inspires awe and worship. He can pass through locked doors and appear and disappear at will. In the risen state, his body expresses and is the complete servant of his being.

Rather than our assessing whether the stories actually happened as described, the stories assess us, for their secret is only fully known as we too allow ourselves to be encountered by the risen Jesus.

The risen Lord continues to guide the disciples through the Holy Spirit. They therefore become able to understand Jesus' attitude and teaching during his ministry. This included understanding his befriending of the needy and the outcasts, and also the stupendous claims he made for himself.

John's chronology in chapters 20 and 21 is greatly condensed when compared with Luke's (Luke 24:50-53; Acts 1:1-12; 2:1-4), where events occupy the fifty days between the Jewish feasts of Passover and Pentecost. In John, the glorification of Christ (that is, the resurrection, the ascension to the Father and the gift of the Spirit) are all present, but not in nearly such dramatic form, and the symbolism used is different. John has been pointing to the resurrection throughout his Gospel. We now pass quietly from the life that has been ("I am not") to the new life enabled by the ongoing presence of the Spirit now freely available to all, and who makes the risen Jesus present to everyone everywhere. This is the new life of being/becoming what God intends each one to be/become: "I am" / "I will be".

Thanks be to God!

Old Testament Abraham Moses Liberator Teacher The Law David The Shepherd King The Covenant Solomon nificent The New Testament St Luke's Gospel Salvation History The Roman Empire Galatians **part five** Ap e Gentiles The Prophets Amos Hosea **literature spun from history** of Creation The Psalms The Wis ature Daniel The Passion Resurrection Jesus The Old Testament Abraham Moses Liberator Law David The Shep The **new testament** The Roman Empire Acts of the Apostles Philippians Paul Apostle of the Gentiles The ament Abraham Moses Liberator Teacher The Law David The Shepherd King The Covenant Solomon the Magnifi

SUGGESTED READINGS AND POINTS TO CONSIDER AS YOU READ

The empty tomb		John 20:1-10
vv. 1-2	John's account emphasises the empty tomb and the evidence it presents. Note the minute, vivid detail, described by an eyewitness, and the use of three different Greek verbs for "seeing".	
vv. 4-5	Mary's only thought is to be close to her dead Lord's body and complete the burial procedures; she imagines (together with the other women, see "we" in v. 2) the body has been removed or stolen.	
vv. 6-7	Who might want to remove the body, and why?	
	John, who is younger, arrives at the tomb first and in awe **looks** in.	
vv. 8-9	Peter, reaching the tomb later, barges straight in. He **observes** how the empty grave clothes lie – the head cloth separate from the rest.	
	John, following Peter in, **perceives** the meaning of what he sees – that the grave clothes have not been tampered with – but the body has vacated them and they have collapsed under the weight of 75 pounds of spices. He grasps the **meaning** and **significance** of what he observes – that the Lord has been raised from death to new life beyond the grave. "He saw and believed."	
Jesus appears to Mary Magdalene in the garden		John 20:11-18
	Mary, peeping into the tomb, sees two angels, one at each end of the slab on which the body had lain. The scene has been compared with the ark of God on which two angels knelt, their arching wings meeting over the empty throne.	
v. 16	Mary recognises Jesus by his so well-loved, tender and characteristic tone of voice, "Mary!"	
vv. 17-18	Mary appears to want to cling to the Jesus she has known – he must not elude her again! But Jesus helps her to recognise she must now move on to a new, more wonderful relationship with him, achieved by letting him go so that he can ascend to the Father. Only then can he be present with her and each one everywhere, all the time; it is a separation for a fuller union.	
	Commissioned by Jesus to bring this news to the disciples (not now "servants", nor "friends", but "brothers"), Mary becomes the apostle to the apostles. Transformed, she now carries the risen Lord within herself and the Good News is spread. "I have seen the Lord!" i.e. not just observed, but seen with the eyes of faith.	

An "angel" means literally God's "messenger".

The ark of the covenant was God's mobile throne in the time of Moses, then housed in the Temple until lost in the destruction of Jerusalem (Exodus 25:20).

*An apostle was one who had **seen** the risen Lord, and had been **sent** by him to preach (Acts 1:21-22).*

part five stament St Luke's Gospel Salvation History The Roman Empire Galatians Christian Paul Ap **literature spun from history** s of Creation The Psalms The Wis ature Daniel The Passion Resurrection Jesus The Old Testament Abraham Moses Liberator Law David The Shep The Covenant Galatians The Roman Empire Acts of the Apostles Philippians Paul Apo **new testament** ament Abraham Moses Liberator Teacher The Law David The Shepherd King The Covenant Solomon the Magnif

The giving of the Spirit		John 20:19-23
v. 19	Why do you suppose the disciples were so terrified?	
	Was each conscious, too, of their own pain and guilt in having failed Jesus in his hour of need?	
	Jesus, aware of their terror, greets them, "Shalom! Peace!" – the usual daily greeting which anticipated God's reign of peace and fulfilment, which Jesus is now pronouncing is here.	
v. 20	The disciples "see" Jesus in a new way. His vulnerability in suffering has touched their own vulnerability. Now, in openness with him and with each other, they can allow themselves to love and be loved and forgiven – cause for the deepest joy (see description of grace on page 138).	
vv. 21-22	Jesus now entrusts to the disciples the continuation of the work the Father had entrusted to him: "**As** the Father has sent me, **so** I send you." The disciples are sent out to transform the world – not in their own strength, but in the power of his Spirit, his very life within them, vitalising and invigorating them.	
v. 23	Giving or withholding forgiveness gives or withholds the opportunity of bestowing new life to others.	
	Who was present on this occasion, and to whom is the commission given?	
v. 19	"The disciples" probably include a wider gathering than just the ten apostles (Thomas was absent), including possibly Jesus' mother and some of the women who had come up from Galilee (and earlier visited the tomb). (See Luke 8:2-3; 23:49; Mark 15:40-41.) In any case, "the disciples" are a representative body, and Jesus' commission through the power of the Spirit is given to the whole community of believers who are "sent out".	
Thomas, the sceptic, becomes convinced that Jesus is risen from the dead		John 20:24-29
	Thomas, full of awe in Jesus' presence, responds with the first complete statement of Christian faith, "My Lord and my God!"	

Jesus' breath resonates with the creation of Adam in Genesis 2:7, where God breathes into Adam the breath of life.

136

Old Testament Abraham Moses Liberator Teacher The Law David The Shepherd King The Covenant Solomon
gnificent The New Testament St Luke's Gospel Salvation History The Roman Empire Galatians **part five** Ap
he Gentiles The Prophets Amos Hosea **literature spun from history** of Creation The Psalms The Wis
rature Daniel The Passion Resurrection Jesus The Old Testament Abraham Moses Liberator Law David The Shep
g The **new testament** The Roman Empire Acts of the Apostles Philippians Paul Apostle of the Gentiles Th
ament Abraham Moses Liberator Teacher The Law David The Shepherd King The Covenant Solomon the Magnif

The conclusion	John 20:30-31
To believe in Jesus as the Christ, the Son of God, is now, after the crucifixion, a more fully developed faith than Martha's (11:27). Only a God who has experienced and encompassed pain and even death can speak to the human situation in all its completeness.	

The Epilogue	John 21
(Possibly added by John the Elder, a close friend and disciple of the beloved disciple.)	

The breakfast on the shore	John 21:1-14
The story illustrates how Jesus is with us in our daily activities, challenging us, guiding us and also feeding us. He works with us and alongside us (both he and the disciples provide fish for the breakfast), and we come to recognise, with awe, his presence among us.	

Jesus cures Peter's hurt over his threefold denial, so reinstating him		John 21:15-19
	(Various Greek words are all translated as "love" in English.)	
v. 15	Jesus first asks Peter if he has a God-like quality of love (*agape*) for him which outstrips that of the other disciples. Peter says Jesus knows he is his friend (Greek = *philia*).	
v. 16	Jesus repeats the question, but without comparison with others. Peter's reply is the same.	
v. 17	Jesus now asks Peter if he is really his friend.	
	Why is Peter so hurt by this question?	
	Why does Jesus throughout this scene address Peter as Simon?	
	Peter replies that he is Jesus' friend. Jesus then puts his full trust in Peter, "Feed my sheep."	
	The cure hurts, but Simon is now on the way to becoming Peter, the Rock, if he keeps Jesus' command, "Follow me."	
	(This led to Peter's crucifixion [upside down, in AD 64 in Rome, according to tradition]; already a past event when John's Gospel was written.)	

What is to be John's future?	John 21:20-23
Peter asks Jesus about the future of John (who, tradition asserts, outlived the other apostles).	
Jesus does not answer the exact question, but focuses the importance onto faithful discipleship for each of us – "Follow me!"	
Why do we so much like speculating about the future?	
Is it helpful?	

"The world itself cannot contain the books…", for these continue to be written in each disciple in whom dwells the incarnate Word	John 21:24-25

POSSIBLE ISSUES FOR DISCUSSION

1   Notice how often in these stories Jesus addresses a person individually by name.

    Do you think God deals with each of us individually in our own needs regarding our faith?

    Can you give any examples?

2   Are there occasions when we know resurrection in our own lives, and life takes on a new and fuller meaning?

3   Jesus said, "As the Father has sent me, so I send you" (John 20:21).

    In what different ways can we respond to this commission?

4   God knows us inside out, yet **still** loves us.

    Like the disciples (especially Judas), we may find God's unconditional love uncomfortable.

    In our market economy, everything has its cash value.

    Why do we find God's **free** grace so difficult to accept?

    > The word **grace** refers to a gift (from God) that is *offered* – in pure generosity and love, and without any pressure for it to be received. It evokes (from the recipient) quite spontaneously a response of love, joy and deep gratitude.
    >
    > from W. H. Vanstone in *Fare Well in Christ*, DLT, 1997

5   What main message does John want each individual to draw from his Gospel?

    What would be your own **brief** summary of his Gospel?

For Pondering

For Pondering

"On the third day the friends of Jesus coming at daybreak to the place found the grave empty and the stone rolled away. In varying ways they realised the new wonder; but even they hardly realised that the world had died in the night.

What they were looking at was the first day of a new creation, with a new heaven and a new earth; and in a semblance of the gardener God walked again in the garden, in the cool not of the evening but the dawn."

G. K. Chesterton (1874–1936), *The Everlasting Man*
(London: Hodder & Stoughton, 1925)

"God became human that we might become divine."
(Literally: "God became what we are that we might become what he is.")

A statement made by both St Irenaeus
(AD 130–200) and St Athanasius (AD 296–373)

"God became human that we might become human."

A twentieth-century theologian's variant on the above

Almighty God,
who wonderfully created us in your own image
and yet more wonderfully restored us
through your Son Jesus Christ:
grant that, as he came to share in our humanity,
so we may share the life of his divinity;
who is alive and reigns with you,
in the unity of the Holy Spirit,
one God, now and for ever. Amen.

Collect for First Sunday of Christmas, *Common Worship*

Appendix
Leader's notes

Appendix
Leader's notes

This section contains some extra material for many of the chapters of the book, and some practical suggestions of ways of facilitating the book's use by groups.

HISTORY EMBEDDED IN LITERATURE: OLD TESTAMENT

Abraham – The Father of Us All

- Abraham is the earliest person in the Bible to whom we can give an approximate date. That's why *A Bird's-Eye View of the Bible* starts here.

- The map of the Fertile Crescent shows the enormous distances travelled by Abraham and his tribe.

- God's threefold promise to Abraham (Genesis 12:1-3) is:

    (a) he will be given a land;

    (b) he will be given a multitude of descendants (even though Abraham is already 75, and his wife, Sarah, is childless);

    (c) through his descendants the whole world will be blessed.

- Abraham's unequivocal response in most biblical versions reads simply "So Abram went". Abraham's response to God forms the critical turning point, enabling God's plan to unfold. (Had others perhaps been called and not responded? We can't say.)

- The name Abraham ("father of a multitude") is used throughout this session, though chapters 11 and 12 use the name Abram ("father of height"). When in 17:5 God renews his promise to Abram, he renames him Abraham, father of a multitude, as an outward sign of the promise.

- The sacrifice of Isaac (Genesis 22:1-19). This is a demanding passage, and people should be encouraged to discuss it. Was God really asking Abraham to sacrifice Isaac?

If (even though Abraham did not know this) God is a God of love and mercy, would he demand such a sacrifice?

If not, how can this passage be understood?

    (a) As a test of Abraham's loyalty?

    (b) Did Abraham think God demanded the offering of his most precious possession?

    (c) Or is Abraham convincing himself he is no less devoted to his God than the heathen around him who offered infant sacrifice to their gods?

Compare the two different tones of God's voice in calling "Abraham!" in 22:1 and 11.

Abraham only learnt the truth contained in this story because of his obedience and readiness to act.

- Throughout the Bible, Abraham is regarded as the man of faith. Faith by definition can't be proved. (Abraham didn't know Isaac would be spared.)

- The three great monotheistic religions (i.e. believing in one God) are Judaism, Christianity and Islam, often called the Abrahamic faiths, and their adherents may all be called "children of Abraham". The title "Father of us all" is the Jewish title for Abraham, but it is equally applicable for Christians.

Moses – Liberator and Teacher

- The dating of the Exodus is notoriously difficult: some scholars say 1450 BC, more say 1250 BC, while many deny that it can be precisely dated at all.

- The name "Passover" derives from the angel of death "passing over" the homes of the Hebrews (Exodus 12:23).

- God's name ("Yahweh", meaning both I AM and I WILL BE) reveals his character: he really exists, now and into the future, and is a God who acts. It was (and is) never spoken by Jews, so it is therefore impossible to know how it was pronounced. This is why it is sometimes written without vowels as YHWH. Written Hebrew had no vowels: the reader inserted vowels to make the word fit the context (which is why sometimes alternative translations appear to be so different).

- Exodus 14:5-29 (but see also page 25 where the different writers are separated out). Note how the earlier (J) text of the ninth century BC gives a natural reason (the strong east wind) for the sea becoming passable. Over the centuries, Moses' stature became enhanced, so that in the Priestly (P) account of the sixth century BC, it is Moses who made the sea passable. (Moses' enhancement is sometimes indicated pictorially by two horns.)

- Can natural phenomena play their part in miracles? Encourage people to think of other "miraculous" things which might also have natural explanations.

- Moses, representing the Law, is one of the twin pillars of the Jewish religion, because of his liberating the Hebrews from slavery and teaching them the requirements (Law) of God. (The other twin pillar is Elijah, representing the prophets.)

David – The Shepherd King

- David spares Saul's life because he respects Saul's status as the anointed king, chosen and consecrated by God. It is not for him to question God's choice.

- His astute political insight is illustrated by his choice of the Jebusite city, Jerusalem, as capital.

  Situated between the ten tribes to the north and the two tribes to the south, Jerusalem belonged to neither territory, so could weld them together. An almost impregnable city, with steep valleys to the east, west and south, and a double wall to the north, David nevertheless captures it by his men entering the city through the water shaft which served it. (Down the ages, the water supply of Jerusalem has always provided a weak point of defence.)

- Hitherto, the ark, the portable throne of God (representing his presence among his people) had travelled with the Hebrews, and been housed in a tent, called the tabernacle, until the ark had been captured in battle by the Philistines (1 Samuel 4:1-11). David recovers the ark and brings it to Jerusalem to sanctify his capital city with God's presence, though he feels the tabernacle is not adequate for it.

Solomon – The Magnificent

- Solomon's prayer at the beginning of his reign for wisdom in the ruling of his people is deeply genuine, and his wisdom became proverbial. Sadly, though, as his reign progresses, power, wealth and majesty gain in importance so that, by the end of his reign, the largest ever united kingdom becomes divided through rebellion, never to be united again.

- The Temple is Solomon's most important (though not his largest) building project. Intended as a permanent dwelling-place for God, no money was spared in its construction, and its gold would have been dazzling. The Temple house contained two rooms: the outer one, the Holy Place, leading into the dark (1 Kings 8:12) inner Holy of Holies. The Holy of Holies symbolised perfection, being a perfect cube (6:19-21) which housed the ark, or throne of God, representing his presence which God promises will not leave his people if they keep his Law (6:11-13). The ark contained only the two stone slabs given to Moses on Mount Sinai, on which were written the Ten Commandments (8:9).

- The cloud which descends as the ark is housed (8:10-11) is the Shekinah, representing the glory of God's presence, which the cloud shields from human vision.

  Other references to this cloud include:

  (a) the pillar of cloud which leads the Hebrews on their escape from Egypt (Exodus 13:21-22);

  (b) the cloud which covers Mount Sinai (Exodus 24:15-16);

  (c) the cloud which overshadows Jesus, Moses and Elijah at the transfiguration (Mark 9:7);

  (d) the cloud which "receives" Jesus at his ascension (Acts 1:9).

- Solomon's forced labour for his building projects and apostasy (precipitated by his foreign wives whom he allows to set up altars to their own gods) are the main causes of discontent which Jeroboam builds on. The prophet Ahijah makes an "enacted" prophecy to Jeroboam that he will become king of the ten northern tribes of Israel on Solomon's death (1 Kings 11:26-40). (See the map of the divided kingdom on page 42.)

HISTORY EMBEDDED IN LITERATURE: NEW TESTAMENT

St Luke's Gospel: Salvation History

- The infancy narratives in chapters 1 and 2 are thought to have been written separately and later placed at the beginning of the Gospel, which seems to start with a powerful six-point date in Luke 3:1-2 to mark the word of God coming to John the Baptist. The infancy narratives are therefore considered separately at the end of St Luke's Gospel.

- As a Gentile, Luke is profoundly aware of how the Gospel (the "Good News") has burst beyond its Jewish origins, and is for all, including most importantly the poor, the outcast and the marginalised.

- Among the parables found only in Luke are two of the best-known, the good Samaritan and the prodigal (wasteful) son.

- Note how many of the central points in Jesus' life Luke places in a context of prayer – his baptism (3:21-22); the choice of the Twelve (6:12-13); Jesus' disciples ask him how to pray (11:1-2); Jesus' prayer for Peter at the Last Supper (22:31-32); Jesus' agony in the garden (22:39-46); Jesus' prayer of forgiveness for his executioners (23:34); Jesus' final blessing of his disciples (24:50-51).

- Bread and wine form the central symbols of the Passover meal, celebrating freedom from slavery in Egypt. Jesus now uses them as life-giving symbols of the new deliverance he is about to offer humanity from the bondage of sin through his death, but of course the disciples could not understand this at the time. (Some Bibles omit 22:20, which is absent in some ancient manuscripts.)

- That Jesus was "in every respect… tested as we are, yet without sin" (Hebrews 4:15) is clearly illustrated in his agony in the garden (22:39-46). Like anyone else, his free will yearns to avoid the cross which looms ahead; but even stronger is his trust in God. (Some ancient manuscripts omit 22:43-44.)

- The Jewish trial for blasphemy carried the death penalty, which required Roman ratification. But Rome would dismiss a charge of blasphemy, so the charge is changed to one of treason, which Pilate has to take seriously, especially with Jerusalem so crowded with pilgrims – though he attempts to delegate responsibility to Herod Antipas (son of Herod the Great), who ruled Galilee under Rome.

- Jesus' elucidation of the scriptures, both on the journey to Emmaus and later in the upper room, shows how they forecast a suffering and rising Messiah, though this had never been understood. So powerful and compelling is Jesus' presentation of the scriptures that it left his hearers in no doubt of its authenticity, and the hearts of the two travelling to Emmaus (Cleopas and his wife, perhaps?) burnt within them (24:32).

Galatians: Charter of Christian Freedom from Paul, Apostle to the Gentiles

- This is the first text to be studied that is not in a story form.

- Refer back to page 50, and read the paragraph on the Letters (Epistles). Note how they were the earliest New Testament documents to be written, as at that time the story of Jesus was passed on orally (so not everyone would know the full story).

- Jesus had sent his disciples out to convert the whole world (Matthew 28:19; Acts 1:8), and so the Gospel was preached to Gentiles. However, it was not clear whether these Gentile converts to Christianity should be expected to keep the Jewish Law. Paul's opponents say that they must. This may represent a conservative way of thinking: if they were Law-keepers themselves, they might have always assumed that Gentile Christians should keep the Law. But the demand to keep the

Law may be an innovation – the earliest Gentile converts were not expected to do so, but now some people are suggesting that they should.

This question was a massive problem, and one which needed speedy resolution. The Council of Jerusalem, consisting of all church leaders, was therefore called in AD 49 (Acts 15).

- Paul reminds his readers that their faith was in Christ, not in "the flesh" (i.e. circumcision representing the Law; Galatians 3:3b; 5:1). The Law can bring them no salvation, because it was impossible to keep it in its entirety (as Paul had himself discovered, Romans 7:14-20). The Law, good in itself, and pointing the way to God, had highlighted sin in his life, but was impotent in helping him to overcome sin.

In contrast, Christ's death on the cross had broken the curse of the Law (Deuteronomy 21:22-23). God has offered us his free gift of Jesus, given out of total love. Union with Christ (through faith and baptism which bestows the gift of his Spirit) offers us a new life of freedom from the Law, and a life of freedom in Christ who, when we repent, gratuitously forgives us all our sins. (Read the definition of grace [at the bottom of page 116], which refers to God's free gift in Christ.)

- Through the Spirit, we recognise God as our loving Father (Galatians 4:6), and hope for a life of righteousness (5:5) and one which demonstrates the fruit of the Spirit described in 5:22-23.

- Though Paul sees the whole issue under discussion as one of "freedom versus slavery", we must recognise that his opponents were good people who were genuine and sincere in their Christian beliefs.

- Paul's defence of his apostleship is necessary for his standing if he is to be able to defend his Gentile converts. Because Paul was converted directly by Christ on the Damascus road, and sent by him to preach to the Gentiles (Galatians 1:15-16; Acts 9:5, 10-17), Paul claims equality of apostleship with Peter, seeing himself and the leaders of the Jerusalem Church as "equals" (2:6-9).

- Peter is also referred to as Cephas (his name in Aramaic). Peter had earlier obeyed God's call and converted Cornelius, a Roman centurion (Acts 10, especially verses 34-35). Initially therefore he happily ate with Gentile Christians in Antioch – but vacillates when emissaries from the strict Church in Jerusalem arrive (Galatians 2:11-14). This passage encapsulates the whole argument of Galatians; it lends itself well to a practical imaginative exercise (role play), as described in detail on page 65, and can produce spectacular results. (But be sure to remember the note on debriefing.)

Cephas is properly pronounced as "Keh-fass", but in English usually as "Sea-fass".

- The word "free" occurs seven times in this letter.

- In "Issues for Discussion", question 2, we meet Pelagius, a fifth-century Briton, who held that salvation can be procured by human effort alone, without divine grace. In complete contrast, Augustine felt that we can only be saved through God's grace freely given and accepted. Pelagius' position represents Paul's opponents who wanted the Law to remain an integral part of Christianity, while Augustine represents Paul's position, that it is through God's grace that we find freedom and peace with God. (You might ask the group which of these two views they think predominates in Britain today? Does Pelagius still rule?)

Acts of the Apostles: The Gospel Becomes Universal in the Age of the Holy Spirit

- In the story of Acts (Luke's second volume), the emphasis is on the third (present) stage of "salvation history". The first stage covers the Old Testament period, and the second stage the ministry of Jesus, described by Luke in his Gospel, volume 1 of "salvation history". The third stage is lived under the guidance and power of the Holy Spirit who, in fulfilment of Jesus' promise, descends on the waiting disciples on the Day of Pentecost (chapter 2). The real "hero" in Acts is not therefore primarily Peter, Paul or any other individual, but the Holy Spirit, and we today continue to live in the age of the Spirit.

- Acts describes how the Gospel becomes universal, for all peoples, in all places. The fact that Rome, the centre of the Empire, represents "the ends of the earth" (1:8) is because travel links throughout the Empire all led to and from Rome. The spread of the Gospel, stage by stage to all peoples, takes place in the steps outlined on page 68, and it would be good to refer to these stages with the whole group.

- Apart from chapter 9 (which describes Paul's conversion), Peter is the leading character up to chapter 12. From chapter 13 onwards, it becomes Paul, as he carries out this Gentile mission from Antioch in Syria, the leading Gentile Church which he was brought into to help (11:19-26). Paul was a well-educated Pharisee and Jew of the Dispersion, who therefore understood the Gentile culture; he had grown up in Tarsus of Cilicia (the south-eastern tip of Asia Minor).

- Paul's missionary strategy in each place is first of all to visit the synagogue where the Jews assemble, for they are the chosen people awaiting the news of the coming of the Messiah. The Jews, however, respond unpredictably. The God-fearers (Gentiles sympathetic to the Jewish religion, but not having become proselytes) are also to be found in the synagogue. They prove more responsive, being "seekers after truth" without being bound by the Jewish Law, and it is likely that these formed the core of many of the churches Paul founded. Only after these approaches does Paul turn to Gentiles outside the synagogue.

- Paul's missionary approach is to relate the Gospel to the background of his audience. Sometimes he falls into the trap of overplaying this approach and short-selling the Gospel, as when he preaches before the learned Areopagus council in Athens without mentioning the crucifixion (17:16-34). However, his next visit was to Corinth (18:1), and 1 Corinthians 2:1-5 shows that he had learnt from his experience in Athens.

- It is not long before Stephen – appointed with six other deacons, all of Gentile background, to ensure fairness towards widows of Gentile background (6:1-6) – becomes the first martyr. His trial and death reflect those of Jesus (6:11-15; 7:54 – 8:1). In his defence before the Jewish council (Sanhedrin), he criticises the way Jews of the past had so often apostasised (7:39), replacing the tabernacle with a Temple, and rejecting both the Law and the prophets who had foretold Jesus (7:44, 47-48, 52-53).

- The ensuing persecution in Jerusalem of Christians by Jews ensures both the costliness of being Christian, and also (as the Christians flee) the spread of the Gospel (8:1-3).

- Note that though the Council of Jerusalem agrees that Gentiles may become Christians directly, on an equal footing with Jews, but without adherence to the Law, it can take a long time for such a ruling at the centre to be accepted by all the scattered churches, and the issue rumbled on locally, as Paul's letters show.

- The "Issues for Discussion", question 1, refers to the many slaves in Rome (especially) who were drawn into the early Church. Having nothing to lose in their status, Paul's teaching that there is no distinction between Christians (see Galatians 3:28) was heady stuff for them. But their numbers may have deterred some of the more well-to-do from becoming Christian, and may thus have made it easier

in AD 64 for the Emperor Nero (falsely) to blame the Christians for having set fire to Rome, resulting in the first Roman persecution of Christians.

- Question 2 refers to how persecution and the martyrdom of Christians result in the spread of the Gospel. The witness of those ready to die for their beliefs (rather than retract) indicates the extent to which they have found a way of life worth living, which death cannot quench.

Joy to the Philippians from Paul, Apostle to the Gentiles

- Philippians is a very special letter, resonating with joy, hope and love. Writing from prison to his favourite church – favourite because they, more than any other church to which he writes, have grasped the meaning of the Gospel which they live out daily – Paul shares with them his own innermost private thoughts. The only aspects he warns them against are those Christians who demand that Gentiles become Jews before becoming Christians (3:2-3), and he implores two women to make up their quarrel (4:2-3).

- Even Paul's imprisonment brings new opportunities to others for evangelism, whether from motives that are genuine or adverse. Either way, the Gospel is preached, so Paul can rejoice (1:12-18).

- Paul's uncertainty as to whether or not he will be put to death is compounded by his personal desire to enter the fuller life of union with Christ beyond the grave, and the thought that there is still work in his churches to do on earth (1:21-26).

- 2:4-11, possibly a very early Christian hymn, is so beautiful and comprehensive that it would be good to read it aloud in the group, and perhaps use it in the prayer time at the end of the session.

- Though in this letter Paul claims that "as to righteousness under the law, [he had been] blameless" (3:6), the Law does not seem to have brought him inner peace; he may indeed have envied Stephen's serenity at his trial and death (Acts 6:15; 7:54 – 8:1). So he had gladly renounced his former life of privilege in order to "know Christ". He regards his former life as valueless compared with gaining Christ and being "found in him", with a righteousness from God based not on the Law, but on faith in Christ. He longs to share in both Christ's resurrection and his sufferings, "by becoming like him in his death" (3:4-11). But he knows he has not yet "reached the goal", towards which he presses on as the "one thing" that matters in his personal life, which is to be "like Christ" (3:12-15).

- Finally, Paul asks the Philippians to "rejoice in the Lord always", and "not [to] worry about anything", but to make their "requests... known to God", and so to know "the peace of God, which surpasses all understanding" (4:4-7). He asks them to ponder on the qualities he lists in 4:8-9, for what one spends time reflecting upon becomes important in one's life.

- Joy is mentioned four times and rejoice ten times in this letter.

- In "Issues for Discussion", question 3, joy has a greater depth than happiness, which may be quite superficial. The joy comes from knowing Christ and being united to him, so can be experienced even in adverse situations, such as bereavement.

- It would be good to discuss in the group the talk on pages 75-76 by Leonard Wilson, Bishop of Singapore during the Second World War, as it illustrates how he found the grace of God, peace and joy while in prison. (The Japanese name, Ogawa, has the accent on the second syllable, pronounced as in "hard".)

A Challenge to Philemon from Paul, Apostle to the Gentiles

- This gem is the only personal letter we have from Paul to an individual, Philemon. It gives us insight into the trouble Paul takes in caring for individual Christians.

- If Philemon became Christian before Onesimus ran away, it is possible Onesimus became Christian then too, along with Philemon's whole household, as the practice often was. If so, he had probably been no more than a nominal Christian.

- But meeting up with Paul, imprisoned for his faith (and whom Onesimus may have remembered had Paul ever visited Philemon), changed all that. Either he then became Christian from a pagan background, or his Christian faith was transformed from a nominal to a live one. Paul shows him that, as a Christian, he must face up to his theft and his escape from Philemon, but he writes a reference on the new person Onesimus has now become for him to hand to Philemon.

- Paul is a caring and skilled pastor, not only to Onesimus, but to Philemon too. The letter starts by congratulating Philemon on his faith, Christian witness and care of his house-church. Because of Philemon's character, Paul approaches him with confidence (as an old man! and prisoner too!) on behalf of Onesimus. Previously useless, Onesimus now lives up to his name (meaning "useful") and Paul would dearly have loved to keep him as a helper, but feels he must first get Philemon's consent and that the past must be amended.

- The survival of the letter suggests Paul's persuasiveness worked. Note, though, that in making his request, Paul avoids commanding Philemon; rather, he appeals to him for a free response of his own accord (verses 8 and 19b). The group may like to consider how free they consider Philemon was in arriving at his decision.

- The extract on page 79 about Eric Lomax and Nagase Takashi is well worth considering in the group after discussing the letter to Philemon. (The emphasis falls on the second syllable of the Japanese names, pronounced as in "hard".)

The session should allow time to reconsider "Attitudes to the Bible".

LITERATURE SPUN FROM HISTORY: OLD TESTAMENT

Amos and Hosea

Note that from Solomon's death (in c. 933 BC), the kingdom has been divided; the map on page 85 illustrates this.

- Both Amos and Hosea prophesy in the kingdom of Israel; conditions there are described on page 85. Amos, however, comes from the southern kingdom of Judah, whereas Hosea prophesies in his native land. Assyria, the power to the north, is a constant threat to a much smaller (especially if troublesome) neighbour, and both prophets foretell the imminent fall of the kingdom of Israel, seeing it as God's judgement on the people's unfaithfulness.

- The introductory note on page 85 is important, as the messages of Amos and Hosea complement each other. Yet this makes for a lot of material for a group to do in one session, even though references for each prophet are fairly brief. As a group, you therefore have a choice:

  either study one prophet more fully, in which case you need to notice the message of the other prophet also (see page 85);

  or cover the two prophets more superficially, so as to get the gist of their messages without getting into too much detail.

- Amos fearlessly castigates both people and priests for their failure to live up to the Covenant in both their social and religious practices. 5:10-12 refers to how elders meted out justice in the city gate. The builder's plumb-line (7:7-9) checks that a building is vertical or "true". It shows society to be split between rich and poor, many of the rich having both a winter and a summer house, while the rich women of Samaria are like fat cattle. Meanwhile, weights and measures are rigged, and the poor are sold into slavery for the price of a pair of shoes. Worship of God is insincere too, because out of kilter with how people are living their lives.

- The core of Amos' message is a call for justice and righteousness (as defined on page 86), because he perceives how these are essential traits of God's being. Israel, though, still remains "special" to God, who has tried, through various disasters, to recall her. But their resistance means that the Day of the Lord will bring only gloom.

- Hosea, who prophesied after Amos in a situation that became increasingly politically unstable (see page 88), bases his prophecy on the tragic circumstances of his own marriage with Gomer, formerly a prostitute, probably with the prophets of Baal (enacting a request for agricultural fertility). This gives Hosea a deep insight into the love God bears for his people, and how distressed and grieved God is at their various malpractices. It makes no difference to the meaning of the text whether Gomer really lived, or is a product of Hosea's prophetic imagination.

- 1:4 is involved and somewhat obscure. At Hosea's call, the reigning king, Jeroboam II, is the last of the royal line founded by Jehu. On the Plain of Jezreel, Jehu had ousted the son of Ahab from being king of Israel because of Ahab having succumbed to his pagan wife, Jezebel, in seizing Naboth's vineyard (1 Kings 21; 2 Kings 9:1 – 10:36). Jehu himself,

however, also ignored the Law (2 Kings 10:30-31), so endangering the kingdom.

- In 3:4, "pillar" refers to a symbol of Baal; the "ephod" is a cultic vestment, and "teraphim" are household gods.

- 2:5 refers to Israel's apostasy to the Canaanite god, Baal, the god of agriculture. The Israelites fail to recognise that agricultural gifts come from their God rather than Baal (2:8). When God lures Israel back into the wilderness (and so back into her initial relationship with him), Israel will know her true God (2:14-21). Hosea's teaching here is similar to that of Amos in Amos 5:14-15.

- 4:1-3 describes the social ills of Hosea's day, followed by religious ills (4:4-6).

- The core of Hosea's message (6:6) is a call for the steadfast love and knowledge of God in both personal and social dealings, if the Covenant relationship with God is to be fulfilled. Hosea therefore builds further on the message of Amos, and his understanding of God's love which balances his judgement is of crucial importance.

- In "Issues for Discussion", question 4, repentance (whether personal or social) is costly because it demands two aspects, both of which are necessary:

  (a) a willingness to admit wrong-doings, whether one's own or those of a group, a nation or a wider conglomerate;

  (b) the intention to amend behaviour in future, whether one's own or those of a group, a nation or a wider conglomerate.

The Exile and the Great Unknown Prophet of the Exile

- The exile was a time of utter devastation for the people of Israel. The Babylonian gods seemed to be more powerful than their God, and they believed that each god had his own territorial area, so their God could not come with them into Babylon. Note, too, that the poor, who were left in a ransacked and devastated Judah, also believed God had finally deserted them – no Temple (so no sacrifice), no city walls (necessary for the self-respect of a city), no Davidic dynasty left. The slough of despair was felt all round.

- There must have been some contact, however minimal, between the poor left in Judah and the Babylonian exiles, even if only through Babylonian officials who travelled the Empire. To enter into this scenario of utter despair, you might like to consider role play with perhaps three groups of people: Babylonian officials, the poor in Judah, and the Jewish exiles in Babylon.

- The exile became a pivotal point in Jewish experience. Out of sheer despair, new hope, accompanied with a wonderful new belief in God and his complete majesty, evolved. This was largely due to a prophet towards the end of the exile, who also foresaw the end of the exile. With his prophecies, we reach the peak of Old Testament prophecy.

- We know next to nothing as to who this prophet was – not even his name. The book of Isaiah has clearly come down to us as a single work, but scholars have long noticed that it contains material of different dates. Some of the prophecies (most of chapters 1 to 39, "First Isaiah") come from the time of Isaiah of Jerusalem at the end of the eighth century BC. Chapters 35 and 40 to 55 ("Second Isaiah") seem to presuppose the later years of the exile, and look forward to the restoration: these are generally attributed to a great prophetic genius of the late sixth century BC whose name we do not know. Chapters 56 to 66 (and 24 to 27?, "Third Isaiah") are still later in date. But although many strands may have gone into making the book of Isaiah over many centuries, it can still be read as a single study of God's dealings with his people. Some Christians, however, believe that Isaiah of Jerusalem wrote the whole book.

- This affects how we think God acts. Are prophets (under God) foretelling a distant future some 200 years or more ahead? Or does critical scholarship (see page 25) mean we use our intellects to perceive the situations which gave rise to certain writings? In other words, is God ready to work through human error, inadequacy and also reason? If so, what does this tell us about God?

- However, the most important thing is that we come to love the prophecies in chapters 40–55 – the peak of the Old Testament prophecies, especially chapter 40 and 52:13 – 53:12. There is no need to overload people unnecessarily with theories about authorship (which is why they are only mentioned here in the Appendix).

Stories of Creation

- The two accounts of creation in Genesis chapters 1 and 2 contain internal contradictions:

  (a) the way in which God is depicted and named;

  (b) too much, or not enough, water before creation (1:2; 2:5);

  (c) the order in which creation takes place, with humanity as the final act of God's creation (1:26) or man as the first of God's creative acts (2:7).

  Yet both stories agree in their religious content, claiming that:

  (a) God is Creator of the whole universe;

  (b) everything God made is good;

  (c) human beings are

  (i) creatures with the rest of creation;

  (ii) made with an affinity to know God, because in some sense akin to him (1:27; 2:7);

  (iii) entrusted to enjoy and look after God's creation (1:26; 2:15).

  The answer to the question, "Which story is true?" is "Both are".

- In exile, the priests (adding their own contributions) re-edited Genesis to Chronicles, so producing the version we now have from scriptures which had been written in different ages. Genesis 1, the majestic Priestly account of the origins of the universe, introduces the whole biblical narrative. It describes God in charge of his creation (in spite of sin which appears in chapter 3); the new creation described at the end of the Bible (Revelation chapters 21–22) resonates with Genesis 1.

- Man and woman are here created concurrently, and it is their complementary relationship that accounts for their being made in God's image. In 1:16, the sun and moon, regarded as "gods" by neighbouring peoples, are not named, but described as "lights". The story gives a divine imperative to the observance of the Sabbath (Exodus 20:11), which had become prominent during the exile as a distinctive feature of Jewish religion.

- *Elohim* (the word used for God in chapter 1) is a plural word (see "us" in 1:26), used possibly in relation to the man/woman union imaging the Godhead. Early Christians saw the name as a proof of the Trinity.

- In the earlier account, from Genesis 2:4 onwards, the whole ethos is more primitive. God is described in anthropomorphic (human) terms (see 3:8, which continues the story in Chapter 2). The word "adam" comes from *adamah*, meaning "ground", and is a collective noun for human beings; adam (humankind) exists alone at first. His helper is taken from his rib, after which adam becomes Adam (the prototype male), and Eve (meaning "life", because she is the childbearer, 3:20) the prototype female. This story undergirds the practice of marriage (2:24).

- Wisdom (a feminine noun) is a particular attribute of God. Proverbs 8:22-31 describes her delighting in God's creative acts, whether as a "master worker" or (in the alternative reading) as "a little child" – or as "darling and delight" (8:30) in the Revised English Bible (REB).

- The book of Job was written in the fifth to fourth century BC.

If short of time, concentrate on the description of the hippopotamus and crocodile in 40:15 – 41:34.

- Wisdom and Job, with Psalm 104, show how God is to be perceived in and through his creation (Psalm 104:24), while Psalm 8 emphasises the unique place of humanity in the created order.

- In question 4, it is important to realise the Hebrews never intended to write a "scientific" account of creation – they knew they hadn't been there to experience it! In any case, both stories offer religious rather than scientific answers.

- If you have time, or if the group has, you may like to look at the rest of Genesis 1–11.

- The garden of Eden (2:10) contains the tree of the knowledge of good and evil, which Adam and Eve are prohibited from eating (2:9, 17). In chapter 3, they both decide unilaterally on what's good and bad, so eat the fruit of the tree, thus declaring moral independence from God, and denying their creatureliness. Their pride declares, "I can go it alone!"

This story, often referred to as "the Fall", answers the questions:

    (a) How do we account for evil in the world?

    (b) Why is livelihood hard?

    (c) Why is childbirth so painful?

    (d) Why are humans not immortal?

(Jews, however, see the story as not so much about morality, but as introducing choice, which is a characteristically human trait.)

The Christian doctrine of "original sin" does not say sexual relationships are unclean, nor does it say that children are born sinful. Rather, it says that all of us have a bias towards evil which shows as we grow and develop. Paul, in 1 Corinthians 15:22, describes "the Fall" as "all [dying] in Adam". Genesis 3 describes a fall "downwards"; perhaps today we may be more inclined to think in terms of a failure (through evolution) to climb upwards.

- The story of the Flood in chapters 6–8 is probably based on an ancient memory of a gigantic flood which covered the "whole world" (6:11-13) in the alluvial plains between the Tigris and Euphrates rivers. The story intertwines sources from P and JE (see page 24), so that either seven or two pairs of animals enter the ark (7:2-3, 8-9). The myth proclaims God's justice (which demands punishment) in the face of evil, but also his mercy, expressed in the magnificent rainbow. The rainbow (God's weapon, now put aside for ever) is the outward symbol of the Covenant that God makes with both humans and all living creatures never to punish the earth like this again (9:8-17).

- The myth of the tower of Babel (11:1-9) answers the question why there are so many languages which divide and confuse humanity. It describes human pride that wants, by building a tower, to reach up to heaven; in other words, humankind has once again forgotten its creatureliness in relation to God. God's response is to "confuse" them by replacing the one language they all share with several languages to divide them. ("Confuse" is a pun on "Babel".)

The New Testament counterpart to this story is Acts 2:1-12 which shows how, with the coming of the Spirit, there is once again unification across and over the language division, since the Holy Spirit is a unifying power.

The Psalms

- All human life and emotion are to be found in the Psalms, which is why they have stood the test of time. They were Jesus' prayer book, so we draw near to his spirituality when we use them (as they have been used down the centuries) in our own worship today.

- Written in Hebrew verse and intended as songs to be sung with musical accompaniment, they have been put to various settings, and sometimes transferred into English verse. Examples of this include the hymns "O God, our help in ages past", based on Psalm 90, and "As pants the hart for cooling streams", based on Psalm 42.

- At one time it was fashionable to place brackets around those verses which hurl curses at enemies, which suggested a "sanitised" approach in prayer. Today, however, these verses are left as they are, because it is so important that we can be frank and open with God, whatever our feelings. God is understanding, and can take whatever we hurl at him; he longs for us to be sincere, rather than present him with a facade when we approach him. (In any case, he already knows us through and through – and still continues to love us.) When we are open, he can begin to relate to us in the way we need most, because of his deep love for us. (You may like to consider in the group how well do those who love you actually know you – warts and all!)

- Notes on some of the Psalms of Ascent (120–134): Psalm 121:1 states that help comes from God, not from the hills used for Baal worship. Psalm 126 is a song of returning exiles. Psalm 133 may refer to priests and Levites.

- In "Questions for Discussion", question 4, Psalm 8:5-7 resonates with the Incarnation which shows the extent to which God was "mindful" of mortals. Even more, it resonates with Jesus himself, and his work in his ministry and passion of achieving salvation for all those who seek it, followed by his glorification. (You can also see in verse 7 a reference to Jesus' ministry when, for example, he stilled the storm [Mark 4:35-41].)

The Wisdom Literature

The Wisdom literature consists of Hebrew poetry. The introductory section on "The Bible as a Library" (pages 8–10) places the Wisdom literature (including Daniel in the Jewish scriptures) under the Writings, the third main category of Old Testament literature. Some of the Wisdom literature is contained in the Apocrypha, which is described on page 10.

- Much of the Bible describes God's self-revelation to us, in which he takes the initiative, and through which we come to know him. But there is also much that we can deduce about morals and about God by observing and reflecting on everyday life, and this is what the Wisdom literature is about. The key to this insight of wisdom, though, is reflection – the insight does not just happen automatically.

- The elderly, with their whole experience of life to ponder over, and with time to reflect on past experiences, were regarded as "wise". They perceived the ways of God in daily life, and were able to hand down their insights

- and wisdom to generations yet to come. (You might like to ask whether any individuals in the group ever quote wise sayings from their parents or grandparents.)

- The Wisdom literature is associated with the name of Solomon, the king of Israel (970–933 BC) renowned for his wisdom. Attachment to the name of Solomon gave the Wisdom texts, spanning the last 400 years of the Old Testament period, a certain authority.

- Note, though, that human wisdom is derived from divine Wisdom (e.g. Wisdom 7:24-26), which is a special attribute of God present before creation began (e.g. Proverbs 8:22), and perceived in the creative works of God (e.g. Job 38–41).

- The Wisdom literature arrives at different answers in its attempt to make sense of life in its divine context. It sometimes therefore questions traditional understanding and breaks new ground. So the book of Job (pronounced with a long o) is a debate, in which Job protests his innocence and questions why the righteous experience undeserved suffering, while his "friends", who champion the traditional way of seeing things, insist he must have sinned to suffer so. Job finds no answer to his question, and recognises that Wisdom is known fully to God alone (28:20-28), while his final vision of the awesome majesty of the Creator God silences him (38:1 – 42:6).

- But Proverbs, though written considerably later, still champions the traditional way of looking at things, maintaining good is rewarded and evil punished. Ordinary things in life are important; so (for example) health is preserved by drinking the fresh flowing water from one's own well, rather than dirty, stagnant water from the street (5:15-23).

- Ecclesiastes, yet later, hangs on to faith in God whilst, in observing life, sees only its futility and its end in death. (The word "vanity" [emptiness] appears 30 times in just twelve chapters. One scholar has suggested that "vanity" would be better translated as "absurdity" – life is not devoid of meaning, it is full of contradictory meanings.)

- In the Apocrypha, Sirach again espouses traditional understanding by identifying the Law with wisdom. Leisure for reflection on the Law is required for a person like a scribe to become wise. Yet the skill of artisans (the bedrock of society, but whose hard work denies them leisure) "is their prayer" (REB 38:24-34).

- The book of Wisdom, written by a Jew of the Dispersion only 50 years before the end of the Old Testament period, seeks to bridge the gap between Jewish and Gentile understanding of life and death. Wisdom, which mirrors God's goodness, is beautiful, and creates "friends of God" who are upright and generous, and "free from anxiety" (7:21 – 8:1).

- In "Issues for Discussion", question 3 invites members to use hindsight. Do they now view any incident in the past in a different way from how they viewed it at the actual time it took place? Can they say why?

- Question 4 illustrates how the early Church sought to explain its experience of Jesus. The passages suggest that, like Wisdom in the Old Testament, Christ is one with God, yet somehow distinct. Colossians

1:15 resonates with Proverbs 8:22. Hebrews 1:1-3a sees the Son, who was incarnate in Jesus, as God's agent in creation, like divine Wisdom in the Old Testament.

Daniel

Daniel belongs to the Old Testament section called the Writings and, in Jewish scriptures, is part of the Wisdom literature.

- The book of Daniel appears to describe certain events that took place during the sixth-century Babylonian exile, and some believe the book was written during this period. Most scholars today, though, see it as a secret, subversive book written during the persecution of the Jews by Antiochus IV from 168 to 164 BC, to encourage those Jews who were resisting him. To preserve the book from destruction if it fell into the wrong hands, it purports to have been written during the exile. Its message is that Daniel resisted all persecution for his faith (though we know the Babylonians actually allowed Jews free religious expression), and that God vindicated him.

- While details of exilic history are frequently inaccurate, the description in 2:31-45 and chapter 7 of the various kingdoms – Babylon, the Medes, Persia, Greece, and finally the Ptolemies and Seleucids (including Antiochus) – is accurate.

- The Jewish Feast of Chanukkah, which marks the rededication of the Temple in 164 BC, falls shortly before Christmas, and is celebrated with the giving of gifts.

LITERATURE SPUN FROM HISTORY: NEW TESTAMENT
St John's Gospel
The Dates of the Four Gospels – A Possible Scheme

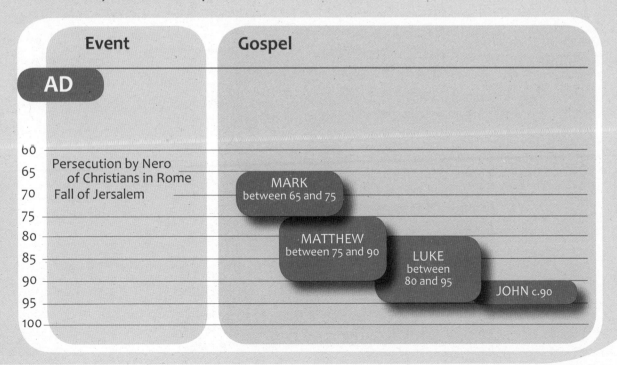

Event	Gospel
AD	

60
65 — Persecution by Nero of Christians in Rome
70 — Fall of Jersalem

MARK between 65 and 75

MATTHEW between 75 and 90

LUKE between 80 and 95

JOHN c.90

60 / 65 / 70 / 75 / 80 / 85 / 90 / 95 / 100

- Notice how often John's Gospel comments on Jesus' human attributes – hunger, thirst, etc. As a completely human being, Jesus has continually to work at being fully open to God. But the channel of communication is kept open, so that Jesus is able to reveal to human beings his intimate knowledge of the Father.

- John knows himself to be fully accepted and loved by God, through Jesus. The astounding thing is that, through Jesus, God in his love longs for us to be his friends (15:12-17)!

    Consider what this means:

    (a) enjoying each other's company;

    (b) enjoying things we share together, including secrets (Jesus reveals his knowledge of the Father);

    (c) enjoying the fact that we're not the same as each other, but different;

    (d) enjoying joint enterprises – God longs for us to be his helpers;

    (e) respect and space for each other, even though we occupy different positions;

    (f) and, especially, a love for each other that permeates the relationship.

- The author of the Gospel is believed to have lived in Ephesus but, though he is referred to as John, his identity is uncertain. The final edition of the Gospel may possibly have been in the early second century. But whoever wrote it was deeply imbued with the thinking of John the apostle, so that in some real sense the Gospel may be said to be his.

- Ephesus: at the time of St John's residence in Ephesus, the city was an important port and commercial centre. But its chief pride was the vast and magnificent Temple of Artemis (goddess of fertility), which was one of the seven wonders of the ancient world. (Paul had founded a church here, and had stirred up a riot by devotees of Artemis; see Acts 19:23-41.)

Pausanias, a second-century Greek traveller, who had seen the other six wonders of the world, wrote:

"I have seen the Hanging Gardens of Babylon, the Statue of Olympian Zeus, the Colossus of Rhodes, the Pyramids of Egypt, the Lighthouse of Alexandria and the Mausoleum of Halicarnassus; but, when I saw the Temple of Artemis towering to the clouds, all of the other wonders diminishingly lost their grandeur. This is the most beautiful work ever created by mankind."

The Prologue and Early Witnesses

- The Prologue introduces various themes found in the Gospel. But if the group finds the Prologue hard going, put it aside for the time being, and return to it as a grand finale at the end of the last session.

- As an introduction to the section on the early witnesses, read the two introductory paragraphs at the top of page 118. The section starts with the further witness of John the Baptist, who witnesses to Jesus as "the Lamb of God who takes away the sin of the world" (1:29), and also as the "Son of God" "who baptises with the Holy Spirit" (1:33-34). The use of the word "lamb" suggests the sacrificial animal offered by Jewish worship in the Temple. The word "sin" is in the singular because it refers to the endemic power of evil in the world, expressed through sins.

- In 1:42, "Cephas" comes from *kepha* (Aramaic for rock), which in Greek is *petra*.

- In 4:4, Jesus passes through Samaria, which lies between Judea and Galilee. Many Jews in Jesus' time preferred to avoid Samaria because of Samaritan unorthodoxy and racial impurity (see the note on page 86); they therefore travelled along the Jordan valley. So Jesus is here declaring his lack of prejudice for people despised by many fellow Jews.

- In 4:6, the woman's manner of life may have led others to shun her, so making it necessary for her to visit the well when others would not be there.

- After considering this whole passage, look at the introductory notes on the woman of Samaria on page 118, especially paragraph (b) and also see (c) and (e). Note how, through our bodies, we can come to know God, because we are not just spiritual beings.

- In "Issues for Discussion", question 4: "naming" affirms and values individuals for what they are and can become (e.g. Simon is renamed Cephas in 1:42). In contrast, "labelling" devalues them and puts them down, so placing obstacles in the way of their growth and development. Our prejudices, some of which we may be unaware of, are expressed in our attitudes towards people; they can do them great damage by despising them and looking down on them.

- The whole of Jesus' relationships with these early witnesses resonates with Isaiah 42:3, which describes the call of the Suffering Servant of God. A "dimly burning wick" can either be quenched (i.e. put out and the flickering light destroyed), or enticed to burn brightly (i.e. affirmed and helped to become what it is meant to be).

The Signs of Jesus

In the Synoptic Gospels, Jesus performs very many miracles (or, more accurately, "mighty works"). In contrast (omitting the draught of fishes in the Appendix, John 21), John's Gospel describes only seven, which, however, he names "signs", which point beyond themselves to a deeper significance. (11:47 and 20:30 suggest, though, that there were many more signs than those recorded. John has presumably selected the signs he describes to convey particular teaching in each instance.)

- The importance of each individual sign is that the central character(s) involved represent us, so the same things can happen to me as happened to the character in the sign. This is especially clear in 9:1, where the blind man appears to represent both an individual and Everyman. I, too, therefore, through an encounter with Jesus, can gain insight in the teeth of those who reject him and remain blind.

- The healing of the paralytic (5:1-18) takes place near the Sheep Gate leading into the northern part of the Temple precincts, which was near the sheep market; these animals were destined for sacrifice. The pool of Bethesda, a double-squared pool, so providing five porticoes, was believed, because of the turbulence of the waters at certain times, to have healing properties. Modern archaeology suggests it was associated with Asclepius, the Greek god of medicine – an interesting adjunct so near the Temple itself.

- Note that in some versions of the Bible, the second half of verse 3 and verse 4 are omitted; ask someone who has these verses to read them out.

- Invite the group to imagine 38 years of becoming (so it seems) a self-imposed invalid; allow time for this. It represents how we often prevent ourselves from living life to the full – perhaps because of the challenges that would then face us.

- Jesus disagrees with his disciples' attitude to the man born blind (9:2): they represent the earlier Old Testament concept that suffering is for sins committed – an attitude still frequently found in our own society today. Instead, the situation offers Jesus an opportunity for God's healing. Jesus claims (9:5), "I AM the light of the world", and the blind man ("I am"), once healed, progresses towards being and becoming the person God intends him to be.

- Note how in John's Gospel, Jesus' very presence precipitates self-judgement depending on the way individuals respond to him (9:39). See the note on page 122.

- In relation to the raising of Lazarus (11:1-53), the modern Westerner asks, "Did it really happen? Could it really happen like this?" This leans towards a negative answer, which then allows the story to be discarded. But the question Jews ask is, "What is the meaning of this passage?", and this is the question we should ask, if we are to understand what John wishes to tell us.

If we ask about the meaning of the story, Lazarus then represents each one of us. Icons (prayerful paintings) in the Eastern Orthodox Church often represent ordinary people like you and me in the tomb with Lazarus, all of us waiting to be restored to new life and to be freed from whatever it is that binds us.

In 11:27, Martha makes a profession of faith which is almost identical to Peter's profession of faith at Caesarea Philippi (Matthew 16:16). Note how this story illustrates the deeply human feelings that Jesus shares with others, and also how Jesus relies on human cooperation (in removing the stone, and unbinding Lazarus) in performing this great sign.

11:45-53 shows how the Jewish council (Sanhedrin) fears Jesus' growing popularity. A popular uprising could well ensue, which they feel might challenge not only their own privileged position under Rome, but possibly also the very Temple itself and the Jewish nation. They therefore decide to destroy Jesus.

- In "Issues for Discussion", question 1 suggests that Jesus can only perform a sign or miracle when there is at least some human cooperation. This can be shown by either the person in need, or someone acting on their behalf, and this enables Jesus' power to take hold of the situation. (Compare Mark 6:6.)

This suggests God's method is not to act unilaterally, but to work in cooperation with others, and so in and through them. In our prayer, therefore, when we offer intercessions for others, and petitions for ourselves, it presupposes that we don't then leave it all to God, but do whatever we are able to in helping to resolve the situation.

The Passion, Death and Resurrection of Jesus

- John devotes five chapters to the Last Supper, which (omitting the Appendix, chapter 21) is a quarter of his Gospel. Clearly therefore this section holds great importance for him.

- John's dating of the Last Supper and crucifixion: John, unlike the Synoptic Gospels, places the Last Supper *before* the Feast of the Passover (13:1; 18:28; 19:31, 42). All four Gospels agree that Jesus died on Friday and was raised on Sunday. So how, in John, does the crucifixion relate to the Passover?

- With regard to the foot washing in John 13, Paul quotes a saying of Jesus not found in the Gospels, "It is more blessed to give than to receive" (Acts 20:35).

But can "giving" on certain occasions make us "feel good" (almost "smug" perhaps), so that we feel "in control"? Whereas "receiving" may possibly require a certain humility and reveal a vulnerability which may make us feel uncomfortable?

May the act of "receiving" before "giving" purify our motives in "giving"?

Is any of this pertinent to the situation Peter finds himself in?

- In 13:19, the more literal translation is "I AM".

- In 13:30, John describes the moment that Judas goes out as "night". This refers not only to physical darkness, but to all the powers of spiritual darkness unleashed by his action.

MIDNIGHT			
THURSDAY	FRIDAY	SATURDAY	SUNDAY
	Jesus crucified/ Passover lambs slain	Feast of Passover	
6pm	6pm	6pm	6pm
The Last Supper	Passover meal		
MIDNIGHT			

- The Last Supper discourses.

  The discourses in chapters 13 to 16 tell us of the final gifts of Jesus to his disciples, who will recognise them when they meet the risen Jesus and receive his Spirit on the evening of Easter Day (20:19-23). The evangelist appears to have placed the discourses in this setting, because they are Jesus' most precious sayings, containing his parting gifts to his followers (even though they are unable to take them in in the context of the Last Supper).

  Because of the nature of these sayings, it is important that the texts suggested for reading are approached in a slow and meditative way, so that members are helped to embrace something of the meaning of these profound gifts of Jesus.

- 13:34 describes Jesus' new command (or "mandate") to his followers to show his love (*agape*). The command gives its name to the day known in the Church's year as Maundy Thursday. Obeying Jesus' commandments will be the outward way in which his disciples share in his love (14:15; 15:10).

- In 14:1-7, Jesus states. "I AM the way, and the truth, and the life. No one comes to the Father except through me." In inter-faith dialogue, this verse can be a stumbling block. But the Christian religion is explicit in believing that Jesus reveals God as Father, who has a profoundly loving relationship with his children, expressed through Jesus. It is God's Fatherhood that Jesus reveals; the verse should not be understood in any way that is judgemental of other faiths.

- All these gifts can be experienced because the disciples will receive the gift of the Spirit, who will indwell, guide and teach them (14:16-17, 26). He will be sent by the Father in the name of the Son. The Spirit therefore reveals the unity of the Godhead, though John has not yet reached any developed doctrine of the divine nature.

- Jesus' prayer in chapter 17 is sometimes called his high-priestly prayer, because in it he offers himself without reserve both to his Father and to his disciples in prayer. In 17:5, the evangelist expresses his belief in the eternal unity of Father and Son. 17:19 shows how Jesus sanctifies himself (i.e. knows this deep union with the Father) for the sake of others, who are always uppermost in his mind.

- Jesus prays for unity among his disciples (17:11b, 21-23), "so that the world may believe" in Jesus.

- After considering the biblical passages, you could explore how many of the distinctively recurring words in the Gospel (that are listed in "Background to St John's Gospel" on page 113) appear in this session on the Last Supper.

- When following this course in our Church, we approached the Last Supper discourses as a collection of Jesus' most treasured sayings valued by his disciples. We then applied this to our own church by inviting each group member to contribute his or her own favourite saying(s) of Jesus from any of the four Gospels. The sayings were then clustered under appropriate headings, and read out in church by group members (not leaders!), balancing men and women, young and old. This replaced the sermon at the Eucharist on Maundy Thursday with great effect and in a way that was deeply moving.

The Arrest, the Trials and the Crucifixion

- Note how the evangelist, in his presentation of this event, repeats the phrase "I AM" (the more accurate translation) three times over (18:5, 6, 8). The soldiers recognise the name of God and, perhaps perceiving something of the glory of Jesus, fall back.

- Jesus uses the opportunity to secure, as he had foretold, the release of his followers as part of his ongoing care and concern for others (6:39; 10:28, and expressed also in his high-priestly prayer in 17:12).

- Throughout the passion story, John emphasises how it is Jesus who, even at his arrest and on the cross, is in charge of his own life (10:18). So Jesus gives himself up in the garden (18:4), and, when on the cross he perceives that all is accomplished, hands over his spirit to the Father (19:28-30). He knows the type of death that awaits him, but is reconciled within himself and with his Father. (The group might find it helpful to look up again the verses introducing the whole of the passion story: 12:23-24, 27-28, 32.)

- Notice, in the Roman trial, Pilate's initial reluctance to try Jesus (18:31). Pilate knows Jesus is innocent, and says so on several occasions (18:38b; 19:4b, 6b, 12a). He therefore makes various attempts to release Jesus, described in 18:39; 19:4-6, 12. Though illegal (because Pilate has not found Jesus guilty), Pilate also orders Jesus to be flogged and mocked as a "king", in the hope of appeasing the chief priests (19:1-3). All he achieves, however, is that for the remainder of the trial and throughout the crucifixion, Jesus is presented as "king".

Pilate, a superstitious man (19:7-11), finds himself ultimately unable politically to risk the (false) Jewish charge of Jesus' treason (19:12); otherwise there might well be widespread Jewish rioting, resulting in Pilate's being censured by Rome for his lack of action. So, Pilate finally gives in to the priests.

- The inscription on the cross is in three languages, so proclaiming Jesus' kingship to the whole world (19:19-22). Pilate finally stands his ground, and refuses any further compromise with the chief priests.

- Breaking the legs of the crucified (19:31-33) brought virtually immediate death, since those crucified could no longer heave themselves up in order to draw breath.

- The burial (19:38-42) has to be handled initially by men, in order to gain Pilate's permission for the release of Jesus' body. There is little time before sunset (6 pm) when the Feast of the Passover begins. Even so, the body is wrapped in linen cloths with the huge weight of spices interweaved in the folds of the cloth.

- The new tomb (i.e. not a recycled one) is a final honour which the evangelist perceives is granted to Jesus in death (19:41).

- In "Issues for Discussion", question 1, the chief priests want Jesus out of the way. This is partly because of their jealousy at the enormous response of the common people to him, but also because they fear a clampdown by Rome on their extensive privileges, should there be an uprising in support of Jesus.

- Question 4: The fact that Jesus has suffered so profoundly (even to death) means we know he identifies with us when disasters occur, and hopefully we can perhaps know of his care, concern and support in our own lives and in those of others involved.

The Resurrection of Jesus

- The resurrection of Jesus is the greatest "sign" of all. Unlike the other signs, though, it is not performed by Jesus, but by the Father.

- Note how, unlike St Luke's chronology, in St John's Gospel the disciples receive the Holy Spirit on the evening of Easter Day through Jesus' "breath" (20:22). (The Greek word, *pneuma*, can be translated as "Spirit", "breath" or "wind".)

- The empty tomb (20:1-10). Finding the stone rolled away from the tomb, Mary Magdalene surmises the body has been removed. The Romans would be unlikely to do this. The most likely persons would be the associates of the chief priests, to ensure the disciples did not invent a story of Jesus rising from the dead. If they possessed the body, they could refute such a rumour by producing it. (The disciples fear this group: see 19:38; 20:19, 26.)

- Jesus' appearance to Mary Magdalene (20:11-18) shows that the full revelation of Jesus' "glory" includes not only his resurrection, but also his return to the Father, accompanied by the outpouring of the Spirit, which are all seen as one great event. This event will also enable Jesus to be present with his disciples always, though in a new way which is based on the mutual love of the disciples and of the Father and Son (14:20-23, 28;

16:5-7; 17:24). The Spirit will enable the disciples to understand the past and will guide them in the future (14:25-26; 16:12-15).

- The Appendix to John's Gospel, chapter 21. The natural climax to the story has been reached at the end of the previous chapter and, in the power of the Spirit, the disciples have been sent out to carry on his work by the risen and exalted Jesus, whose ascension to the Father has ended his earthly appearances.

Chapter 21 is an addition, set in Galilee, and from a later date. The story of the breakfast on the shore, also called the miraculous draught of fish (21:1-14), has many similarities with the story in Luke 5:1-11, at the beginning of Jesus' ministry. There is, however, no reason why two different stories of this nature should not be independent of each other.

The reference to 153 large fish (21:11) is taken by some as the actual number of fish caught, but for others the number is symbolic, though the nature of the symbolism is disputed. There were believed to be 153 species of fish; the catch might therefore illustrate the universality and variety of the Christian mission (see John 10:16; Luke 5:10). If so, the fact that the net did not break might suggest the unity of these diverse believers in contrast to the divisions over Jesus during his ministry among the unbelieving crowds (e.g. 7:43; 9:16; 10:19).

As well as a resurrection appearance, the story emphasises the joint meal of Jesus with his disciples as they eat fish and bread, similar to that used to feed the five thousand (6:1-14). The story in chapter 21 appears to refer to the shared meal of the breaking of bread in the Church, through which the disciples recognise the presence of the risen Jesus.

The threefold question put to Peter by Jesus (21:15-19) not only reinstates Peter after his earlier denial (though the cleansing balm, emphasised by the use of his name "Simon" rather than the name that Jesus gave him, Peter [the Rock], stings the wound). The story also sees Peter as a shepherd and overseer in the Church of Christ.

Peter's question about the destiny of "the beloved disciple" (21:20-23) suggests that, though living to a great age, this disciple has already died, and that a rumour (which appears to have circulated in the Church) that he would not die was false. Yet the narrator of this chapter believes he lives on through the Spirit-filled Gospel which is based on his testimony and bears his name.

- The Prologue (1:1-18). If you omitted this at the beginning, you may like to read it now in the group with the help of the notes on pages 114 and 115.

A Suggestion for Prayer Time

In relation to Jesus' command to Peter to "Follow me" (John 21:19b, 22b), you may like to consider using as a prayer these final words from *The Quest of the Historical Jesus* (published in English in 1910), by Albert Schweitzer (1875–1965). The passage needs to be read slowly and meditatively.

(The language has been very slightly modernised.)

He [i.e. Jesus] comes to us as one unknown, without a name, as of old by the lakeside he came to those who knew him not. He speaks to us the same word, "Follow me", and sets us to the tasks which he has to fulfil in our time. He commands. And to those who obey him, whether they be wise or simple, he will reveal himself in the toils, the conflicts, the sufferings which they will pass through in his fellowship, and, as an ineffable mystery, they will learn in their own experience, who he is.